WORLD WAR II
AT SEA

WORLD WAR II AT SEA
By Jeremy Harwood

First published in North America in 2015 by Zenith Press, an imprint of
Quarto Publishing Group USA Inc, 400 First Avenue North, Suite 400,
Minneapolis, MN 55401 USA, by arrangement with Quid Publishing
© Quid Publishing 2015

Zenith Press titles are also available at discounts in bulk quantity for
industrial or sales-promotional use. For details write to Special Sales
Manager at Quarto Publishing Group USA Inc., 400 First Avenue North,
Suite 400, Minneapolis, MN 55401 USA.

To find out more about our books, visit us online at www.zenithpress.com.

ISBN: 978-0-7603-4765-2

Set in Akzidenz Grotesk and New Century Schoolbook

Printed and bound in China

Conceived, designed and produced by
Quid Publishing
Level 4 Sheridan House
Hove BN3 1DD
England

Design and illustration: Simon Daley

JEREMY HARWOOD

WORLD WAR II
AT SEA

A NAVAL VIEW OF THE GLOBAL CONFLICT: 1939 TO 1945

ZENITH
PRESS

CONTENTS

◄ Japanese aircrew crowd onto the flightdeck of the aircraft carrier *Kaga* to attend a pre-attack briefing the day before Japan launched its surprise aerial assault on the US Pacific Fleet at Pearl Harbor on December 7, 1941. The stunning Japanese success confirmed that the days of the battleship as queen of the seas was finally over, a fact confirmed by the sinking of the British battleship *Prince of Wales* and battlecruiser *Repulse* from the air off Malaya three days later.

TIMELINE

1940

MAY | JUNE | JULY | AUGUST | SEPTEMBER | OCTOBER | NOVEMBER | DECEMBER | JANUARY | FEBRUARY | MARCH | APRIL | MAY | JUNE | JULY | AUGUST | SEPTEMBER | OCTOBER

SEPTEMBER 17, 1939
Aircraft carrier *Courageous* torpedoed and sunk by U-29 southwest of Ireland.

OCTOBER 14, 1939
U-47 sinks battleship *Royal Oak* at anchor in Scapa Flow and escapes undetected. ❶

APRIL 10, 1940
Six British destroyers surprise ten German ones in Narvik fjord, sinking two of them. The British return three days later—this time with the battleship *Warspite* in support—and sink seven more destroyers and a U-boat. ❷

SEPTEMBER 4, 1939
Liner *Athenia* sunk by U-31 off Ireland. The unescorted and unarmed vessel was torpedoed without warning; 19 of her crew and 95 passengers (28 American) died.

DECEMBER 13, 1939
Graf Spee is forced into action by three British cruisers off the River Plate and seeks shelter in neutral Uruguay. She scuttles herself off Montevideo harbor on December 17.

MAY 28–JUNE 4, 1940
Royal and French Navy warships and hundreds of small civilian vessels evacuate British, French, and Belgian troops from Dunkirk.

JULY 3, 1940
Force H attacks French fleet at anchor in Mers-el-Kébir, sinking the battleship *Bretagne* and seriously damaging *Provence* and the battlecruiser *Dunkerque*.

1941

1942

NOVEMBER | DECEMBER | JANUARY | FEBRUARY | MARCH | APRIL | MAY | JUNE | JULY | AUGUST | SEPTEMBER | OCTOBER | NOVEMBER | DECEMBER | JANUARY | FEBRUARY | MARCH | APRIL

NOVEMBER 11, 1940
British carrier-borne torpedo-bombers attack the Italian battle fleet in its base at Taranto, putting half of it out of action.

MARCH 28, 1941
Italian naval squadron sailing to attack British convoys sailing between Alexandria and Greece is intercepted by the Mediterranean Fleet off Cape Matapan. The Italian battleship *Vittorio Veneto* is crippled and three heavy cruisers and two destroyers are sunk.

MAY 24, 1941
Bismarck and *Prinz Eugen* sink the battlecruiser *Hood* and cripple the battleship *Prince of Wales* in the Denmark Strait.

MAY 17, 1941
German battleship *Bismarck* and heavy cruiser *Prinz Eugen* sail from their Baltic base Gotenhafen (Gydansk) for Norway to attempt a breakout into the North Atlantic.

MAY 27, 1941
After her steering is disabled by British carrier-borne torpedo bombers, the crippled *Bismarck*, which had been steaming for the French port of Brest, is brought to bay by the Home Fleet and sunk 400 miles from her destination.

NOVEMBER 19, 1941
Australian light cruiser *Sydney* and German commerce raider *Kormoran* sink each other off Western Australia. There are no survivors from *Sydney*.

DECEMBER 10, 1941
Prince of Wales and the battlecruiser *Repulse* are sunk off the northeastern coast of Malaya by Japanese bombers operating from air bases at Saigon.

DECEMBER 7, 1941
Two waves of Japanese carrier-borne aircraft launch a surprise attack on the US Pacific Fleet at Pearl Harbor.

FEBRUARY 11, 1942
Scharnhorst, *Gneisenau*, and *Prinz Eugen* begin their "Channel Dash" up the English Channel from Brest to German home waters and arrive two days later.

JANUARY 11, 1942
Operation Drumbeat, the first coordinated U-boat attack on shipping along the USA's eastern seaboard, is activated.

1943

MAY · JUNE · JULY · AUGUST · SEPTEMBER · OCTOBER · NOVEMBER · DECEMBER · JANUARY · FEBRUARY · MARCH · APRIL · MAY · JUNE · JULY · AUGUST · SEPTEMBER · OCTOBER

JUNE 4, 1942
The battle of Midway starts with a Japanese air strike on the island. Admiral Nimitz, however, had foreknowledge of the attack and had her carriers in place to counter it. The Japanese lost all four of their crack aircraft carriers. The Americans lost just one, *Yorktown*.

MAY 7, 1942
The battle of the Coral Sea begins. It lasted for three days and ended in tactical stalemate. Though the Americans lost more ships, the Japanese had to abandon their plan to land invasion troops at Port Moresby.

MAY 24, 1943
Dönitz withdraws his U-boats from the North Atlantic. His losses were now unsustainable —41 U-boats were sunk in May alone.

NOVEMBER 8, 1942
Operation Torch, the Allied amphibious invasion of French North Africa, begins. Task forces landed near Casablanca on the Moroccan Atlantic coast, near Oran in western Algeria and near Algiers itself.

JULY 9, 1943
Operation Husky, the Allied amphibious invasion of Sicily, is launched. The landings triggered the overthrow of Mussolini by the Fascist Party's Grand Council.

JUNE 27, 1942
Convoy PQ-17 sails from Iceland for Archangel. Mistakenly ordered to scatter by the Admiralty after its escort had been withdrawn, it suffered catastrophic losses; 24 out of its 35 ships were sunk by U-boats and Luftwaffe aircraft.

AUGUST 10, 1942
Operation Pedestal, the last-ditch attempt to get a convoy through to Malta before the island was forced to surrender, is launched. Out of the 14 merchant ships which sailed from Gibraltar, 6 made Valetta. The tanker *Ohio*, the last to arrive, had to be towed by three ships into harbor.

SEPTEMBER 26, 1943
Scharnhorst is sunk by a vastly superior British force in the Barents Sea. Only 36 of her 1,839-strong crew survive.

SEPTEMBER 9, 1943
Italian fleet steams from Spezia in northern Italy for Malta, where it surrenders to the Royal Navy.

NOVEMBER
DECEMBER
1944
JANUARY
FEBRUARY
MARCH
APRIL
MAY
JUNE
JULY
AUGUST
SEPTEMBER
OCTOBER
NOVEMBER
DECEMBER
1945
JANUARY
FEBRUARY
MARCH
APRIL

**JUNE 6,
1944**
Operation Overlord, the Allied invasion of northern France starting with landings on the Normandy beaches, is launched.

**OCTOBER 23,
1944**
The battle of Leyte Gulf was Japan's last naval effort to change the course of the Pacific war. The Japanese lost 4 carriers, 3 battleships, 6 heavy and 4 light cruisers, 11 destroyers, a submarine, and some 500 aircraft.

**JANUARY 30,
1945**
Wilhelm Gustloff, a one-tine German cruise ship, is sunk in the Baltic by a Soviet submarine. Out of the 10,000 service personnel and civilian refugees crammed onboard, more than 6,000 perished. It still holds the record as the single worst disaster in maritime history.

**MARCH 25,
1945**
US Navy starts the pre-invasion bombardment of Okinawa, firing more than 500,000 shells and rockets at the island in a week.

**APRIL 27,
1944**
An S-Boat flotilla intercepts a convoy taking part in Operation Tiger, the dress-rehearsal for the D-Day landings, as it heads across Lyme Bay for Slapton Sands.

**JUNE 19,
1944**
The battle of the Philippine Sea begins. The Japanese lost so many aircraft in it that US pilots referred to their downing as a "turkey shoot."

**APRIL 7,
1945**
Japan's last super-battleship *Yamato* is sunk by US planes while on a one-way suicide mission to Okinawa.

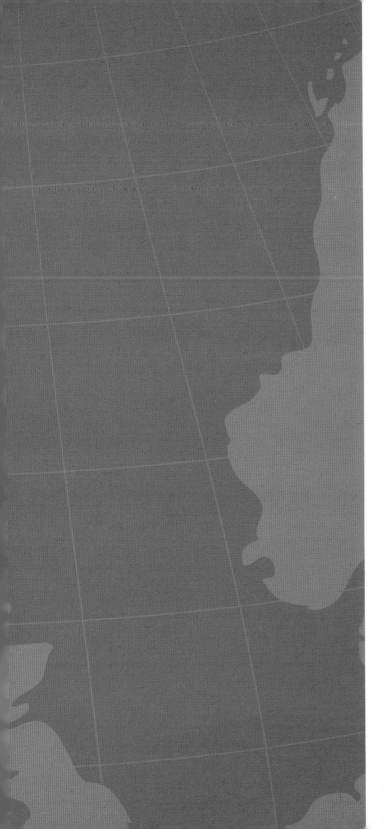

BEGINNINGS

At the start of World War II, Britain, and France between them enjoyed supremacy at sea. Although the ships of Hitler's Kriegsmarine were modern and well armed, German naval strength—at least when it came to surface vessels—was demonstrably inferior to that of the two Allied navies. Nor could the Third Reich look to its Axis partners to redress the balance. Both Italy and Japan decided to remain neutral.

By the end of July 1940, the situation had been transformed. France had capitulated—ironically, much of its fleet had been destroyed by the Royal Navy at Mers-el-Kébir when it refused to sail for a British port. Italy was now in the war on the Axis side, and the Regina Marina was preparing to battle the British for Mediterranean naval supremacy. In the Atlantic, U-boats were a constant menace. Meanwhile, in the Far East, the Imperial Japanese Navy was on the watch, waiting for an opportune moment to strike.

NAVAL STRENGTHS

When Britain went to war with Nazi Germany in September 1939, it was believed that the Royal Navy was more than ready for action. In terms of manpower, the fleet had a total strength of 129,000 officers and men, plus 73,000 reservists, at its disposal. Including the vessels serving with it from Australia and New Zealand, it fielded 317 operational warships. These broke down into 12 battleships and battlecruisers, 8 aircraft carriers, 58 cruisers, 100 destroyers, 101 escort vessels, and 38 submarines.

BRITISH UNPREPAREDNESS

On the surface, this looked like a formidable naval array, but apparent strength concealed several underlying weaknesses. One problem was probably unsolvable. It had proved patently impossible to keep up a world-class fleet given the limited budgets the British Admiralty had made available to it as a consequence of the hard times the country went through in the years after World War I. Another problem, however, was self-inflicted.

In 1922, Britain signed up to the Washington Naval Treaty, which, at the USA's instigation, imposed strict limits on the number of battleships and battlecruisers the British, US, Japanese, French, and Italian fleets could contain. The ratio the treaty laid down was 5:5:3:1.67—that is, the Royal Navy and the USA were given parity, while the Japanese, in return for other concessions in the Far East, accepted a slight numerical inferiority. The French and Italians bottomed out with equal numbers. The treaty also imposed a ten-year naval holiday, during which time no new capital ships would be laid down by any of the treaty's signatories. Any built after that would be limited to a displacement of 35,000 tons.

Over the next few years, successive Conservative and Labour governments hacked at the naval building program time and again. In 1929, ignoring expert advice, Labour proposed to reduce the number of cruisers in the Royal Navy from 70 to 50. The decision was formalized during the London naval conference the following year, when the British accepted parity in cruiser tonnage with the USA. The Japanese stuck out for a ratio of 70 percent. Destroyers and submarines were now also to be subject to the Washington provisions, while the naval holiday was extended until 1936.

It was a sad story. In April 1931, Admiral of the Fleet Sir Frederick Field, the First Sea Lord, surveyed the cumulate effect of ten years of cutbacks. "The British Commonwealth," he wrote, "has accepted a naval strength which, in certain circumstances, is definitely below that required to keep our sea communications open in the event of our being drawn into war. In defensive material, in the modernisation of ships … we are below the standard of the other powers."

Field went on to spell out specific British weaknesses. "The number of our capital ships is now so reduced," he wrote, "that should the protection of our interests render it necessary to move our fleet to the East, insufficient vessels of this type would be left in home waters to ensure the security of our trade and territory in the event of any dispute arising with a European power." The 50 cruisers the navy was allowed under the terms of the London naval treaty was "definitely insufficient," while, in destroyers, too, it was dangerously weak. In 1918, the navy had a total of 433 destroyers under command, all of which had been needed. The figure in 1931 was some 120. By 1936, 55 of these would be overage.

The consequences were stark. When naval rearmament at last got back underway in 1936—the same year that Britain concluded the Anglo-German naval agreement, which gave the Kriegsmarine the right to expand to 35 percent of the size of the Royal Navy's surface fleet—there was a huge amount of ground to be made up after years of neglect.

The majority of Britain's capital ships were too old— only two postdated World War I—too slow, or

HMS *Nelson* seen at anchor. She was one of two battleships the British built in the 1920s, her sister-ship being *Rodney*. Both were the only Royal Navy battleships to be fitted with 16-inch guns as their main armament. Both were also unique in having the three main gun turrets fitted forward of the superstructure. The design was a compromise. To comply with the terms of the Washington Naval Treaty, signed in 1922, *Nelson* could displace no more than 35,000 tons. This meant cutting back on her speed and her protective armor plating.

insufficiently armored, while the five *King George V*–class battleships under construction suffered from an unfortunate design compromise. While the Germans and Americans opted for 15-inch and 16-inch guns—and the Japanese for 18-inch ones—for their main armament, the British stuck to the terms of the Washington Treaty and chose 14-inch guns. It had been planned to install 12 of these, but this proved impossible without unacceptable sacrifice of speed and defensive armor. Accordingly, the number was cut back to ten, mounted in two quadruple turrets and a twin one.

FRENCH SEA POWER

With 7 old and new capital ships, and with a further 2 under construction, an aircraft carrier, 19 cruisers, and 66 destroyers, the French navy was an invaluable adjunct to British naval power, especially in the Mediterranean, where most of the French fleet was based. The French and British Mediterranean fleets—one concentrated in the west and the other in the east—were together just about strong enough to deal with the Italian battlefleet should Italy decide to honor its treaty commitments to Germany. Mussolini, however, elected to remain neutral.

The situation changed for the worse in June 1940. With France forced out of the war and Mussolini entering it, the naval balance of power swung heavily against the British. A powerful squadron had to be detached from the Home Fleet to attempt to replace in some measure the French presence in the western Mediterranean. This dangerously reduced the Home Fleet's ability to protect the Atlantic convoy routes from marauding German surface raiders. At the same time, the absence of the French fleet placed Britain's position in the Far East and the Pacific in jeopardy, always assuming that the Japanese would decide to take advantage of the British predicament.

MERS-EL-KÉBIR

Originally, the plan had been for the British Mediterranean fleet to sail via the Suez Canal to Singapore, while the French remained behind to hold the Italians in check. With France's capitulation, this eastward switch became impossible unless the Mediterranean was abandoned. Churchill, only a few weeks into his premiership, refused to countenance such a move.

There was an even worse possibility. The British, rightly or wrongly, believed that there was a real risk the French fleet would be handed over to the Germans as part of the armistice terms. Churchill and his war cabinet decided to take drastic action. On June 27, the premier ordered that all French ships be prevented from returning to their home ports.

In Alexandria, where Force X—a battleship, four cruisers, three destroyers, and a submarine—was anchored alongside the British Mediterranean fleet, things proceeded peacefully. The French agreed to their ships being demilitarized. The same was not the case at Mers-el-Kébir, a major French naval base three miles (4.8km) west of Oran in Algeria, where Admiral Sir James Somerville's Force H, sailing post haste from Gibraltar, arrived on the morning of June 3.

Somerville's force included the battlecruiser *Hood*, the battleships *Valiant* and *Resolution*, the aircraft carrier *Ark Royal*, 2 light cruisers, and 11 destroyers. The French battleships *Bretagne* and *Provence*, the battlecruisers *Dunkerque* and *Strasbourg*, the seaplane carrier *Commandant Teste*, six destroyers, and a motley collection of submarines, torpedo boats, sloops, patrol boats, and minesweepers crowded the harbor.

Somerville gave Admiral Marcel Gensoul, the French commander, four choices. He and his fleet could fight on from a British harbor, steam to a British port after which his sailors would be repatriated to France, sail to a French port in the Caribbean where the fleet would be entrusted to US supervision for the rest of the war,

The French battleship *Richelieu* passing Brooklyn Bridge in New York's East River, heading for repairs at a US Naval yard in 1943. The largest battleship ever constructed by France, *Richelieu* had a checkered wartime career. Torpedoed and then further damaged by shellfire when British and Free French forces tried unsuccessfully to capture the West African port of Dakar in September 1940, she served under Vichy colors until 1942 when, following the German occupation of Vichy France, she finally passed into Free French hands.

or scuttle itself. Gensoul, like many senior French naval officers of time, was profoundly suspicious of the British. Ordered by Vichy to fight if necessary, he played for time while his ships raised steam and prepared for action. Somerville warned him that he would open fire at 7:30 p.m. that evening if he did not receive a satisfactory answer to his demands.

The British started to shell the French as soon as the ultimatum expired. *Bretagne* exploded and capsized, *Dunkerque* was disabled, and *Provence* ran aground. The destroyer *Mogador*, its stern blown off, managed to anchor in the shallows. Miraculously, *Strasbourg*, shielded by five destroyers, managed to escape, as did *Commandant Teste* and another seven destroyers. Together with six cruisers from Algiers, they all managed to steam back to Toulon and safety. *Richelieu*, one of France's newest battleships was not as fortunate. She was heavily damaged by Fleet Air Arm torpedo bombers at her moorings at the West African port of Dakar and put out of action for a year.

The whole action lasted no more than half an hour. Around 1,300 French sailors were killed. Though MPs in the House of Commons cheered Churchill to the echo after he justified the attack, it was, as *The Times* wrote, a "melancholy victory." Most of the remainder of the French fleet remained in port in Toulon until November 1942. As the Germans marched into Vichy France, following the Allied invasion of North Africa, it put into effect the secret orders Admiral François Darlan, its commander-in-chief, had given it to cover such an eventuality. It sunk itself.

REBUILDING THE KRIEGSMARINE

France was not the only great power to lose practically its entire navy. Back in 1919, the German Imperial High Seas Fleet, having surrendered to the Royal Navy, had been scuttled by its own crews as it lay moldering at anchor in the great British naval base at Scapa Flow.

The victorious Allies had already determined that Germany should be prohibited from ever again being a great sea power. The Treaty of Versailles limited the size of its fleet to no more than 6 obsolete battleships, 6 light cruisers, 12 destroyers, and 12 torpedo boats. Any new capital ships built as replacements were to be no heavier than 10,000 tons. The Germans were also forbidden to build naval aircraft or construct submarines.

By the time Hitler came to power in 1933, the Kriegsmarine had already laid down *Deutschland* (later renamed *Lützow*), *Admiral Hipper*, and *Admiral Graf Spee*, its first three modern warships. Though limited in tonnage by the Versailles restrictions, their 11-inch main armament outgunned all contemporary cruisers, while thanks to their MAN diesel engines, which were capable of producing speeds of up to 28.5 knots, they were faster than most battleships. The Germans called them "Panzerschiffen" (armored ships)—it was the British who christened them pocket battleships. Admiral Erich Raeder, who had been commander-in-chief of the Kriegsmarine since 1928, intended them to be commerce raiders.

Two 32,000-ton battlecruisers—*Scharnhorst* and *Gneisenau*—were launched in 1936, followed by three heavy cruisers, starting with *Admiral Hipper* and ending with *Prinz Eugen*. Two more were planned, but never completed. Nor was *Graf Zeppelin*, the first of Germany's projected aircraft carriers. Her construction had been ordered as part of Plan Z, which Hitler authorized in January 1939.

Plan Z was the blueprint for a massive naval expansion. By 1944, the Kriegsmarine was to consist of 12 battleships, 15 pocket battleships, 4 aircraft carriers, 5 heavy cruisers, 36 light cruisers, and 249 U-boats. Raeder, who had been agitating for such a construction program for years, was delighted to have secured the Führer's backing, but it was not to last. Goering opposed it from the start, and the outbreak of war that September led to its postponement and then

cancellation in favor of an all-out effort to step up U-boat production. All that survived of it were the two great sister battleships *Bismarck* and *Tirpitz*. The former was launched in February 1939 by Hitler himself and commissioned in August 1940. *Tirpitz* followed in February 1941.

THE REGIA MARINA

Though relatively small, the Kriegsmarine was extremely efficient. The Italian fleet was far larger, but poorly commanded. On paper, the Regia Marina was the fifth largest navy in the world, behind the navies of Britain, the USA, Japan, and France, but bigger than those of Germany and the Soviet Union.

After France's capitulation in 1940 and the consequent neutralization of the French fleet, the Italians fielded what they claimed was the most formidable navy in the Mediterranean. It included six battleships—two of which, *Littorio* and *Vittorio Veneto*, were faster and better armed than anything Admiral Cunningham's Mediterranean fleet could put up

against them—around 20 cruisers, 7 of which were over 10,000 tons, 61 destroyers, 70 torpedo boats, and more than 100 submarines. There was one significant gap, though. The Regia Marina lacked aircraft carriers. Admiral Domenico Cavagnari, the Chief of Naval Staff from 1932 until Mussolini sacked him in 1940 following the successful Fleet Air Arm torpedo-bomber attack on the anchored Italian fleet at Taranto, vetoed their construction.

Like Mussolini, his admirals counted on only having to fight a short war. Like him, they were to be disappointed. The fleet they commanded, though numerically imposing, was technologically backward and unimaginatively led. Admiral Franco Maugeri, the head of naval intelligence from 1941, was quick to blame the Duce for the deficiencies. Mussolini, he said, had created nothing more than "a show navy, a great, glittering toy that lent added prestige and lustre to his regime." In fact, the navy's leadership was just as culpable. They seemed to suffer from a collective inferiority complex as far as the Royal Navy was concerned.

The resulting paradox was that the more their fleet increased in strength, the less Italy's combat-shy admirals appeared willing to risk it in battle. When, under German pressure, they did reluctantly take the offensive, the results were disastrous.

THE SINKING OF *ATHENIA*

In the late afternoon of September 3, 1939—the day that Britain and France declared war on the Third Reich—the first shots were fired in the Battle of the Atlantic. Oberleutnant Fritz-Julius Lemp, the 26-year-old commander of U-30, a Type VIIa submarine on patrol about 250 miles (402km) northwest of the coast of Ireland, was the man responsible for initiating what was to become the longest-fought campaign of the entire war. It lasted for nearly six years, almost up to the moment of Germany's final capitulation.

On August 22, the U-30 had been one of 14 German submarines that had sailed from Wilhelmshaven to take up position on their war stations. Over the next week, as the Polish crisis escalated, war seemed more and more likely to break out with the Western powers. On September 3, the inevitable happened. At 12:56 p.m. Berlin time, U-boat High Command radioed a top-priority coded message. It read simply: "Hostilities with England effective immediately."

PLAYING IT BY THE RULES

Two more transmissions followed in short order. The first of them authorized attacks on enemy shipping to commence, but warned that the so-called Prize Regulations must be observed. These had been incorporated in the 1930 London Naval Agreement. Though Germany had not signed up to them at the time, she had agreed to abide by them in 1936.

According to the rules, a U-boat could not attack an unarmed, unescorted merchant ship without warning. Surfacing and firing a warning shot across the bows was the standard procedure. The ship in question then had to heave to and allow itself to be searched by a boarding party checking for the presence of contraband. If none was found, the ship was free to proceed. If contraband was detected, the ship could be sunk, but only after its crew and passengers had been given time to take to the lifeboats.

Warships, troopships, and vessels escorted in convoys, on the other hand, could be sunk without warning. Attacks on passenger liners were prohibited. The third signal told all Kriegsmarine vessels that they were free to begin hostilities without waiting for what the signal termed "provocations."

ATTACKING *ATHENIA*

Lemp was fully aware of what the Prize Regulations stipulated—indeed, he, like his fellow U-boat commanders, had been reminded of them before he sailed from Wilhelmshaven. However, they were of little immediate use when, at 4:30 p.m., the U-30's bridge watch sighted a large ship looming in the distant horizon. U-30 was at the northern limit of its patrol zone, sailing on the surface and well away from the normal shipping lanes.

Lemp increased speed to close the distance on his potential target and then dived as he neared it for a closer periscope inspection. It was now around 7 p.m. Peering through his periscope in the fading light, Lemp noticed that the ship he was observing was blacked out and zigzagging at high speed. Though she was large enough to be a passenger liner, Lemp concluded that she must be a British Armed Merchant Cruiser, a converted passenger liner kitted out with guns and so fair game for immediate attack. He ordered his crew to battle stations.

At exactly 7:40 p.m., Lemp fired his first torpedo. It struck his target squarely amidships, stopping her dead in the water. He fired a second torpedo, but this malfunctioned and ran wild. Fearing that it might circle around and hit his own submarine, he dived deep to avoid it, surfacing again only after the danger had passed.

By that time, it was twilight. From the bridge of U-30, Lemp observed his listing target through his binoculars. She did not appear to be in danger of sinking, so he fired a third torpedo. It, too, ran wild.

▼ BELOW AND OPPOSITE Fritz-Julius Lemp (below), commander of U-30, the submarine that sank the 13,500-ton passenger ship *Athenia* (right), in conversation with Admiral Karl Dönitz after the later has just decorated him with the Knight's Cross in August 1940. Lemp died the following May after failing to scuttle U-110 when she was forced to surface after a depth-charge attack by two British destroyers and a corvette escorting a North Atlantic convoy. Some of his surviving crew claimed that the British had shot him swimming in the water, but it is more likely that he allowed himself to drown because of his failure to sink his submarine. He always claimed that his attack on *Athenia* had been an honest mistake. Because she was blacked out and was zigzagging, he had taken her for an armed merchant cruiser and so a legitimate target.

Exasperated by the repeated torpedo failures, Lemp edged closer to finish off the kill. Keeping the moon behind him to help conceal his approach, he was now able to make out the silhouette of the darkened ship. He checked it against his copy of the Lloyd's Register of shipping.

What Lemp discovered horrified him. He had made a monumental error. Instead of attacking an Armed Merchant Cruiser, he had just torpedoed *Athenia*, a 13,580-ton British passenger liner of the Donaldson Line en route from Glasgow to Montreal. Any doubts he might still have had about the vessel's identity vanished when his wireless operator picked up the distress call *Athenia* was transmitting. It confirmed her identity, gave her position, and concluded with the three-letter code SSS, meaning she was being attacked by a submarine.

What Lemp did not know was that *Athenia* was jam-packed with around 1,100 passengers, including 311 Americans. Fortunately, the sea was calm and the weather good, giving passengers and crew ample time to take to the lifeboats. She managed to stay afloat until the next morning, by which time three rescue ships and two British destroyers had arrived on the scene. Out of the entire ship's complement, 118 perished—many of them as a result of a tragic accident during the rescue.

Knute Nelson was a Norwegian tanker, which, together with *City of Flint*, an American freighter, and the Swedish steam yacht *Southern Cross*, had raced to *Athenia*'s assistance. In the dark, one of her lifeboats was struck by the tanker's propeller and capsized. Out of the 52 female passengers and 8 seamen onboard, only 8 survived.

COVERING UP THE SINKING

Onboard U-30, Lemp was in a state of near panic. Rather than attempting to help in the rescue—understandably enough with British destroyers nearby—he slipped quietly away undetected. Nor did he inform U-boat High Command of the attack. Instead he kept radio silence until September 14, 11 days after the sinking. He broke it only to report that U-30 had been severely damaged after being depth charged by British destroyers following his sinking of the freighter *Fanad Head* and to ask permission to disembark a badly wounded crewman in Iceland for medical attention. He still did not mention *Athenia*. He also failed to record the attack in the submarine's war log and swore his crew to secrecy.

When the BBC broke the news of the attack, it came as a total shock to Commodore Karl Dönitz, the commander of the U-boat arm, and to Raeder himself. Even after Lemp confirmed Dönitz's suspicions that he had sunk *Athenia* after U-30 had limped back to port on September 27, Dönitz, Raeder, and the entire German propaganda machine continued to deny that any U-boat had been involved in the sinking.

Raeder denounced the story as "an abominable lie." Dönitz believed that the truth was best swept under the carpet. U-30's log was hastily doctored to place her 200 miles (322km) away from the scene. Goebbels, for his part, claimed that Churchill was responsible for the sinking. It was a deliberate British plot, the Propaganda Minister fulminated, to try to drag the USA into the war. The full extent of the cover-up was not uncovered until the Nuremberg Trials were held after the war. There, it and the accusations that the British had staged the sinking came back to haunt Raeder, who was accused of committing deliberate fraud.

MAGNETIC MINES: HITLER'S DEADLY WEAPON

▼ A German C-type magnetic mine, photographed at Shoeburyness, Kent, where it was dropped on the mudflats by a Luftwaffe aircraft in November 1939. After the mine's discovery, it was disarmed and rendered safe by experts from the Enemy Mines Section, HMS *Vernon*, Portsmouth. In this picture, the protective nose cone has already been removed to expose the electrical and mechanical workings of the mine. Unlike conventional contact mines, magnetic mines were almost impossible to detect and equally hard to sweep. Luckily for the British, their experts discovered how the mines worked and then devised effective countermeasures.

At the start of the war, Hitler boasted that his scientists had developed a secret weapon that could sink enemy ships undetected, leaving his opponents guessing as to what was causing their loss. It was a new type of mine—a magnetic mine. Distinct from the conventional floating contact mine, the magnetic mine lay in wait on the sea bottom for its unsuspecting victim to pass overhead to trigger its explosion.

Magnetic mines claimed their first victim on September 10, 1939, when the steamship *Magdepur* blew up and sank in Orford Ness as the result of the devastating blast of a mysterious underwater explosion. The *City of Paris* met the same fate six days later. The number of victims steadily mounted as the Germans stepped up their efforts, dropping mines by parachute from low-flying aircraft off British ports and harbors as well as laying them from U-boats and destroyers. Over the next months, a total of 76 ships were sunk.

TAKEN BY SURPRISE

The British were caught completely off guard by the mysterious new weapon. Winston Churchill, the newly appointed First Lord of the Admiralty, later conceded, "the terrible damage that could be done by large ground mines had not been fully realised." He feared that this new menace might "compass our ruin." Addressing the problem became a top naval priority. Churchill ordered the navy to locate and salvage an unexploded, undamaged mine regardless of cost.

Luckily for the British, chance came to their aid. On the night of November 21, a Luftwaffe Heinkel 111 bomber dropped the mine it was carrying short of its target. Instead, it landed on the mudflats in the Thames Estuary near Shoeburyness. The tide was on the ebb and the mine looked intact.

DISARMING A MINE

This was the opportunity for which the Admiralty had been waiting. Mine expert Lieutenant Commander John G. D. Ouvry, one of the staff of the Mines Department of HMS *Vernon* (the shore-based Torpedo and Mining School at Portsmouth, England), later recorded the story of what happened: "I was awakened at 3 a.m. the following day and instructed to catch the first available train from Portsmouth to London. I went direct to the Admiralty, where I was informed that I was required to remain at immediate notice to endeavour to discover the type and mechanism of these mines. Speed in this task was of the very greatest

importance, for our sea traffic was in danger of being brought to a standstill."

Later the next night, tired out with the strain of waiting, Ouvry checked into a hotel to get some sleep. He was woken abruptly soon after midnight by an urgent message from the Admiralty, ordering him to return at once. When he got there, he was told of the Shoeburyness discovery. His orders were to locate the mine, attempt to make it safe, and then, if successful, transport it back to Portsmouth for further investigation.

Ouvry immediately left by fast car—first for Southend and then for Shoeburyness itself. There, he and Lieutenant Commander Roger Lewis joined up with the working party Commander Maton, another naval officer attached to the Experimental Department, had already assembled. "Together we headed seaward, filled with excited anticipation," Ouvry wrote. "Guided by torches, we slithered for about 500 yards [457m] over slimy mud and sand. Occasionally, we splashed knee deep through pools. We strained our eyes in the darkness. Suddenly one of the guides, a private soldier who had seen the airborne object drop into the water in the early hours of the night, shouted, 'There it is, sir!'

"It was a very thrilling moment when the light from the torches, concentrated in the direction he indicated, revealed a glistening object with horns," Ouvry continued. "It was our intention to carry out a preliminary examination, take flashlight photographs, then lash the mine down until the daylight low-water period, when we would do our best to render it safe."

DEFUSING THE MINE

Ouvry went on to explain how he and his colleagues dealt with defusing the mine.

"We decided that Chief Petty Officer Baldwin and I should endeavour to remove the vital fittings; Lieutenant Commander Lewis and Able Seaman Vearncombe to watch from what was considered to be a safe distance and make detailed notes of our actions

and progress for reference in case of accidents," he recollected. "There was a possibility that the mine had devices other than the magnetic one, which added to the hazard. If we were unlucky, the notes which the two watchers had taken would be available for those who would have to deal with the next available specimen.

"I first tackled an aluminium fitting sealed with tallow. In order to use one of the special spanners which had been rushed through (by Commander Maton) in the local workshops for us, it was necessary to bend clear a small strip of copper. That done, we were able to

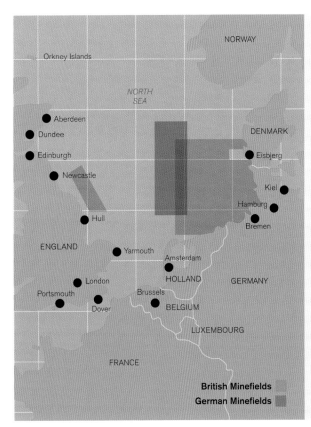

MINEFIELD LOCATIONS

Both Germany and Britain started laying minefields in the North Sea shortly after the outbreak of war in 1939. Vast numbers of mines were laid in an attempt to restrict access to British and German ports except through clearly defined channels and, more generally, to hinder the movements of all potentially hostile surface vessels and submarines. There were three types of minefield: defensive, offensive, and tactical. Defensive minefields were generally laid by surface vessels fairly close to the coast in shallower areas; offensive ones were laid farther out to sea by aircraft and submarines. Both sides were well equipped with contact mines; the Germans soon augmented these with magnetic mines and, later in the war, acoustic and pressure varieties.

extract this first fitting. Screwed into its base when we drew it clear, we found a small cylinder—obviously a detonator, for in the recess from which the fitting had been withdrawn were disks of explosive. These I removed. This mysterious fitting proved to be a delayed-action bomb fuse; it was necessary for the airman to tear off the copper strip referred to (before releasing his load) if bomb, not mine, was the requirement.

"Before we could proceed further, we had to call on Lieutenant Commander Lewis and Able Seaman Vearncombe for assistance to roll the mine over, this being firmly embedded in the hard sand and held fast by tubular horns. The fact that the mine did not, and was not intended to, float explains the non-success of our minesweepers in their efforts to secure a specimen. Lieutenant Commander Lewis and Able Seaman Vearncombe from then onwards lent a hand with the stripping down.

"Dr Wood, chief scientist of the Mine Design Department, HMS *Vernon*, arrived in time to witness the later stages. We were somewhat startled to discover yet another detonator and priming charge. Having removed all the external fittings, we signalled for the caterpillar tractor and soon had the mine ashore. We had a shock—and a laugh when the shock wore off—before we had stowed away all the removed gadgets. We stopped for a breather on the foreshore, and one of the helpers carrying a rather heavy fitting put it down on a stone. It immediately began to tick noisily. The company dispersed like lightning!"

"WIPING" AND DEGAUSSING

With the mysterious mine safely dismantled, its casing and the various components Ouvry and his team had removed were sent to HMS *Vernon*. Responsibility for discovering exactly how the device worked now passed to Wood and his two assistants. They worked night and day until they finally found what they were looking for. Deep inside the case, they located an intricate piece of

electromagnetic apparatus. When activated by a ship's steel hull passing above it, the apparatus triggered a detonator, which, in turn, set off the 660lb (299kg) of high explosive with which the mine was armed.

Once the way in which the mine worked had been discovered, devising effective countermeasures took priority. The answer was degaussing, a process in which antimagnetic cables were passed up and down a ship's side to induce a permanent antimagnetic state. This was known as "wiping." By April 1940, ten wiping stations were operational; by June, around 1,000 ships of all kinds had been wiped successfully. Hitler's much vaunted secret weapon had been rendered ineffective.

HOW MINES WERE LAID

The diagram here shows how contact mines were laid by submarine during the early part of the war. Once a mine and its sinker had been launched from the submerged submarine, its plummet released and the sinker detached itself. A windlass inside the sinker started to unwind. When the plummet struck the seabed, the windlass locked. The weight of the sinker then pulled the mine just below the sea's surface, ready to detonate if

and when a ship broke one of its horns. Such mines were also fitted with delayed-action fuses, which did not activate until the U-boat was well clear of the area. Minelaying was not popular among U-boat crews. This was because the mines were normally laid close to shore in what were usually extremely hostile waters. If detected there, the U-boat was in great danger of being attacked and sunk.

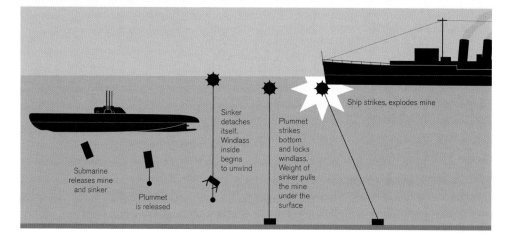

Submarine releases mine and sinker

Plummet is released

Sinker detaches itself. Windlass inside begins to unwind

Plummet strikes bottom and locks windlass. Weight of sinker pulls the mine under the surface

Ship strikes, explodes mine

THE SINKING OF THE *ROYAL OAK*

It was hardly the victorious start to the war the Royal Navy wanted. On September 17, 1939, the aircraft carrier *Courageous* was sunk, torpedoed by U-29 while carrying out an ill-advised antisubmarine sweep about 150 miles (241km) west-south-west of Mizen Head, Ireland. Captain William T. Makeig-Jones, the aircraft carrier's commander, and 519 members of the crew went down with their ship.

This was bad enough, but worse was to come. On the night of October 12, Kapitänleutnant Günther Prien, in command of U-47, penetrated Scapa Flow, Britain's great naval base in the Orkneys, and sank the battleship *Royal Oak*. The news of this second sinking was received with jubilation in Berlin and consternation at the Admiralty. The question on everyone's lips was how had a solitary U-boat manage to break through Scapa Flow's supposedly impregnable defenses?

THE VIEW FROM BERLIN

William Shirer, an American journalist based in Berlin, wrote a vivid account of how the Germans broke the news of the sinking. "The place where the German U-boat sank the British battleship *Royal Oak* was none other than Scapa Flow, Britain's greatest naval base," he noted in his diary. "It sounds incredible. A World War submarine commander told me last night that the Germans tried twice to get a U-boat into Scapa Flow during the last war, but both attempts failed and the submarines were lost."

Shirer went on to describe Prien's unexpected appearance at a hastily convened press conference. "Kapitänleutnant Prien, commander of the submarine, came tripping into our afternoon press conference at the Propaganda Ministry this afternoon, followed by his crew—boys of 18, 19, and 20," he recorded. "Prien is 30, clean-cut, cocky, a fanatical Nazi, and obviously capable. Introduced by Hitler's press chief, Dr. Dietrich,

who kept cursing the English and calling Churchill a liar, Prien told us a little of how he did it. He said he had no trouble getting past the boom protecting the bay. I got the impression, though he said nothing to justify it, that he must have followed a British craft, perhaps a minesweeper, into the base. British negligence," Shirer concluded, "must have been something terrific."

UNREADY AND UNPREPARED

Shirer was right in one respect. Scapa Flow was not as secure as British officialdom fondly believed. In fact, it was dangerously unready to serve as the Home Fleet's main anchorage. The defenses built during World War I had been allowed to fall into disrepair. The old steel underwater netting guarding Scapa Flow's main points of entry had rotted and rusted. The rest of the defenses were just as decrepit.

In May 1939, despite the sinking of an old merchantman to act as a blockship in Kirk Sound two months previously, a naval survey showed that it and Skerry Sound were still navigable. Admiral Sir William French, commanding Orkney and Shetland, confirmed this the following month. After sailing through Kirk Sound himself in a picket boat, he reported that a submarine or destroyer could make it through easily at slack water. The Admiralty decided to ignore this prescient warning. Though, soon after he was appointed First Sea Lord at the start of the war,

ROYAL OAK

Class *Revenge*-class battleship

Displacement 33,500 tons (full load)

Length 624ft 7in (190.4m)

Beam 88ft 5in (26.9m)

Draft 28ft 6in (8.7m)

Speed 21 knots

Armament Eight 15-in guns mounted in 4 turrets; 14 single 6-in guns; 25 single 3-in anti-aircraft guns; 4 single 3-pdr guns; 4 torpedo tubes

Crew 997–1,150

One of five *Revenge*-class battleships built during World War I—the others were *Revenge*, *Resolution*, *Royal Sovereign*, and *Ramillies*—*Royal Oak* fought at the battle of Jutland in 1916. It was to be her only major fleet action. Unlike some British battleships, few attempts were made to modernize her; by 1939, her slow speed rendered her obsolescent. Like the other members of her class, she was relegated to what were thought to be safer second-line duties. *Royal Oak* was torpedoed and sunk by a U-boat while at anchor in the Scapa Flow naval base in October 1939.

Royal Oak photographed peacefully, probably off Gibraltar, in 1937 while serving with the Mediterranean Fleet. She was at anchor in Scapa Flow on the night of October 13, 1939 when, having penetrated the anchorage undetected, Günther Prien, commander of U-47, launched his surprise attack at 1 a.m. the next morning. His first torpedo salvo went undetected, though one caused minor damage to the battleship's bow. The crew thought there had been some sort of internal explosion. His second, fired 20 minutes after the first, scored three perfect hits and proved fatal. She sank within ten minutes of the attack.

Churchill ordered more blockships to be sunk and new nets and booms to be installed, little or nothing had been done by the middle of October.

DÖNITZ PREPARES

For Grand Admiral Raeder, commander-in-chief of the Kriegsmarine, and Commodore Karl Dönitz, commander of its U-boat arm, Scapa Flow was particularly significant. A vision of row upon row of capital ships, taken by surprise at anchor by a U-boat attack made both men's mouths water. Even if the attacking submarine itself was lost, if it was able to sink a single British battleship, the trade-off would be more than worth it. Dönitz did not hesitate. On October 1, he summoned Prien to see him. He respected him as a skillful and daring submarine commander.

SINKING OF HMS *ROYAL OAK*

It took skilled seamanship to steer U-47 in and out of Scapa Flow in the face of its fast tides and unpredictable currents. The U-boat also had to find its way past the blockships the British had sunk in Scapa Flow's four access channels. Taking Kirk Sound and then Holm Sound as his best option, Prien took advantage of a fast incoming tide to navigate through a gap and into the calm waters of Scapa Flow itself. Having sunk *Royal Oak*, he calmly made his way out again without his U-boat being spotted.

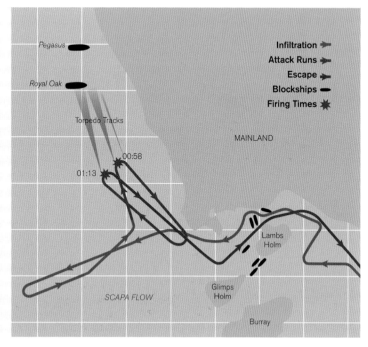

Now he had decided to entrust him with the execution of Special Operation P, one of the most daring naval missions of the entire war.

Dönitz had been planning the attack on Scapa Flow for some time. He handed over all the documentation that he had assembled for Prien to study. Aerial reconnaissance photographs, taken by the Luftwaffe as early as September 6, showed the entire British Home Fleet at anchor with antisubmarine booms and blockships notionally blocking Scapa Flow's seven entrances. Or were they? In Kirk Sound, the three blockships the British had sunk there lay just far enough apart for a U-boat to zigzag through between them in the still water just after high tide.

It would require skillful seamanship. Even in daylight, let alone at night, navigation would be tricky—14, which Dönitz had sent to scout the approaches to the Sounds, had had to battle against 10-knot riptides. Nevertheless, he concluded that "a penetration at this point (Kirk Sound) on the surface at the turn of the tide would be possible without further ceremony." The Commodore gave Prien 48 hours to say whether or not he considered the operation practical.

Prien assessed the wealth of information Dönitz had provided at home that evening. "I worked through the whole thing like a mathematical problem," he later wrote. The next day, he reported to Dönitz again. The Commodore was sitting at his desk. "He did not acknowledge my salute," Prien recalled. "It seemed he hadn't noticed it. He was looking at me fixedly and asked me 'Yes or no?'"

Prien answered simply "Yes, sir." Dönitz stood up and shook his hand. "Very well," he said. "Get your boat ready." U-47 sailed from Kiel on October 8, heading out into the North Sea, traveling on the surface at night and submerged by day.

PRIEN STRIKES

At 7:15 p.m. on October 14, U-14 cautiously surfaced off the Orkneys and edged herself forward with the tide, heading northwest toward Holm Sound. For the next four hours, the submarine battled the tide as it made its way up the sound and on into Kirk Sound, where Prien steered carefully for the elusive gap between the sunken blockships. At 12:27 a.m. precisely, U-47 entered Scapa Flow.

Prien began cruising west and then north, looking for a target. Eventually, he struck lucky. He caught sight of the dark silhouette of a battleship anchored some way off. It was *Royal Oak*, one of five *Revenge*-class battleships that had seen service during World War I. Though attempts had been made to modernize them over the years, by the start of World War II they were generally considered obsolescent, if not actually obsolete. This was largely due to their slow speed—at best they could steam at 22 knots. For this reason, Churchill dismissed them as "coffin ships."

U-47 closed in on its target. Prien fired a salvo of three torpedoes from his bow tubes, but only one of them struck home. He tried another shot from his stern tube, but this, too, missed. Then he fired another three torpedoes. This time all three hit their mark. Three monster explosions followed.

Tons of water leapt the height of *Royal Oak*'s mast, while clouds of black smoke gushed from a colossal hole in her starboard side. Her lights went out and she immediately began to heel over. "Flames shot skyward, blue … yellow … red," Prien later recalled. "Like huge birds, black shadows soared through the flames, fell hissing and splashing into the water … huge fragments of the mast and funnels." Onboard, the only light came from blazing cordite searing through the vents—"like looking into the muzzle of a blow lamp" was how a Marine survivor put it—illuminating a hellish scene of screaming, horribly burned men, stumbling about like lost souls in the flickering maze.

Prien decided to make for home. *Royal Oak* was obviously doomed—in fact, it took just minutes for the battleship to sink. With the tide now falling, U-47 had

U-BOAT TYPE VIIB

Class Attack U-boat

Displacement 753 tons (surfaced), 857 tons (submerged)

Length 211ft 7in (67.5m)

Beam 19ft (5.8m)

Draft 14ft 5in (4.4m)

Speed 16 knots (surfaced), 8 knots (submerged)

Armament Four 21-in bow torpedo tubes, one rear tube, one 88-mm deck cannon, one 20-mm anti-aircraft gun

Draft 144

The Type VIIB U-boat commanded by Günther Prien when he sank *Royal Oak* was one of seven variants. Type VIIAs were the first to enter service in June 1936; the Type Bs that followed in 1938 had a slightly lengthened hall and larger saddle tanks. Range was increased from 4,300 to 6,500 miles; Type Bs could also carry 14 torpedoes as opposed to the earlier boats' 11. Twin rudders improved maneuverability and turning radius. All in all, 709 Type VII U-boats of all variants were built during the war—more than any other submarine built by any other power.

to battle against the fierce current, but eventually she was in the open sea. Prien and his crew reached Wilhelmshaven and safety on the morning of October 17. They were immediately flown to Kiel to be welcomed by Dönitz, now promoted to the rank of Rear Admiral, and Raeder. From Kiel, they were flown to Berlin, where Prien was decorated by Hitler himself.

LOOKING FOR SCAPEGOATS

Immediately after the sinking, the search for scapegoats began. Why, for instance, had the crew of *Royal Oak* failed to realize that they were under attack as soon as Prien's first torpedo struck the ship? It appeared that many thought that the explosion had been a minor one—probably in the paint store—and that the ship's fire crew could be trusted to deal with it. Many of the ship's open portholes were never shut, with the result that seawater was free to pour through them as *Royal Oak* began to list. No one ordered the watertight hatches or doors to be closed. Nor was the order to abandon ship ever given. Out of *Royal Oak*'s 1,146-strong crew, 833 died.

It was useless blaming Rear Admiral Henry Blagrove—he had gone down with his ship. Captain William Benn and the *Royal Oak*'s other officers were exonerated by a Board of Enquiry. French was less fortunate. He was censured for the poor state of Scapa Flow's defenses and forcibly retired. British counter-intelligence was also blamed. The Admiralty was convinced that a German spy in the Orkneys must have provided the information that enabled Prien and his U-boat to reach their target. MI5 agents were rushed to the islands to flush out the elusive Nazi spy. Their search failed. Major-General Vernon Kell, the head of MI5, paid the price for failure. He, too, was forced to resign. As for Churchill, he probably only escaped blame because he was new to the job.

THE *GRAF SPEE*'S LAST VOYAGE

U-boats were not the only weapon the Kriegsmarine had at its disposal to attack Allied shipping. The *Deutschland*-class pocket battleships had been designed specifically as long-range commerce raiders. The trouble was that, as the Polish crisis escalated toward open war, only two were ready for action. *Admiral Scheer* was lying off Wilhelmshaven with much of her internal machinery dismantled for a major refit.

Admiral Graf Spee and *Deutschland* were able to sail, even though their diesel engines were due for an overhaul. This was postponed. They left German waters on September 21 and 24 respectively for their designated war stations in remote parts of the Atlantic, where they would lurk until the signal came ordering them to start their raiding activities. *Graf Spee* made for the south, while *Deutschland* stayed closer to home in the north. The former reached her destination

without being detected. *Graf Spee*, on the other hand, narrowly escaped being sighted by the cruiser *Cumberland* on passage from Rio de Janiero to Freetown. The pocket battleship's reconnaissance aircraft spotted the approaching cruiser and signaled *Graf Spee* and *Altmark*, her accompanying fuel tanker, to alter course to avoid premature discovery.

THE RAIDERS STRIKE

The order to start raiding activities came through on the night of September 25. By this time both ships had used up one quarter of their fuel and provisions, while the need to carry out the postponed engine overhaul was becoming more pressing. Nevertheless, both readied themselves for action.

Graf *Spee* was the first to strike. On September 30, she sank the British steamer *Clement*. To ensure the

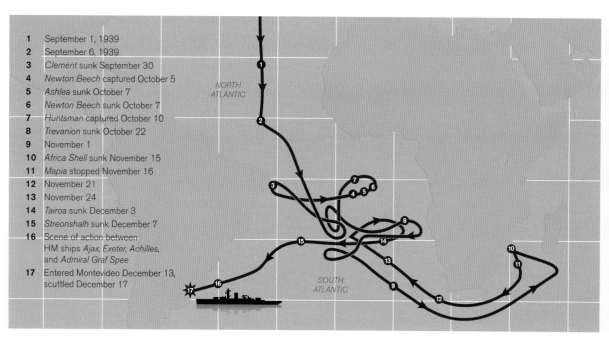

1   September 1, 1939
2   September 6, 1939
3   *Clement* sunk September 30
4   *Newton Beech* captured October 5
5   *Ashlea* sunk October 7
6   *Newton Beech* sunk October 7
7   *Huntsman* captured October 10
8   *Trevanion* sunk October 22
9   November 1
10   *Africa Shell* sunk November 15
11   *Mapia* stopped November 16
12   November 21
13   November 24
14   *Tairoa* sunk December 3
15   *Streonshalh* sunk December 7
16   Scene of action between HM ships *Ajax, Exeter, Achilles,* and *Admiral Graf Spee*
17   Entered Montevideo December 13, scuttled December 17

NORTH ATLANTIC

SOUTH ATLANTIC

GRAF SPEE AT WAR

Admiral Graf Spee, one of Germany's three so-called pocket battleships, sailed from Wilhelmshaven, her home port, on August 21,1939, shortly before the outbreak of war. Her destination was the South Atlantic, where, if war came, her mission was to attack British merchant shipping. She received the order to commence hostilities on September 26. Between then and December 17, when she scuttled herself off Montevideo harbor in the River Plate estuary, *Graf Spee* sank nine British merchant ships and captured two others in the South Atlantic and during a two-week sortie into the Indian Ocean. She also stopped and then released a neutral Dutch vessel. Her clash 240 miles off the eastern coast of Uruguay with the British cruisers *Exeter, Ajax,* and *Achilles* proved her undoing.

crew's safety, Captain Hans Langsdorff, her commander, radioed the Brazilian naval authorities to inform them of his attack. Alerted to the presence of a German raider in the South Atlantic, the Royal and French Navies formed eight task forces with orders to hunt Langsdorff down.

It was a formidable collection of naval power, consisting of 2 battleships, 1 battlecruiser, 4 aircraft carriers, and 16 cruisers. Force F (the cruisers *Berwick* and *York*) patrolled between North America and the West Indies; Force G (the cruisers *Exeter*, *Cumberland*, *Ajax*, and *Achilles*) was assigned to the east coast of South America; Force H (the cruisers *Sussex* and *Shropshire*) patrolled the Cape of Good Hope; Force T (the aircraft carrier *Eagle* and the cruisers *Cornwall* and *Dorsetshire)* was in the southern Indian Ocean; Force K (the battleship *Renown* and the aircraft carrier *Ark Royal*) patrolled off the Brazilian coast; Force L (the battleship *Dunkerque*, the aircraft carrier *Bearn,* and the cruisers *Georges Leygues*, *Gloire,* and *Montcalm*) operated in the Atlantic from Brest; Force M (the cruisers *Dupleix* and *Foch*) in West African waters; and Force N (the battleship *Strasbourg*, the aircraft carrier *Hermes,* and the cruiser *Neptune*) in the West Indies.

With thousands of miles of sea to patrol, locating the pocket battleships was like looking for the proverbial needle in a haystack. On October 5, *Graf Spee* captured the cargo ship *Newton Beach* and, two days later, sank the freighter *Ashlea*. She then captured *Huntsman* on October 10. After sinking *Trevanion* on October 22, she made for the Indian Ocean, where she sank the tanker *Africa Star* on November 15. She then doubled back into the Atlantic to meet *Altmark* and refuel.

The only success the Allied task forces had to show for all their efforts was the sinking of the supply ship *Emmy Friedrichs* while she was on her way to rendezvous the pocket battleship. They still had no clue as to the *Graf Spee*'s whereabouts. *Deutschland*, in the meantime, after sinking just two ships, had been

Graf Spee photographed from the air in April 1939 while underway in the English Channel en route to take part in Atlantic naval maneuvers with her two sister-ships *Admiral Scheer* and *Deutschland*, the cruisers *Leipzig*, *Kruizer,* and *Kiln*, a destroyer, submarine flotillas, and their accompanying U-boat ship. Laid down in 1932 in Wilhelmshaven and launched two years later, she was designated the Kriegsmarine's new flagship after she had completed her sea trials successfully.

recalled to Germany, managing to make her home port without ever having been sighted.

BROUGHT TO BAY
This left *Graf Spee* as the only pocket battleship still at sea. She scored another success when she intercepted and sank the cargo ship *Doric Star*, but this proved to be her undoing. Despite being warned not to attempt to transmit a distress call, the *Doric Star*'s wireless operator pluckily managed to send out an RRRR

(raider alert) call, at the same time giving his ship's position.

At last, the Allies had something firm to go on. Though Langsdorff sunk two more ships—*Tairoa* on December 3 and *Streonshalh* four days later—the net was starting to close in on him. It was Commodore Henry Harwood, commanding Force G, who successfully anticipated Langsdorff's decision to shift operations to the River Plate estuary. Accordingly, Force G's one heavy cruiser and two light cruisers (*Cumberland*, Harwood's second heavy cruiser, was refitting in the Falkland Islands) steamed toward the South American coast. They arrived off the River Plate on December 12, the day before *Graf Spee*—cruising at a reduced speed of 15 knots to save fuel—reached the area.

Spotting smoke on the horizon, Harwood ordered *Exeter*, his heavy cruiser, to investigate. She signaled that she had sighted "what appears to be a pocket battleship." The British ships readied themselves for action. Langsdorff, for his part, believed he was facing a group of destroyers, probably escorting a convoy. He ordered *Graf Spee* to accelerate to its maximum speed of 22 knots in order to close with the enemy. This proved to be a critical mistake. Had the German captain realized that he was up against British cruisers, he would probably stood off them and used his 11-inch main armament to shell them mercilessly before they could get within range. *Exeter* was equipped with eight-inch guns, while *Ajax* and *Achilles* carried only six-inchers.

Graf Spee opened fire on *Exeter* at 6:18 a.m., the British ship replying two minutes later. *Ajax* and *Achilles* struggled to shorten the range enough to join in the fight. For the next 30 minutes, the German gunners hammered *Exeter*, putting both its forward gun turrets out of action and starting several fires onboard. In return, *Exeter* succeeded in seriously

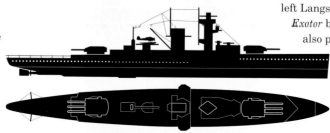

ADMIRAL GRAF SPEE

Class *Deutschland*-class pocket battleship

Displacement 16,200 tons

Length 610ft (185.9m)

Beam 70ft (21.3m)

Draft 19ft (5.8m)

Speed 28 knots

Armament Six 11-in guns in three main turrets, eight 5.9-in guns, 16 105-mm dual purpose cannon, nine 37-mm and ten 20-mm anti-aircraft guns

Crew 1,150

Supposedly built to meet the stipulations of the Treaty of Versailles, which limited her displacement to 10,000 tons, *Graf Spee* topped 16,000 tons when completed, even though her designers had tried to save as much weight as possible during her construction. To this end, her hull was electrically welded rather than riveted, while, instead of conventional boilers and steam turbines, she was powered by eight MAN diesel engines producing 56,000 horsepower between them. Diesel power also extended *Graf Spee*'s operational range, allowing her to travel 12,500 miles without the need for refueling.

damaging *Graf Spee*'s fuel processing system; its loss left Langsdorff with only 16 hours of usable fuel.

Exeter battled on until her last eight-inch turret was also put out of action. To stop *Graf Spee* moving in for the kill, *Ajax* and *Achilles* launched their own attack. The two sides continued the fight until around 7:25 a.m., when, a torpedo attack having been unsuccessful and *Ajax* and *Achilles* damaged, both ships pulled back. Harwood decided to shadow *Graf Spee*—now steaming westward under the cover of a smoke screen—until nightfall, his plan being to resume the attack after dark.

TRAPPED AND SCUTTLED

Harwood was determined to resume the battle, even though, as he wryly admitted, despite the hits his six-inch guns had inflicted on *Graf Spee*, "we might as well have being throwing snowballs at her." In fact, the British ships had done more damage than they realized—enough for Langsdorff to decide to head for the nearest neutral port to make repairs. On December 14, he dropped anchor at Montevideo in Uruguay.

The battle continued—this time on the diplomatic front. The Germans asked for two weeks to make repairs; the British demanded that Uruguay stick to the terms of the Hague Convention and expel *Graf Spee* after 24 hours. They also set their undercover agents to work. Rumors spread like wildfire that Force H, including the battlecruiser *Renown* and the aircraft carrier *Ark Royal*, was about to arrive to reinforce Harwood's battered squadron. In fact, it was still 1,000 miles (1,609km) away. *Exeter*, too, was out of the fight. Listing heavily to starboard and still burning forward, she made for the Falkland Islands 1,200 miles (1,931km) away. *Cumberland*, which had cut short its refit, arrived to replace her.

Langsdorff believed the rumors. He was now faced with three possibilities. He could sail out and resume the battle, allow his ship to be interned, or scuttle her. Hitler ruled out internment as an option. Langsdorff believed that *Graf Spee* faced certain destruction if she was left out to sea. He decided to sink her himself.

On the late afternoon of December 17, *Graf Spee*, manned by a skeleton crew, steamed slowly out of Montevideo harbor. When she reached the end of Uruguayan territorial waters, she stopped and the skeleton crew disembarked. Captain Henry Daniels, the special correspondent in Montevideo for the *Daily Telegraph*, described the scene:

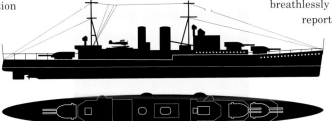

EXETER

Class	*York*-class heavy cruiser
Displacement	10,500 tons (full load)
Length	540ft (164.6m)
Beam	58ft (17.7m)
Draft	20ft 6in (6.2m)
Speed	32 knots
Armament	Six 8-in guns in three main turrets, four 4-in anti-aircraft guns, two 2-pdr anti-aircraft guns, six torpedo tubes
Crew	630

Exeter differed from her sister-ship *York* in a number of significant ways. Her bridge was more compact and lower, while her funnels were upright and not raked. After war broke out, her anti-aircraft armament was also improved by equipping her with quadruple ½-inch machine gun mountings. Heavily damaged by *Graf Spee* during the battle of the River Plate estuary, she underwent a major reconstruction on her return to the UK before being despatched to the Far East, where she was sunk in the Java Sea by the Japanese on March 1, 1942.

▲ Hitler is taken aback as a rock labeled "*Graf Spee* Defeat" is thrown at him through a window, smashing his coffee cup, labeled "Bremen Escape." When the crack German transatlantic liner *Bremen* successfully ran the British blockade to reach Hamburg, its home port, German propaganda immediately claimed this as a significant victory. The decision to scuttle *Graf Spee* to avoid her potential sinking by the Royal Navy or her forced internment in a neutral South American port was seen by the outside world as a major Nazi defeat.

"All Montevideo's quays, piers, breakwaters, and adjacent coastline were densely crowded with people breathlessly watching the German corsair," Daniels reported. "The crowds stood silent as the great ship passed to sea. Suddenly she turned, not as they expected to seaward where the ships of Britain watched, but westward towards the setting sun … Her speed dropped to dead slow, then she stuck her nose into a mud bank and stopped and her anchor was dropped.

"The hour was 8 p.m. and the sun was dipping below the river's western rim. Suddenly, there was a flash of flame and a double explosion which shook the air, and the centre of the ship was blotted from view by a cloud of dense black smoke. The concussion had not died away before a blinding burst of flame shot from the after part of the ship high above her masthead, and a thunderous roar deafened the ears of the watching crowds. The whole ship seemed to light and crumple as though inferno itself had burst forth from her vitals.

"Sheets of flame spread over the tranquil sea as the oil from the bunkers of the riven ship came to the surface and caught fire. Dense clouds of smoke rose in the air, and soon the wreck was a blazing inferno from stem to stern. It was the end of the tragedy."

It was not quite the end, however. Taken to Buenos Aires with his surviving crew, Langsdorff shot himself in his hotel room on December 19, lying prone on the *Graf Spee*'s battle standard. In a last letter he wrote: "I alone bear the responsibility for scuttling the pocket battleship *Admiral Graf Spee*. I am happy to pay with my life for any possible reflection on the honors of the flag. I shall face my fate with firm faith in the cause and future of the nation and of my Führer." He was the battle's last victim.

LEFT AND OPPOSITE It took the fires onboard *Graf Spee* four days to burn out after Hans Langsdorff, her captain, had ordered her to be blown up and scuttled in the estuary of the River Plate. The German commander believed, thanks to a British intelligence deception, that he faced certain destruction if he put out to sea to fight again. In fact, *Renown* and *Ark Royal*, the battlecruiser and aircraft carrier Langsdorff was convinced had joined the two cruisers still lying in wait for him, were hundreds of miles away. He signaled Berlin: "Close blockade at night; escape into open sea and breakthrough to home waters is hopeless. Request decision on whether the ship should be scuttled in spite of insufficient depth in the estuary of the Plate, or whether internment is preferred." The terse reply read: "No internment in Uruguay. Attempt effective destruction if the ship is scuttled."

Graf Spee's last captain made his ship's last moments as dramatic as possible. The first explosion onboard her took place exactly as the sun set, while the pocket battleship's skeleton crew, lining the deck of the German merchant ship *Taconna*, gave the Nazi salute. An estimated 500,000 spectators were watching from the shore.

INVASION OF NORWAY

A few months into World War II, Hitler took a huge strategic gamble. He and his military advisers knew that unimpeded access to Norwegian coastal waters was vital for the transport of Swedish iron ore via Narvik to fuel the Third Reich's blast furnaces. And, more generally, they appreciated that gaining control of Norway's ports and harbors would make breaking the British naval blockade of Germany a little easier.

Grand Admiral Erich Raeder, commander-in-chief of the Kriegsmarine, had started pressing the Führer to take action as early as October 1939. He argued that Germany's failure to extend its northwest flank in World War I had led to the bottling up of the Imperial High Seas Fleet in its bases and to the famine caused by the Allied blockade, which had contributed so greatly to eventual German capitulation.

THE *ALTMARK* INCIDENT
The meeting Raeder brokered between Hitler and Vidkun Quisling, the leader of the Norwegian Fascist Party, was one of the two factors that persuaded the Führer that an Allied intervention in Norway was one of the cards. The other was the so-called *Altmark* incident.

Altmark, the German tanker which had been supplying *Graf Spee* with fuel, had been ordered to head for home from the South Atlantic where she had been skulking since the pocket battleship's scuttling, on January 22, 1940. She had 299 prisoners from the British merchant ships *Graf Spee* had sunk onboard. Avoiding the usual shipping lanes, she made her way through the Denmark Strait between the Faroe Islands and Iceland to reach Norwegian territorial waters on February 14. Captain Heinrich Dau, *Altmark*'s commander, planned to creep stealthily down the coast to avoid British interception.

"THE NAVY'S HERE!"
The Norwegians inspected *Altmark* briefly three times, each time accepting Dau's assurances that she was unarmed and trading peacefully. They never checked the holds despite all the efforts the prisoners made to try to attract their attention. The British were not so easily fooled. After *Altmark* was sighted by an RAF search plane off Bergen on February 16, Captain Philip Vian, commander of the 4th Destroyer *Flotilla*, was ordered to intercept her.

Later that afternoon, the light cruiser *Arethusa* spotted *Altmark*, escorted by two Norwegian torpedo boats, and two of Vian's destroyers started to close on her. Ignoring orders to heave to, the tanker dodged into Josing Fjord, while the torpedo boats blocked off the entrance. The Norwegians refused the British demand to be allowed to board the tanker and search her themselves.

It looked like a standoff. Then Churchill personally intervened. He ordered Vian to go ahead with or without Norwegian cooperation. At around 11:20 p.m., *Cossack*, Vian's command vessel, moved in on *Altmark*, which unsuccessfully tried to ram her before running aground. The boarding party swarmed onto the tanker. After a brief struggle, in which four of *Altmark*'s crew were killed and five wounded, the British had control of the ship. Opening the hatch of one of the holds, a sailor called down, "Are there any Englishmen down there?" Upon hearing a positive answer, he called again, "Then come up. The navy's here!"

OPERATION WESERUBUNG
Hitler's reaction was predictably violent. It was as if someone had trodden on a particularly painful corn on his foot. He ordered planning to start immediately for the simultaneous invasion of Norway and Denmark. The date for the operation to start was set for April 9. It looked to the Führer as if he had acted in the nick of time. The day before, British warships mined the waters around Narvik. The race to secure Norway had started.

In Denmark, the invasion went almost without a hitch—the only hiccup was when the old battleship *Schleswig-Holstein* ran aground. The Germans crossed

One of three Coastal Command Hudson reconnaissance aircrafts photographed the German oil tanker *Altmark* sheltering in a Norwegian fjord where she had taken refuge after her attempted interception by the light cruiser *Arethusa* and Captain Philip Vian's 4th Destroyer *Flotilla* off the southern cost of Norway. *Altmark* had been *Graf Spee*'s supply ship and was now trying to take advantage of Norwegian neutrality to sneak her way back to Germany with 299 of the British prisoners the pocket battleship had captured onboard. Her captain had successfully managed to conceal their presence from the Norwegians when he entered neutral waters, but Vian was not so easily fooled. Following direct orders from Winston Churchill, he followed *Altmark* into the fjord.

The destroyer *Cossack* steamed straight for *Altmark*, with a boarding party standing by ready to board. *Altmark* attempted to ram her, but only succeeded in running aground. The boarding party took control of the tanker, locating and freeing all the prisoners, who were quickly transferred to *Cossack*. Having completed his mission, Vian steamed for home at full speed. The incident was the catalyst that led Hitler to order planning for an invasion of Norway to be intensified.

the frontier at 5:30 a.m. on April 9; at 7:30 a.m., the Danish government ordered a ceasefire. In Norway, however, the invaders encountered stiffer resistance.

In Oslo Fjord, the brand-new heavy cruiser *Blücher* was sunk by a single shell from a Norwegian coastal battery, which hit her in the magazine as she passed through the narrows near Oscarsborg. The accompanying ships were forced to turn back, so delaying the occupation of the capital and allowing the members of the Norwegian government and royal family to escape the Germans. Her sister-ship, *Admiral Hipper*, was also damaged when she was rammed by

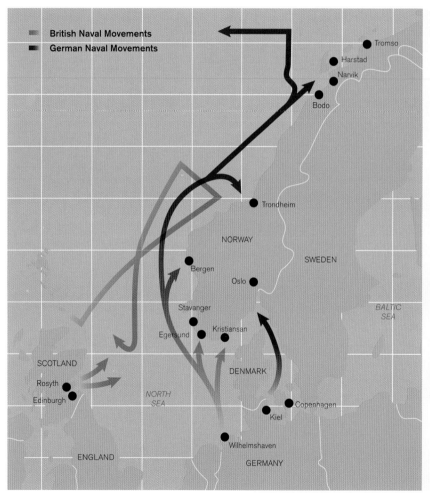

INVADING NORWAY

This map charts British and German naval movements at the start of Germany's invasion of neutral Norway in April 1940. Hitler was prepared to risk a confrontation with the British Home Fleet in order to reinforce the bridgeheads his airborne troops quickly established in the country, reasoning that the Luftwaffe's total air superiority would more than counterbalance the Kriegsmarine's numerical inferiority. Despite the loss of the cruiser *Blücher*—sunk by a Norwegian shore battery as she neared Oslo—and the extensive damage inflicted on *Admiral Hipper* when a British destroyer rammed her, the Führer was proved right. The Kriegsmarine succeeded in landing troops at Bergen, Stavanger, Egersund, Kristiansand, Arendal, Horton, Trondheim, and Narvik virtually unopposed.

the British destroyer *Glowworm*, but she was still able to help take the city of Trondheim.

The light cruiser *Karlsruhe* led the assault on Kristiansand, but was sunk later the same day by the British submarine *Truant*. Her sister-ship, *Königsberg*, having been damaged by Norwegian shore batteries at Bergen, was finished off by British Skua dive bombers flying from the Orkneys. She was the first major warship ever to be sunk from the air.

INTO ACTION AT NARVIK

In the far north at Narvik, the most important strategic objective of the entire campaign, ten German destroyers managed to land the Alpine troops they were transporting, sinking two coastal defence vessels in the process. Captain Bernard Warburton-Lee, commanding a five-ship-strong destroyer flotilla, was ordered to attack them. At 4 a.m. on April 10, with a blinding snowstorm raging, *Hardy* led *Hotspur*, *Havoc*, *Hunter*, and *Hostile* into the harbor.

A torpedo from *Hardy* blew off the stern of the German flagship *Wilhelm Heidkamp* and killed Commodore Friedrich Bonte, the flotilla commander. A second destroyer was sunk by two torpedoes and three more were damaged by gunfire. Six out of the eight German merchant ships in the harbor were sunk.

If Warburton-Lee's intelligence had been accurate, there should have been only one German destroyer left. In fact, there were five of them. They swiftly steamed back from the adjacent fjords to launch a counterattack. In it, *Hardy* was badly damaged, and had to be beached. *Hunter* was sunk outright and *Hotspur*, too, was badly damaged, but the two other British destroyers managed to rescue her. As for Warburton-Lee, he was mortally wounded by a shell which hit *Hardy*'s bridge. His last signal was "Continue to engage the enemy."

The British were not done with Narvik yet. Vice-Admiral William Whitworth onboard the battleship

Warspite, together with nine destroyers, resumed the attack three days later. *Kuinne*, *Ludemann*, *Zenker*, and *Armin* were quickly sunk. The remaining German destroyers were pursued by *Eskimo*, *Bedouin Forester*, *Hero*, and *Icarus*. Only U-51 made it to the open sea.

SEA POWER CONFRONTS AIR POWER

Whitworth had one crucial advantage; the Luftwaffe, as yet, was unable to provide effective air cover for the Kriegsmarine ships at Narvik. Whitworth himself— this time in the battlecruiser *Renown*—had also fought a brief engagement off Narvik with the battlecruisers *Scharnhorst* and *Gneisenau*, but the Germans, though hit several times, were able to use their superior speed to disappear into a snow squall.

▲ Grand Admiral Eric Raeder, commander-in-chief of the Kriegsmarine, inspects a guard of honor. He had been urging Hitler to intervene in Scandinavia since the previous October. Churchill might thunder that the invasion of Norway was "as great a strategical error as the one Napoleon made when he invaded Spain" but, like the Führer, Raeder was prepared to take the risk, even though he privately admitted in his diary that his fleet was "in no way sufficiently armed for the great struggle against England."

Further south, it was a different story. Admiral Sir Charles Forbes, commander-in-chief of the Home Fleet, was not as lucky. He first came up against the Luftwaffe on the afternoon of April 9 off southern Norway. There he only lost the destroyer *Gurkha* to air attack, he considered that the risks were too great to continue trying to operate in those waters. *Furious*, the aircraft carrier sailing with him, had no fighters onboard. Nor could the fleet's anti-aircraft defense

provide it with sufficient protection. Rather than taking the offensive against German transport shipping as had been the original attention, Forbes instead was reduced to convoying Allied troops to Namsos and Andalsnes, where they were landed with the intention of launching a two-pronged attack on Trondheim.

The land campaign was an unmitigated disaster from start to finish. Though Narvik was finally recaptured on May 28, the German blitzkrieg in the

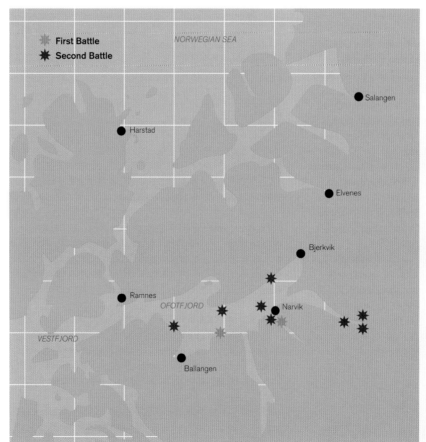

CLASHES AT NARVIK

Though caught off guard by the German invasion—the Admiralty had thought the Kriegsmarine was concentrating for an Atlantic breakout—the British navy was quick to respond. On April 10, a flotilla of five destroyers, commanded by Captain Bernard Warburton-Lee, took on the ten German destroyers that had arrived at Narvik the previous day. After landing the troops they had been transporting, the Germans had dispersed. Five destroyers remained in Narvik, two deployed in a neighboring fjord to the west and the remaining three to the north.

Warburton-Lee managed to destroy 2 destroyers and sink 11 German merchantmen and a supply ship before withdrawing. He and Commodore Friedrich Bonte, his German opposite number, were both killed. Three days later, the British returned to the attack with the battleship *Warspite* and nine more destroyers. They sank three more of their opponents—the remaining five destroyers, after suffering crippling damage, were scuttled by the Germans themselves.

Low Countries and France made its abandonment inevitable. Indeed, the decision to withdraw from it was made even before it was taken. Mercilessly bombarded from the air, Namsos and Andalsnes had already been forcibly evacuated.

LOSS OF *GLORIOUS*

The Admiralty assembled a large convoy with covering warships—including *Glorious* and *Ark Royal*—to undertake the evacuation. Once they were well out at sea, Captain Guy D'Oyly-Hughes, commanding *Glorious,* asked and received permission to leave the convoy and make independently for Scapa Flow.

It is unclear why D'Oyly-Hughes left the safety of the larger force and *Ark Royal*. Possibly fuel shortage demanded that he sail a more direct route; or possibly he was anxious to get on with the court-martial proceedings he had instigated against one of his officers after an earlier action. Whatever the reason, it was a fateful decision for *Glorious* and her two escorting destroyers. What is clear is that none of the ships was in a high state of readiness when they were intercepted by *Scharnhorst* and *Gneisenau*.

First contact was reported on *Scharnhorst* at 4:46 p.m.; at 5:01 p.m., *Glorious* picked up the Germans on her radar. The aircraft carrier desperately tried to increase her speed by firing up all her boilers, while getting her Fairey Swordfish torpedo bombers up onto her flight deck. As *Scharnhorst* and *Gneisenau* were to windward of her, she had to steam toward them in order to launch her planes.

Acasta and *Ardent* were steaming either side of *Glorious* and slightly ahead of her. Being nearer the two battlecruisers, *Ardent* valiantly interposed itself between *Glorious* and the German warships and started laying a smokescreen. *Acasta* started to make smoke as well. On *Glorious*, the first Swordfish were on deck, armed with torpedoes, by 5:34 p.m.

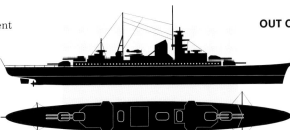

SCHARNHORST

Class *Scharnhorst*-class battlecruiser

Displacement 38,900 tons (full load)

Length 741ft 6in (226m)

Beam 100ft (30.5m)

Draft 32ft (9.8m)

Speed 32 knots

Armament Nine 11-in guns in three main turrets, 12 5.9-in guns (four each in two turrets and four in one turret), 14 4.1-in guns, 16 37-mm anti-aircraft cannon

Crew 1,800

Together with her sister-ship *Gneisenau*, *Scharnhorst* redefined conventional battlecruiser design. Traditionally, such ships had been fast, heavily armed, but only lightly armored. The two German ships, by contrast, were given heavy armor protection. To avoid the reduction in speed this otherwise would have entailed, their main armament was reduced in weight by the employment of nine 11-inch rather than 15-inch guns. These proved adequate for most purposes. In the early months of the war, both ships enjoyed considerable operational success, making two sorties into the Atlantic, where their victims included the armed merchant cruiser *Rawalpindi*. During the Norwegian campaign, they intercepted and sank the aircraft carrier *Glorious*.

OUT OF ACTION AND SINKING

Just three minutes later, *Scharnhorst*'s third salvo struck home, smashing through *Glorious*'s flight deck and starting a fire in the hanger beneath it. Another salvo struck the bridge, killing D'Oyly-Hughes and almost all of the bridge personnel. After the main engine room was hit, *Glorious* slowed, started to list, and began circling to port. She sank at 6:10 p.m. *Ardent* had preceded her, sinking at 5:25 p.m. *Acasta* finally went down at 6:20 p.m. The total death toll for the three ships amounted to 94 officers, 1,380 ratings, and 41 RAF personnel.

The Germans did not get off scot-free. *Acasta* managed to torpedo *Scharnhorst* before she sank, inflicting substantial damage on her. Shortly afterward, *Gneisenau* was also torpedoed by the British submarine *Clyde*. These were by no means the only German naval casualties. Raeder had deployed practically the entire strength of the Kriegsmarine in the battle. By the end of the campaign, it had only three cruisers and four destroyers fit for combat. In addition to their other losses, the British cruisers *Suffolk* and *Effingham* were put out of action and the anti-aircraft cruiser *Curlew* sunk. A French cruiser was seriously damaged and seven British destroyers, one French destroyer, and one Free Polish destroyer were lost.

On the surface, it looked like a clear-cut German victory. In practice, the naval casualties the Germans incurred meant that, when the time came later that summer, the Kriegsmarine was unable to contest the command of the English Channel and incapable of covering a cross-Channel invasion. Its weakness meant that, had Operation Sealion ever been launched, it would almost certainly have been doomed to fail.

THE DUNKIRK EVACUATION

In May 1940, as Hitler's victorious panzers thrust forward toward the English Channel, threatening to encircle the Allied armies in Flanders, General Lord Gort, commander-in-chief of the British Expeditionary Force (BEF), was on the horns of a dilemma. He could follow Churchill's orders and attack southward, attempting to bludgeon his way through the so-called "panzer corridor" to join up with the French on the Somme. Or he could fall back toward the Channel coast, from where it was hoped the navy might be able to extricate the BEF successfully.

Gort chose the second alternative. Lieutenant-Colonel Robert Bridgeman, the BEF's acting Director of Operations, was ordered to draw up a plan for the withdrawal. Pouring over his maps, Bridgeman decided that the best bet was the 27-mile (43-km) stretch of coast between Ostend and Dunkirk. The latter was to be the linchpin of the entire evacuation.

LOOKING FOR A MIRACLE

As the BEF's troops began their fighting retreat back toward the Flemish coast, Admiral Operation Dynamo, the code name for the evacuation, was hastily set in motion. Vice Admiral Sir Bertram Ramsey, in charge of Dover Command, was put in charge of the operation.

No one believed that more than a handful of the BEF would be evacuated successfully. The Admiralty told Ramsey that the immediate aim was to rescue up to 45,000 men of the BEF within two days "at the end of which it was probable that the evacuation would be terminated by enemy action." General Sir Edmund Ironside, Chief of the Imperial General Staff, reckoned privately that the British would be lucky to evacuate 30,000 men. "God help the BEF," he raged in his diary, "brought to this state by the incompetence of the French Command." General Sir John Dill, Ironside's successor, stated bluntly that "militarily, there is only a remote chance that any considerable formation of the BEF will be able to extricate itself in the encircled position."

Gort was just as pessimistic. "I must not conceal from you," he signaled Anthony Eden, Churchill's new Secretary of State for War, "that a great part of the BEF and its equipment will inevitably be lost even in the best circumstances." Lieutenant-General Henry Pownall, Gort's Chief of Staff, was similarly resigned to disaster. "And so here we are back on the shores of France on which we landed with such high hearts over eight months ago," he lamented. "I think we were a gallant band who little deserves this ignominious end to our efforts." Even the ever-optimistic Churchill braced the House of Commons to expect the worst. He told MPs "to prepare themselves for hard and heavy tidings." It seemed that nothing but a miracle could save the BEF from complete and utter disaster.

THE EVACUATION BEGINS

Operation Dynamo got off to a shaky start. By the evening of May 27, only 7,669 men had been embarked. Ramsey had been gathering together as many destroyers and suitable merchant vessels together as quickly as he could—he stipulated that the latter must be capable of ferrying at least 1,000 men at a time back across the Channel. It all took time—and this was a luxury the British did not possess. So, too, did establishing the best sea routes to use.

There were three of these—Routes Y, Z, and Y. The last, with a length of 87 nautical miles, was the longest, but the safest, Route X, which was only 39 nautical miles long, was the shortest, but, because it was in range of German artillery at Gravelines and near Calais, could not be used during the hours of daylight after May 27. Route X, which was 55 nautical miles in length, supplemented it from 29 May.

As if this was not enough, Dunkirk was coming under increasingly heavy aerial attack by the Luftwaffe. Though Hitler's sudden and inexplicable decision to halt his panzers short of the town won the BEF the breathing space it needed to reinforce its perimeter

Allied troops patiently await evacuation from Dunkirk between May 27 and June 4, 1940. The Royal Navy was tasked with getting as many of these as troops possible off the beaches and back to safety before the Germans panzers moved in on the port. At the start, military experts doubted 50,000 would be lucky enough to be evacuated; by the time Operation Dynamo, as it was called, came to an end, 338,226 British, French, and Belgian troops had been snatched from the shore, rescuers and rescued defying almost constant Luftwaffe bombardment. They were forced, however, to leave all their heavy equipment behind.

defenses, Goering assured him that his bombers would put a stop to any attempt at evacuation. The Luftwaffe's most impressive series of attacks targeted ten British ships, which, during the afternoon of 29 May, were moored alongside Dunkirk's harbor mole. They put three of them out of action.

The destroyer *Jaguar* was one of them. She had taken onboard around 1,000 soldiers and was steaming out of the harbor when the Luftwaffe struck. Though no bombs actually hit the ship, one landed in the sea just a couple of yards away and exploded. Following the explosion, there was a terrifying roar, as steam escaped from *Jaguar*'s shattered steam-pipes. Then her engines

stopped. What one of her officers described as "a deathly hush" followed. Fortunately, another destroyer was able to come to her assistance. *Grenade* was not as fortunate. She suffered a direct hit while she was tied up to the mole. The crew were forced to abandon her. She sank while being towed clear of the harbor entrance after a massive internal explosion. *Crested Eagle*, a paddle steamer moored to the other side of the mole, was the third casualty.

Out at sea, too, ship after ship was sunk or put out of action. When the news reached London, the Admiralty decided the losses were insupportable. It withdrew the seven fleet destroyers that Ramsey had remaining,

▲ The destroyer *Jaguar* drops a depth charge to deter U-boat attack while on her way to pick up troops awaiting evacuation at Dunkirk. Previously, she had helped to rescue survivors from the coastal steamer *Abukir*, which had been sunk by a German S-boat while carrying more than 200 BEF soldiers, a party of Belgian nuns, and a group of British schoolgirls, from Ostend to safety. The S-boat proceeded to machine gun the survivors in the water before *Jaguar* and two other destroyers arrived on the scene.

leaving him with just 15 smaller and less modern ones at his disposal. He got them back only after warning his superiors that there was no way of completing the evacuation without them

THE SCENE ON THE BEACHES

Onshore, the situation frequently looked like descending into near chaos. P. D. Elliman, a young Royal Artillery Second Lieutenant, compiled a vivid description of the scene on the beach between the eastern Jetty and Malo-les-Bains after he and his men arrived there during the early afternoon of May 29. "The tide was fairly low," Elliman wrote. "A steamer lay on her side at the water's edge. The sandy beach was about 100 yards [91m] wide. Down the centre stood the line of men three abreast. The smoke from the burning oil tanks drifted eastwards over the town. A few officers walked up and down. All was quiet.

"And then it started! A formation of high flyers came up from the west and dropped stick after stick of bombs. This first attack was most unnerving. You felt so completely exposed on the beach. For a time some of us huddled under the hull of the wrecked steamer, but as nothing happened for some time I called in all my men and formed them up in the queue again for fear we should lose our place."

It was a protracted game of cat and mouse between the Luftwaffe and the troops on the beaches, with the men scattering each time planes passed overhead, then rushing back to form up at the end of each attack.

EVACUATION ROUTES

Vice Admiral Sir Bertram Ramsey, in charge of Operation Dynamo from his headquarters at Dover, established three evacuations routes to and from Dunkirk across the English Channel. Route Y was the longest. It was joined by Route X, which passed to the southwest of the point where German U-boats and S-boats were now patrolling, on May 29. That was the day the evacuation reached crisis point; the Luftwaffe succeeded in either sinking or putting out of action no fewer than ten destroyers, eight personnel ships and paddle steamers in addition to a number of smaller vessels. These losses were so perturbing that seven fleet destroyers were withdrawn from Ramsey's command. It was only the following afternoon he was allowed to deploy them again. Route Z had its problems as well. After May 27, it could not be used during daylight because it was now within range of artillery batteries at Gravelines and near Calais.

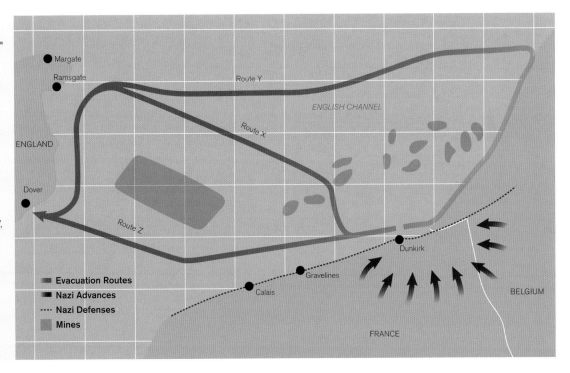

The Ju 87 dive bombers were a particular menace. "The Stukas were diving, zooming, screeching and wheeling over our heads like a flock of huge infernal seagulls," Elliman recorded.

THE DUNKIRK ARMADA

The navy was doing its best, but it was not enough, especially after Hitler rescinded his previous order and the panzers started to roll forward again. Smaller boats with shallow drafts were desperately required to lift men directly off the beaches. Some 588 of them were commandeered by the Admiralty during the evacuation; hundreds more were volunteered by their civilian owners.

The first "little ships," as they became known, arrived off Dunkirk at around noon on May 29. It was not long before their crews saw what they were up against. Arthur D. Divine was one of those manning the boats involved in the rescue.

"The picture will always remain sharp-etched in my memory—the lines of men wearily and sleepily staggering across the beach from the dunes to the shallows, falling into little boats, great columns of men thrust out into the water among bomb and shell splashes," Divine wrote. "The foremost ranks were shoulder deep, moving forward under the command of young subalterns, themselves with their heads just above the little waves that rode in to the sand. As the front ranks were dragged aboard the boats, the rear ranks moved up, from ankle deep to knee deep, from knee deep to waist deep, until they, too, came to shoulder depth and their turn.

"The little boats that ferried from the beach to the big ships in deep water listed drunkenly with the weight of men. The big ships slowly took on lists of their own with the enormous numbers crowded aboard. And always down the dunes and across the beach came new hordes of men, new columns, new lines."

Though the outlook still looked bleak, Rear Admiral William Wake-Walker, in charge of shipping off Dunkirk, was filled with renewed confidence. "I saw for the first time that strange possession of craft of all kinds that has become famous," he later recollected, "tugs towing dinghies, lifeboats and all manner of pulling boats, small motor yachts, motor launches, drifters, Dutch schoots, Thames barges, fishing boats and pleasure steamers." Divine summed it up. Not only was it "the queerest, most nondescript flotilla that ever was," but it was "manned by every kind of Englishman, never more than two men, often only one, to each small boat. There were bankers and dentists, taxi drivers and yachtsmen, longshoremen, boys, engineers, fishermen and civil servants."

Not everyone made it back home safely. Jimmy Dench, skipper of the cockle-boat *Letitia*, recorded how *Renown*, another of the "little ships" taking part in the evacuation, was lost early in the morning of June 1. "Soon we saw another boat coming up behind us," Dench wrote. "It was *Renown* and, yelling that they had engine trouble, they made fast to our stern."

A trawler was already towing *Letitia* and she, in turn, took *Renown* in tow. Dench continued: "Tired out, the engineer, seaman and signaller went to turn in as our work seemed nearly done. We were congratulating ourselves when, at about 1:50 a.m., a terrible explosion took place and a hail of wood splinters came down on our deck. In the pitch dark, you could see nothing and we could do nothing, except pull in the tow rope which was just as we passed it to *Renown* about three-quarters of an hour before."

Renown had been blown to smithereens by a mine. The same day, nine destroyers and personnel ships were sunk or put out of action, plus numerous other smaller craft. The tug *St Abbas* was one of the Luftwaffe's victims. She was literally split in two by four delayed-action bombs dropped into the water just ahead of her. It took just 45 seconds for her to sink.

Troops onboard the destroyer *Vanguard* moored alongside the mole at Dunkirk. The tide was low at the time, making it hard for them to embark; at high tide, the destroyer's deck was at the same level as the quay. Like other ships, *Vanguard* was subject to heavy air attacks, but, unlike them, she escaped virtually unscathed. *Crested Eagle*, a paddle steamer moored to the other side of the mole, was hit by four bombs in succession as she attempted to get underway. She eventually had to be beached near Bray-Dunes where she became a landmark for small ships striving to find the beach.

THE END OF THE EVACUATION

The evacuation was now entering its final stages. On June 2, shortly before 11 p.m., the last ships carrying 7,208 British and 19,803 French troops sailed for home. In all, between May 26, when a mere 3,373 members of the BEF had been evacuated, to June 2, 288,572 men had been rescued, according to Ramsey's figures.

It was not quite the end. Although Operation Dynamo had been officially terminated, Ramsey signaled the next day: "I hoped and believed that last night would see us through, but the French, who were covering the retirement of the British rearguard, had to repel a strong German attack, and so were unable to send their troops to the pier in time to be embarked. We cannot leave our allies in the lurch, and I must call on all officers and men detailed for further evacuation tonight, and let the world see that we never let down an ally." The British evacuated a further 26,995 Frenchmen. The next day, Dunkirk surrendered.

The evacuation was not confined to French troops, as Ordinary Seaman Stanley Allen, serving on the destroyer *Windsor,* recalled. "There was a little dog, a terrier-type mongrel, which came onboard with some of the soldiers. He only understood French. When I spoke to him he wouldn't leave me. He didn't understand any English, which rather tickled some of the soldiers. After Dunkirk was all over, he was collected by a PDSA van to go into quarantine for six months before he was taken on to the staff of the parish where our sub-lieutenant's father was vicar. All of us cheered the old dog off. It was a very nice human touch amongst all that carnage of Dunkirk—as although people, in spite of all, were still caring."

OPERATION SEALION

It took just six weeks of fighting before France was forced to yield to the Nazi invaders. After the French armistice was signed on June 22, 1940, Britain was left alone in the field. Hitler confidently expected that the British would swiftly follow France into capitulation.

Surrender, however, was the last thing on the vast majority of Britons' minds. Much to the Führer's disbelief, they scornfully rejected his "last appeal to reason," offering them peace terms. They were determined to continue fighting. Hitler decided to force the issue. On July 16, he issued Directive Number 16, authorizing the start of planning for the invasion of Britain. The preamble read: "As England, despite her hopeless military situation, still shows no sign of willingness to come to terms, I have decided to prepare, and if necessary to carry out, a landing operation against her. The aim of the operation," the Directive went on, "is to eliminate the English motherland as a base from which war against Germany can be continued and, if necessary, to occupy it completely."

On August 1, Hitler issued Directive Number 17, spelling out in detail what would be the first steps in Operation Sealion, as the invasion was now code-named. The Luftwaffe, he decreed, would have to drive the RAF out of the skies and win aerial supremacy over the Channel and the subsequent battlefield. A few days later, William Joyce, the renegade broadcaster whom the British had derisively nicknamed Lord Haw-Haw, warned that the Führer was determined. "I make no apology for saying again that invasion is certainly coming soon, but what I want to impress upon you is that while you must feverishly take every conceivable precaution, nothing that you or the government can do is really of the slightest use," he ranted. "Don't be deceived by this lull before the storm, because, although there is still the chance of peace, Hitler is aware of the political and economic confusion in England, and is only waiting for the right moment. Then, when his moment comes, he will strike, and strike hard."

The Führer reiterated the message when addressing a near-hysterical audience at Berlin's Sportsplatz on September 4. "In England, they are filled with curiosity and keep asking 'Why doesn't he come?,'" he taunted. "Be calm. He is coming! He is coming!"

RAEDER'S DOUBTS

The Kriegsmarine stole a march on the other two armed services when as early as October 1939 Grand Admiral Erich Raeder unilaterally instructed his Naval Operations Staff to secretly compile a feasibility study for a projected invasion of Britain. Raeder was anxious to avoid being taken by surprise in case Hitler should suddenly decide such an attempt should take place.

Though the two men had discussed the possibility of an invasion briefly several times earlier that summer, it was not until July 11, 1940 that the Grand Admiral formally put forward his views to the Führer. He told him bluntly that in his view such a landing was something that should be undertaken only as a last resort. Raeder was convinced that, without running the risk of an attempted invasion, Britain could be brought to heel by U-boat and Luftwaffe attacks on convoys and an all-out aerial bombardment of Britain's key industrial centers.

The Naval Operations Staff concurred with their commander-in-chief. "The task allocated to the Navy in Operation Sealion," they warned, "is out of all proportion to the Navy's strength." The Kriegsmarine had sustained heavy losses in the Norwegian campaign. One heavy cruiser, 2 light cruisers, 10 destroyers, 8 U-boats, 1 torpedo boat, and 13 troops transports had been sunk, while a pocket battleship, the Kriegsmarine's two battlecruisers, another heavy cruiser and one more light cruiser had been heavily damaged. This left Raeder with one heavy cruiser, two light cruisers, and four destroyers with which to contest naval command of the English Channel with the Royal Navy. The Home Fleet could field 5 battleships, 11 cruisers and 30 destroyers against him, reinforced

INVASION 1940

The original plan for Operation Sealion, the projected German invasion of Britain, was drawn up by Grand Admiral Raeder's naval staff in November 1939 and presented to Hitler for approval on May 31, 1940. He and the army high command rejected it. It took until the end of August to produce a revised plan that the Führer considered practical. The invasion was now to be launched on a narrower front than originally proposed, stretching between Beachy Head and Dover. It was to start only when the Luftwaffe had wiped out RAF Fighter Command and achieved absolute air superiority. Its failure to do so led Hitler to postpone Sealion until the following year on September 17, and then to abandon the idea of an invasion completely on January 9, 1941. For his part, Raeder told the Führer he regarded invasion as a last resort in order to bring the British to the negotiating table.

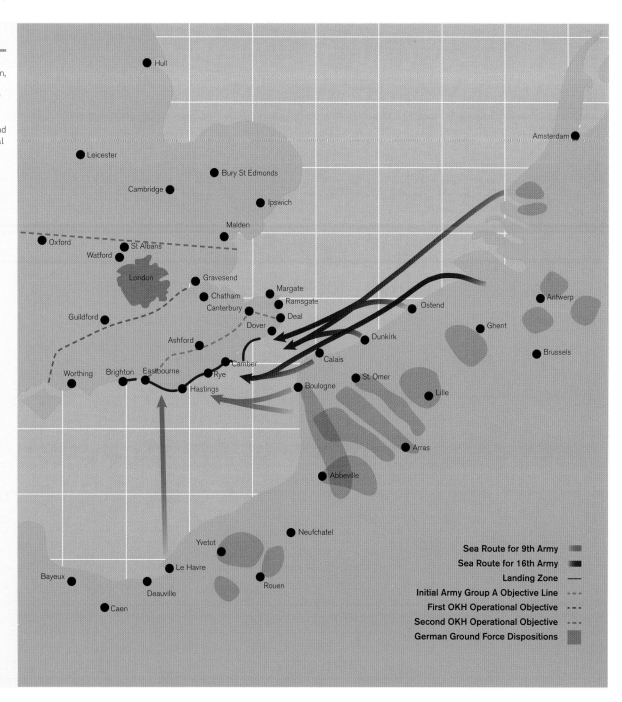

Sea Route for 9th Army
Sea Route for 16th Army
Landing Zone
Initial Army Group A Objective Line
First OKH Operational Objective
Second OKH Operational Objective
German Ground Force Dispositions

if necessary by Force H, which consisted of 2 battleships, 2 battlecruisers, 3 aircraft carriers, and 5 cruisers all based at Gibraltar.

It was clear that the British enjoyed a commanding naval superiority. To overcome this, Raeder insisted that the Luftwaffe had to establish complete dominance of the skies above the English Channel before Operation Sealion was launched. If the Luftwaffe failed, Sealion would have to be delayed or, at worst, abandoned completely.

CONFUSION AT THE TOP

Even the Führer had his doubts about Sealion's feasibility. He conceded that it was "an exceptionally bold and dangerous operation," warning that, "even if the way is short, this is not just a river crossing, but the crossing of a sea which is dominated by the enemy." Nevertheless, he ordered invasion preparations to be intensified.

Above all, Hitler was determined to keep all his options open. Air attacks, he ordained, should begin immediately. "If the results of air warfare are unsatisfactory," he told his subordinates, "invasion preparations will be stopped." If, on the other hand, "we have the impression that the English are crushed and that effects will soon begin to tell, we shall proceed to the attack." On August 2, the long-expected order went out to the Luftwaffe "to overpower the English air force in the shortest possible time." The RAF, Hitler decreed, "must be beaten down to such an extent that it can no

◀ Dornier Do 17 bombers in flight at low altitude over the English Channel in July 1940. The Luftwaffe started attacking shipping there and in the outer reaches of the Thames estuary on July 10 as a preliminary to launching an all-out assault. Its aims were twofold. The first was to block the Channel to the small coastal convoys the British favored. If the Luftwaffe could do this, it was argued, it was likely it would be able to deny the Royal Navy access to the Channel if and when it came out to fight in strength. The second was to draw out British fighters from their bases so that the Luftwaffe could assess the RAF's strength and see how quickly and efficiently Fighter Command could deploy its squadrons.

longer muster any power of attack worth mentioning against the German crossing." Goering, the Luftwaffe's commander in chief, confidently predicted that, given good weather, the RAF would be driven out of the skies in four days.

While the Battle of Britain started to mount toward a crescendo, a debate about how best to implement Operation Sealion raged between the Kriegsmarine and Army High Commands. Raeder insisted that the navy simply was not strong enough to land the invading troops on the 237-mile-long (381-km) front the army was demanding. The most he would countenance was a much less ambitious set of landings between Folkestone and Brighton. A meeting between the Planning Staffs on August 7 revealed how irreconcilable the differences were between the two. "I utterly reject the navy's proposals," exclaimed General Franz Halder, the army's Chief of Staff. "I might just as well put the troops through a sausage machine."

THE FÜHRER'S INDECISION

Hitler intervened to broker a compromise. By the end of August, it was agreed, as the Kriegsmarine had hoped, that the invasion should be launched on a less ambitious front. However, the Führer told his general that he would not attempt to invade Britain at all if, at the end of the day, the task was too risky. In the meantime, preparations for the invasion were to continue.

The Kriegsmarine had estimated that 1,722 barges, 471 tugs, 1,161 motorboats, and 155 transports would be needed to get the first wave of the invading troops across the narrowest part of the Channel. Slowly but surely, the invasion barges started to gather. On August 31, RAF photoreconnaissance revealed that 56 barges from Amsterdam and another 100 from Antwerp were finally on the move toward the Channel ports. On the same day, 18 more were spotted at Ostend. Soon, 255 of them had been counted at Calais, 192 at Dunkirk, 230

at Boulogne, 140 at Flushing, and 227 at Ostend, while at Antwerp another 600 barges and 200 larger ships were assembling. The numbers rose and rose. In secret session on September 17, Churchill told the House of Commons that "upwards of 1,700 self-propelled barges and more than 200 seagoing ships, some very large ships, are already gathered at the many invasion ports."

It seemed to Churchill and his advisers that the invasion must be imminent. In fact, as early as September 3, after persistent prodding by Raeder, the date for the launch of the invasion was put back until September 21. It was then delayed again for a further week. The Kriegsmarine warned that, given the army's demand that the landings should take place at dawn on an ebbing tide and the navy's need for partial moonlight during the Channel crossing, this was the last practical launch date until after the end of the year. It also pointed out that the Luftwaffe seemed still far away from gaining air superiority over the RAF.

Hitler dithered until September 14, the eve of the original deadline for the launch of the attack. He summoned a meeting of the leaders of his armed forces, only to concede that "on the whole, despite all our successes, the preconditions for Sealion are not yet there … A successful landing means victory, but this requires total command of the air." Despite all Goering's promises, this clearly had not been achieved.

Accordingly, Operation Sealion was postponed indefinitely. On October 21, Hitler told his commanders that it was definitely cancelled until at least the following spring. In fact, the plan was never to be revived. For the first time, Hitler had lost a major battle. The consequences were to be far-reaching in the extreme.

"THE HAPPY TIME"

The Kriegsmarine's U-boat crews christened the 18 months from October 1939 *die Glückliche Zeit* (the happy time). As the amount of shipping the U-boats sank continuously rose, it seemed as though they might well succeed in severing Britain's vital transatlantic lifeline, cutting the British Isles off from the armaments, foodstuffs, and all the other supplies the British needed in order to be able to continue waging war. Between September 1939 and June 1940, the U-boats sunk 224 merchant ships totalling 1.3 million tons—and there was much more to come.

It literally became a fight for survival. Winston Churchill himself claimed in retrospect that "the only thing that ever really frightened me during the war was the U-boat peril." He was right to be so concerned. If the British had lost the Atlantic battle, their country might have been starved into submission. Her armed forces, too, starved of the American-built tanks, guns, planes, and other armaments they so desperately needed, might have been forced to lay down their arms.

REBUILDING THE U-BOAT ARM
Mindful of the damage U-boats had inflicted during World War I, when they sank more than 11 million tons of shipping, the victorious Allies in the Treaty of Versailles specifically prohibited German possession of submarines in perpetuity. The ban lasted until 1935, when, by the terms of the Anglo-German Naval Agreement, Britain gave Germany the "right to possess a submarine tonnage equal to the submarine tonnage possessed by the British Commonwealth of Nations." It was an amazing—and improvident—act of appeasement.

Hitler and Grand Admiral Raeder, commander-in-chief of the Kriegsmarine, were quick to take advantage of this far-reaching concession. Raeder chose Karl Dönitz, who had distinguished himself as a submarine commander in World War I, for the task of creating the Kriegsmarine's U-boat fleet.

As the new U-boats slowly started to come off the slipways, Dönitz set about molding them into an efficient fighting force. He estimated that in the event of war with Britain, he would need 300 of them to force the British into submission. By the time it came to actual war in September 1939, he had only 57 U-boats at his disposal, of which just 27 were ocean-going submarines. Of these, only 11 to 12 were on patrol at sea at any one time. The reasons for the shortfall were obvious. The army and Luftwaffe between them voraciously devoured the majority of the Third Reich's rearmaments expenditure; the Kriegsmarine was a poor third. Raeder's proposed naval construction program—Plan Z, as it was termed—also favored capital ships over submarines.

WOLF PACKS IN ACTION
Dönitz might not have anywhere near the number of U-boats he needed to wage an all-out maritime war, but he was determined to do his best. The battle tactics he devised were based on a personal World War I experience. "In October 1918," he recalled, "I was the captain of a submarine in the Mediterranean near Malta. On a dark night, I met a British convoy, with cruisers and destroyers. I attacked and I sank a ship. But the chance would have been very much greater if there had been a lot of submarines. That's where the idea of a wolf pack—to put the submarines together, to attack together—came from. In all the years from 1918 until 1935, when we had submarines again, I never forgot this idea."

During the first year of the war, Dönitz refined the new tactics. Firstly, pack attacks against convoys, he concluded, were best carried as far out in the Atlantic as possible to give his U-boats several days to press home their assault. Secondly, any U-boat making contact with a convoy should shadow it rather than immediately attacking it to give time for reinforcing submarines to arrive on the scene. Once the entire wolf pack had

With the fall of France, British naval resources were stretched to the limit, which was why Winston Churchill appealed to President Roosevelt for the "loan" of 50 of the USA's old World War I destroyers. *Walker*, seen here steaming at speed, was one of the existing destroyers that the Royal Navy was relying on to protect its Atlantic convoys against the U-boat menace. Among her successes was the part she played in the destruction of U-100 and U-99 in March 1941. The latter was commanded by Otto Kretschmer, the Kriegsmarine's most successful U-boat ace of that time.

assembled, it should attack simultaneously, launching one massive blow with the aim of overwhelming the convoy's escorts and forcing it to scatter.

The U-boats generally went into action by night at high speed on the surface. A surfaced Type VIIC submarine could make a maximum speed of around 17 knots as opposed to only 7.5 knots when submerged. U-boat ace Kapitänleutnant Otto Kretschmer recalled how successfully the tactic was employed when he and U-99 joined one of the first real wolf packs while on patrol in the Atlantic in October 1940. "I remember that there was a signal that there was a convoy coming in from America to England, and its position was not known," he recalled. "Dönitz ordered all submarines to the west of Ireland to form a sort of reconnaissance line to let the convoy pass through. When the first submarine was sighted and the convoy made a contact signal, this line was dissolved automatically and every boat was free to move into the attack."

TWO U-BOAT ACES

Kretschmer was already well on the way to becoming the most successful U-boat commander of the entire war. He had sunk a total of 47 ships before he was captured in March 1941 while attacking Convoy HX112, when a depth-charge attack by the British destroyer *Walker* forced the badly damaged U-99 to the surface.

Chief Petty Officer William Begg, onboard *Walker*, recalled what happened after that. "As we swung round again," he wrote, "the submarine suddenly broke the surface and, as her gun's crew ran towards their gun, I ordered our gun's crew to open fire. The U-boat started sinking stern first. Suddenly the captain called across in plain English 'Please save my crew!' Captain Macintyre said 'Let the bastards sink!' Don't forget we were in the heat of battle and had lost good men and ships and some of them to a horrible death. Then he ordered us to throw over the scrambling nets and we drifted over towards the submarine, ourselves now a

sitting duck for any other U-boat in the vicinity. We were off Iceland, and death was quick in those waters."

Another U-boat ace was not as fortunate. Kapitänleutnant Joachim Schepke lost his life on U-100 while attacking the same convoy. Fred Chilton, who served on *Vanoc*, the destroyer that sunk him, recorded the event. "The sleek destroyer headed straight for the conning tower of U-100," he wrote. "Cries of alarm sounded thinly in the night air as the U-boat crew saw the knife-edge bows of the destroyer coming at them in a cloud of spray. Some of them jumped overboard and tried desperately to swim out of the way.

"On *Vanoc*'s bridge they heard the roar of Schepke's voice as he shouted in German 'Don't panic, they are going to miss us! They will pass astern!' Then came the rending, grinding crash as *Vanoc* struck U-100 amidships by the conning tower, throwing the remainder of the crew into the water. Her bow cut both Schepke's legs off at the trunk and jammed him behind the periscope casing. *Vanoc*, carried forward by her speed, ran right over the stricken U-boat before coming to a halt, straining to release herself with both engines pulling astern. Eventually she came clear with a sharp jolt and U-100 rose high in the air.

"Schepke, still alive, was jerked free from the conning tower and his body thrown into the air to fall helplessly into the sea. He was still wearing his white-covered cap with all its rakish dash as he thrashed wildly for a few seconds and then sank beneath the heavy swell to be followed a few minutes later by U-100. Despite his weaknesses, Schepke had died like an ace—on his bridge."

THE LOSS OF U-47

Günther Prien, who had sunk *Royal Oak* at Scapa Flow on October 14, 1939, had gone to the bottom in U-47 earlier the same month while leading an attack on Convoy OB-293. Though the convoy's escorts sank one of Prien's accompanying submarines and drove off the other two, Prien continued to dog the convoy on his

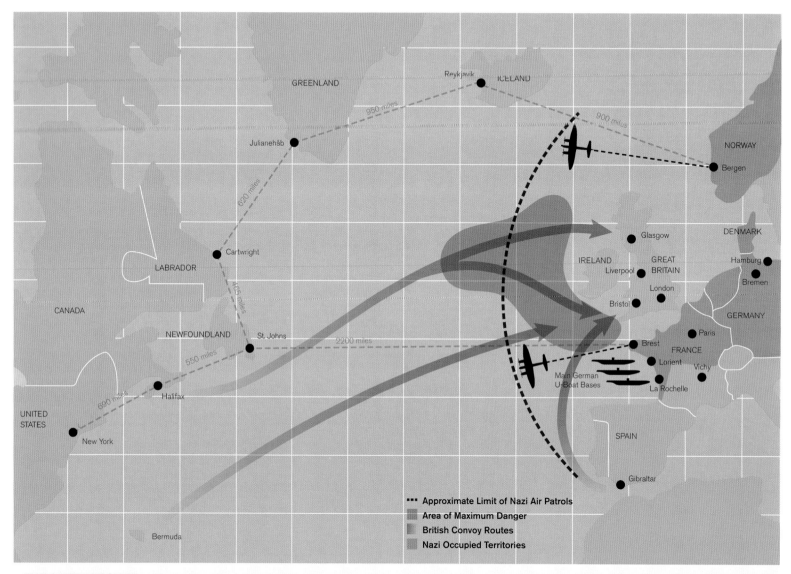

Approximate Limit of Nazi Air Patrols
Area of Maximum Danger
British Convoy Routes
Nazi Occupied Territories

THE BATTLEGROUND

Spurred on by the loss of *Athenia*, the first ocean-going convoys sailed from the Thames and Liverpool on September 9, 1939; a week later, homeward sailings commenced from Halifax, Nova Scotia; Kingston, Jamaica, and Freetown, Sierra Leone. Convoys from Gibraltar were started at the end of the month. The shortage and the range of their escorts meant that they could be escorted only to or from points 200 miles west of the Irish coast, southward to just below Ushant in the Bay of Biscay, or similar short distances off the Canadian coast. It was almost two years before transatlantic convoys could be escorted all the way across the ocean. Dönitz's U-boats operated in isolation at this time, rather than attacking in wolf packs. He also had an insufficient number of submarines available to wage the kind of all-out attack of his ambitions. This was to come later as the strength of the U-boat fleet increased.

own, heavily damaging the 20,638-ton *Terje Viken*, which sank a week later.

Surfacing at dusk on March 7 under the cover of rain, Prien was closing in on the convoy for the kill when the wind changed and the skies cleared to reveal the old World War I destroyer *Wolverine* bearing down on him. Prien hastily crash-dived. During the night, he surfaced once more—his last reported radio transmission to U-boat headquarters was timed at 3:54 a.m. local time on the morning of March 8—but *Wolverine* soon caught up with him, forcing U-47 back under the waves.

The British used ASDIC—the forerunner of sonar—to locate Prien, tracking of U-47s propellers. Finally, *Wolverine* dropped a full salvo of depth charges directly over the point of contact. A tremendous explosion lofted seawater skyward, while lookouts on *Wolverine* reported spotting an orange light appearing below the surface.

Wolverine was credited with the kill. After the war, however, fresh evidence indicated that the U-boat she had attacked might not have been the U-47 but another submarine altogether. If she did not sink U-47, what did? One theory is that Prien's submarine was hit by own of its own malfunctioning torpedoes. Another is that she was the victim of a diving accident, her pressure hull rupturing thanks to the underwater battering the submarine had received. What is clear is that the fate of U-47 remains a mystery. No trace of her wreck has ever been found.

The Kriegsmarine delayed announcing Prien's death for ten weeks—even his wife was kept in the dark. Coupled with the capture of Kretschmer and the loss of Schepke, it was a major blow to U-boat morale. He was posthumously awarded the Oak Leaves to his Knight's Cross; while a statement from the Wehrmacht High Command noted, "He and his brave crew will live forever in German hearts." The "happy time" was starting to draw toward a close.

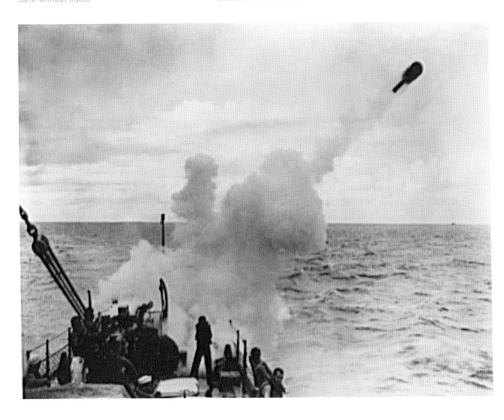

BATTLE IN THE MEDITERRANEAN: TARANTO

The fall of France in June 1940 had radical consequences for the balance of naval power in the Mediterranean. Not only was Italy now belligerent, but the Royal Navy could no longer look to the French fleet for support.

On paper, the Regia Marina outnumbered and outgunned Britain's Mediterranean Fleet, even though the latter could call on Force H, stationed at Gibraltar, for reinforcement. The Italians could field 6 battleships, 7 heavy and 12 light cruisers, 61 destroyers, 33 old and 35 modern torpedo boats, and over 100 submarines. Their two most modern battleships, *Littorio* and *Vittorio Veneto*, which entered service in August 1940, were faster and better armed than any of their British counterparts, while two older battleships—*Duilio* and *Dora*—were in the process of being modernized and

updated. Their *Zara*-class and *Bolzano*-class heavy cruisers were also considered formidable opponents.

Should Mussolini's admirals decide to take the offensive, they stood every chance—at least in theory—of scoring a decisive victory. Paradoxically, this was exactly what they declined to do. They argued, for instance, that sorties into the Eastern Mediterranean would be of little or no strategic benefit. Even taking Suez, could it be seized, "would gain nothing of decisive importance."

The admirals seemed to lack any kind of aggressive instinct. As opposed to the breezy, confident Admiral Sir Andrew Cunningham, the commander-in-chief of the Mediterranean Fleet, it was almost as if they expected to be defeated right from the start. Certainly, in some major aspects, the fleet they commanded was

▼ BOTTOM LEFT *Littorio*, the most modern battleship in the Italian fleet, was one of the ships that Fleet Air Arm Fairey Swordfish torpedo bombers badly damaged when they attacked Taranto by night in October 1940. Both she and her consort *Duilio* had to be beached to prevent thems from sinking. Together with La Spezia, Taranto was the principal dockyard of the Regia Marina.

BELOW Admiral Inigo Campioni is pictured on the bridge of his flagship *Giulio Cesare* while serving as commander-in-chief of the Italian battlefleet. Before the war, he had been regarded as the most promising commander in the navy, but his seeming unwillingness to risk his ships in battle against the British Mediterranean Fleet infuriated Mussolini, who had him relieved of command in December 1940.

technologically behind the times. Though the naval communications at Livorno had been experimenting with radar and sonar since 1935, their efforts were decried as "futuristic" by the Naval High Command. The admirals regarded aircraft carriers and torpedo planes as luxuries that could well be dispensed with, which meant that, when war came, the fleet was reluctant to operate beyond the range of land-based air support. Finally, they dreaded loosing ships in battle. Italy's lack of raw materials and inadequate industrial base meant that the nation's ship-building industry was incapable of replacing the inevitable war losses. As if this was not enough, a shortage of fuel oil kept much of the fleet more or less immobilized in port as the war progressed.

INITIAL CLASHES

As early as July 9, 1940, the Italian navy's lack of confidence was demonstrated in battle. Italian naval intelligence officers had intercepted and deciphered a coded radio transmission from the Mediterranean Fleet's base Alexandria, which alerted them to the fact that a British squadron was approaching Punta Silo off the coast of Calabria. The Italians decided to lay a trap for the British, utilizing powerful capital ships that outgunned their opponents, submarine ambushes, and land-based air attack.

The results were not what the Italians had anticipated. Though they were fighting almost within sight of their own shores, timid tactics and botched coordination between their attack's various elements led to failure. The turning point came when *Giulio Cesare* was hit by a single salvo from *Warspite*'s 15-inch guns. Though fired at extreme range, the salvo put four of her boilers temporarily out of action, so reducing her speed to 18 knots. Vice Admiral Inigo Campioni immediately ordered his fleet make for home as fast as it could under the cover of a thick smokescreen.

LITTORIO

Class *Littorio*-class battleship

Displacement 46,000 tons (fully load)

Length 762ft (232.3m)

Beam 107ft (32.6m)

Draft 32ft (9.8m)

Speed 30 knots

Armament Nine 15-in guns in three main turrets, 12 6-in guns in four turrets, 12 3½-in anti-aircraft guns, 20 37-mm and 20 20-mm anti-aircraft cannon

Crew 1,900

Littorio and her sister-ship *Vittorio Veneto* were both laid down on October 28, 1934 and joined the Italian fleet in 1940. *Roma* was launched on June 9, 1940 —the day before Italy entered the war— and was commissioned in June 1942. *Impero*, the last of the class, though launched in 1939, was never completed. *Littorio* was torpedoed again in June 1942 while attacking a Malta-bound convoy, further damaged by ARF air attack while in La Spezia harbor the following year, and then hit by a German Fritz X glider bomb while on passage to Malta to be interned following the Italian surrender. *Roma* was sunk by the Germans on the same passage, the first warship ever to be destroyed by a guided missile.

Cunningham pursued the Italians to within 25 miles (42km) of the coast before turning for Alexandria.

Despite repeated appeals for air support, the Regia Aeronautica failed to come to Campioni's assistance. When Italian aircraft finally turned up to harass Cunningham as he retired, they failed to inflict any significant damage on his ships.

Cunningham concluded that adopting offensive tactics against the Italians would pay dividends. His belief was reinforced by what happened off Cape Spada in northern Crete barely a week later, when Rear Admiral Ferdinand Casardi, in command of the light cruisers *Giovanni Delle Bande Nere*, and *Bartolomeo Colleoni*, took on five British destroyers and the Australian light cruiser *Sydney*.

Four of the destroyers—*Hyperion*, *Ilex*, *Hero*, and *Hasty*—were engaged in an antisubmarine sweep when they sighted the Italians. As the latter could outrun and outgun them, they turned and worked up to maximum speed, steaming for *Sydney* and *Havoc*, the fifth British destroyer. *Sydney* maintained radio silence until she was within range. Then, unspotted by the Italians, she opened fire. Taking Casardi completely by surprise, a salvo from her six-inch guns straddled *Bande Nere* almost immediately.

The panicking Casardi assumed that *Havoc* was another British cruiser. He ordered his ships to make smoke as he started to zigzag southeast in an attempt to disengage from the action. *Sydney* closed the range, concentrating her fire on *Colleoni*, now the nearest and rearmost target.

Her steering and engine room badly damaged, *Colleoni* slowed to a crawl and then stopped dead in the water. After a momentary hesitation, her consort abandoned her, disappearing around the island of Agna Grabusa and heading south as fast as she could steam. Leaving *Hyperion*, *Ilex*, and *Havoc* to finish off *Colleoni*, *Sydney* continued the pursuit with *Hasty* and *Hero*, but

Bande Nere was too fast for them and they were forced to abandon the chase. Meanwhile, the defenseless *Colleoni*, torpedoed by both *Ilex* and *Hyperion*, capsized and sank, her crew having abandoned ship. The destroyers were able to save 555 of them, though rescue operations were hampered by the belated appearance of some Italian aircraft, which bombed their own men in the water.

BLITZING TARANTO

What Cunningham wanted to do was to force the entire Italian battle fleet into action at a time and place of his choosing. Since the Italians resolutely refused to come out and fight, he decided to take the battle to the enemy. A devastating aerial attack on Taranto, the Regia Marina's most important base, by carrier-born Fairey Swordfish torpedo bombers was the result.

By November 1940, Taranto was playing host to six Italian battleships, three heavy cruisers, and three destroyers, all of which were moored on the shoreward side of the Mar Grande, the outer harbor. Four more heavy cruisers, 2 light cruisers, 21 destroyers, 16 submarines, 9 tankers, and other smaller craft were anchored in the Mar Piccolo, the inner harbor. Mar Piccolo was completely landlocked with the exception of a single narrow entrance channel. It was also too shallow to accommodate large capital ships. The Mar Grande was bigger and deeper. Long breakwaters protected it from surface attack.

Cunningham's plans for Operation Judgement, as the assault on Taranto was code-named, were based on ones formulated in 1935, when tensions between Britain and Italy were in crisis as a result of Italy's invasion of Ethiopia and revised three years later by Captain Arthur St George Lyster, when he was in command of *Glorious*, then the only British aircraft carrier in the Mediterranean. This time, *Illustrious* and *Eagle* were to carry out the attack. A fire in *Illustrious*'s hanger, which destroyed or damaged a number of her

aircraft, and serious defects in *Eagle*'s fuel system, forced the postponement of the attack. Only *Illustrious* was repaired in time to take part in it.

THE TWO WAVES

On November 11, the operation finally went ahead, when *Illustrious*, stationed about 40 miles (64km) off the Greek island of Cephalonia and 170 miles (274km) southeast of Taranto, launched 21 Swordfish in two waves. The first, consisting of 12 aircraft, was airborne at 8:40 p.m., with the second, which was 9 aircraft strong, following 56 minutes later. Six of the first wave and four of the second were armed with 250-lb (113-kg) bombs and flares; the others carried Mark XII torpedoes, set to run at 27 knots at a depth of 33 feet (10m).

The first wave approached Taranto around two hours later to be greeted by a hail of Italian anti-aircraft fire. They had failed to achieve the hoped-for surprise.

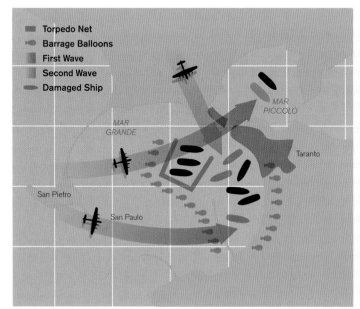

- Torpedo Net
- Barrage Balloons
- First Wave
- Second Wave
- Damaged Ship

MAR PICCOLO

MAR GRANDE

Taranto

San Pietro

San Paulo

SURRENDER ATTACK

Flying from the aircraft carrier *Illustrious* in two waves about an hour apart in November 1940, 21 Fleet Air Arm Fairey Swordfish torpedo bombers put the Italian battlefleet out of action, taking the naval base's defenses by surprise. It was a major reverse for the Italians, who had confidently believed that torpedoes could not be launched effectively in the harbor's relatively shallow waters. By the end of the attack, Italy's battleship strength had been reduced from six to two for the cost of only two Swordfish shot down.

Regardless of that, they went ahead with their mission. The flare-carrying aircraft broke formation to lay their flares in a line to silhouette the battleships in the outer harbor, while the others, skimming just 30 feet (9m) above the water, located their targets and went into the attack.

Conte di Cavour was the first battleship to be hit. A single torpedo struck her toward her bow and her forecastle promptly erupted in flames. She sank shortly afterward. A minute or so later, *Littorio* was torpedoed twice. The second wave carried on where the first had left off. This time, *Duilio* was badly damaged; *Littorio* was hit by a third torpedo. All the Swordfish bar two—one in each wave—got back to *Illustrious* safely.

A NOTABLE VICTORY

Cunningham had intended to repeat the attack the following night, but bad weather meant that *Illustrious* could not launch her aircraft. Nevertheless, he was more than satisfied with the result of the attack, claiming that he had delivered a decisive blow that altered the balance of naval power in the Mediterranean. "In a

total flying time of about six hours," he wrote, "20 aircraft had inflicted more damage on the Italian fleet than was inflicted on the German High Sea Fleet in the daylight action at the battle of Jutland."

The Kriegsmarine High Command, which had already written the Italian admirals off as incompetent and unreliable, concurred. Its official war diarist wrote: "The English attack must be regarded as the greatest naval victory of the war. At a stroke, it has changed the strategic situation at sea in the entire Mediterranean decisively in England's favor. Even more than before, the enemy will move throughout the Mediterranean, taking no account of the Italian Fleet." As for the Italians, they were left to count the cost and try to make good the damage. *Conti di Cavour*, though eventually salvaged, never went to sea again. *Duilio* and *Littorio* were put out of action for six months while they were undergoing repairs. The rest of the fleet was moved to Naples to protect it from similar attacks.

BATTLE IN THE MEDITERRANEAN: CAPE MATAPAN

If the defeat at Taranto was not bad enough, Mussolini's ill-judged invasion of Greece quickly turned into a major disaster. Though the Duce had told Count Ciano, his Foreign Minister, that he would "send in his resignation as an Italian if anyone objected to him fighting in Greece," Hitler, who had been deliberately left in the dark about the attack, was furious that it had been launched in the first place and even more enraged at its consequences.

Nor was the situation in North Africa any better for the luckless Italians, where General Sir Archibald Wavell's Army of the Nile had driven them out of Egypt and was remorselessly pursuing them across Libya as they fell back in headlong retreat. Grimly, the Führer prepared to intervene to back up his faltering ally on both fronts. Meanwhile, the Italian battlefleet skulked in port.

OPERATION GAUDO

Hitler insisted that, before he would commit the Wehrmacht to action, the Regia Marina had to sortie to stop British convoys ferrying troops, supplies, and equipment between Alexandria and Greece. Operation Gaudo was the result. The plan was for the Italians to divide their battle fleet into two and sweep the waters north and south of Crete clear of British shipping. The convoys would be caught in a pincer movement and sunk piecemeal. If the Regia Marina could destroy or damage any Royal Navy squadrons it encountered as well, it would be so much the better.

Vice Admiral Angelo Iachino was put in command of the operation. Though he had a formidable force at his disposal—it consisted of the brand new battleship *Vittorio Veneto*, 6 out of the navy's 7 heavy cruisers, 2 light cruisers, and 17 destroyers—he was reluctant to embark on the mission with which he had been entrusted. Though Luftwaffe air reconnaissance assured him that two out of the Mediterranean Fleet's three battleships had been put out of action as had its

sole aircraft carrier, he argued that success depended on him being provided with adequate air cover right from the start. This was something neither the Regia Aeronautica nor the Luftwaffe was prepared to guarantee.

In fact, all three of Admiral Sir Andrew Cunningham's battleships—*Warspite*, *Barham*, and *Valiant*—were ready for combat, while the aircraft carrier *Formidable* had arrived at Alexandria to take the place of the damaged *Illustrious*. Even more significantly, Ultra intelligence had alerted Cunningham to the likelihood of the Italian sortie. Diverting his convoys away from the danger zone, he prepared to take to sea to intercept the unsuspecting Iachino. He and his fleet would be steaming into a carefully baited trap.

▼ A Fairey Albacore torpedo bomber takes off from *Formidable*. Like other *Illustrious*-class aircraft carriers, she was more heavily armored than her predecessors, although this did not save her from substantial damage when the Luftwaffe successfully blitzed her off Crete at the end of May 1941. She had been dispatched to the Mediterranean that February to take the place of the damaged *Illustrious*; the following month, she played a major part in the battle of Cape Matapan, her aircraft crippling the Italian battleship *Vittorio Veneto*.

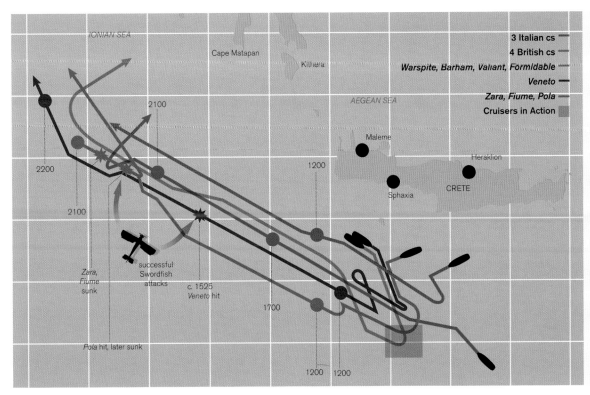

IONIAN SEA

Cape Matapan

Kithera

AEGEAN SEA

Maleme

Heraklion

CRETE

Sphaxia

2100

2200

1200

2100

Zara,
Fiume
sunk

successful
Swordfish
attacks

c. 1525
Veneto hit

1700

Pola hit, later sunk

1200 1200

3 Italian cs
4 British cs
Warspite, *Barham*, *Valiant*, *Formidable*
Veneto
Zara, *Fiume*, *Pola*
Cruisers in Action

THE FLEETS SAIL

Iachino sailed from Naples on March 26, 1941 on *Vittorio Veneto*. He was escorted by four destroyers. He steamed initially for the Straits of Messina, where he rendezvoused with the three cruiser squadrons assigned to the operation. Rear Admiral Carlo Cattaneo's 1st Cruiser Division from Taranto consisted of the heavy cruisers *Pola*, *Zara*, and *Fiume* plus four destroyers, while Rear Admiral Luigi Sansonetti's 3rd Cruiser Division from Messina was made up of the heavy cruisers *Trieste*, *Trento*, and *Bolzano*, and three destroyers. The 8th Division, from Brindisi and commanded by Rear Admiral Antonio Legnani, consisted of the light cruisers *Garibaldi* and *Abruzzi* and two destroyers.

At around nightfall a day later, Cunningham sailed from Alexandria with his three battleships and *Formidable*, screened by nine destroyers. As he steamed for Crete, he ordered Vice Admiral Henry Pridham-Wippell, with four light cruisers—*Orion*, *Ajax*, *Gloucester*, and *Perth*—and four destroyers, to sail south from the Aegean to rendezvous with him. If Pridham-Wippell were to encounter the Italians first, he was to lure them south toward the main battlefleet.

BATTLE STATIONS

Cunningham and his fleet headed northwest throughout the night toward a position south of Gardo Island, while Pridham-Wippell and his cruisers steamed out of the Aegean via the Kithera Channel to arrive west of Crete. *Vittorio Veneto* and its escorts were steering eastward toward the same area, with Sansonetti's three cruisers 20 miles (32km) off the Italian flagship's port bow. Cattaneo's and Legnani's squadrons were twice that distance away, heading on the same bearing.

The British battlefleet was still 150 miles (241km) away when reconnaissance aircraft from *Formidable* first spotted the three Italian cruiser squadrons. Pridham-Wippell's cruisers were closer to the enemy. At 7:45 a.m. on March 28, he sighted *Trieste*, *Trento*, and *Bolzano* as they appeared on the horizon astern of him. As instructed, he altered course and headed for the battlefleet, the Italians steaming after him. The pursuit lasted for about an hour before the Italians suddenly turned northwest. Iachino's plan was to lure the British cruisers toward *Vittorio Veneto* and the rest of his fleet, so that he could catch them between two fires. The ruse worked. Under heavy bombardment from the Italian flagship, Pridham-Wippell hastily turned back toward Cunningham again.

Formidable's torpedo bomber crews now took a hand. Flying their new Albacores, they carried out two air strikes against *Vittorio Veneto*. She managed to dodge the torpedoes the first strike launched, but the Albacore leading the second one scored a direct hit on her port side, heavily damaging her port screws. The great battleship rocked as the torpedo exploded and then stopped dead. The crew managed to get her underway again, but the maximum speed she could now make was only 12 knots. Iachino's frantic radio calls for air support went almost totally ignored—the single flight of Messerschmitts that actually reached him managed to remain on station for barely ten minutes before shortage of fuel forced them to return to base. RAF Blenheim bombers from Crete continued to harass the Italians from high altitude, though they did not score any hits.

TAKEN BY SURPRISE

As dusk fell that evening, Cunningham's reconnaissance aircraft, now flying 50 miles (80km) ahead of his fleet, spotted the Italians again, steaming

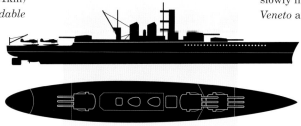

VITTORIO VENETO

Class	*Littorio*-class battleship
Displacement	45,750 tons (fully loaded)
Length	780ft 1in (237.8m)
Beam	107ft 7in (32.8m)
Draft	31ft (9.4m)
Speed	31.2–31.4 knots
Armament	Three triple 15-in turrets, two fore and one aft, four triple 6-in gun turrets, four 4.7-in guns, 12 3.5-in guns, 20 37-mm and ten 20-mm anti-aircraft cannon
Crew	1,830

Vittorio Veneto saw more action than any other Italian battleship during World War II, being hit twice by torpedoes and once by bombs. The first time the battleship was torpedoed was in the run-up to the battle of Cape Mataplan in March 1941. A single torpedo dropped by a Fairey Albacore from the British carrier *Formidable* hit her abaft T turret on her port side. Serious flooding and a loss of power to the port propeller shaft resulted, but she nevertheless was able to make port under her own steam. She was torpedoed a second time that December by the British submarine *Urge* southwest of Sicily. She was again hit on the port side—this time under the rear 15-inch gun turret—but the damage was minor.

slowly in five columns to protect the stricken *Vittorio Veneto* as she limped back toward Taranto. Another Albacore air attack—this time launched from Maleme in Crete—followed. This time, the Albacores hit the heavy cruiser *Pola* dead amidships. She shuddered to a halt, her boiler rooms flooded, and all her electrical circuitry was put out of action.

Iachino ordered Cattaneo's 1st Cruiser Division to turn back and go to *Pola's* assistance while the rest of the Italian fleet continued to make for home. Unbeknown to the Italian admiral, the British battlefleet, which had picked up the motionless *Pola* on its radar, were also steaming straight for it. As Cunningham's ships closed in for the kill, hoping that the vessel they had detected was *Vittorio Veneto*, other ships were spotted about two miles (3km) to the front. They were the heavy cruisers *Zara* and *Fiume*, together with a destroyer escort. Blinded by lack of air reconnaissance and absence of radar, they were blissfully unaware of Cunningham's presence. They were approaching in line, led by a single destroyer, followed by the two heavy cruisers and then by the three remaining destroyers.

Cunningham's ships swiftly deployed, their gun turrets rotating to bear on the dark shapes ahead. The unfortunate Italians, their guns pointing helplessly fore and aft, never knew what hit them as *Warspite* and *Valiant* opened fire. In his autobiography, *A Sailor's Odyssey*, Cunningham vividly described what happened:

"In the dead silence, a silence that could almost be felt, one heard only the voices of the gun-control personnel putting the guns on to the new target," he recorded. "One heard the orders repeated in the director tower behind and above the bridge. Looking forward, one saw the turrets swing and steady when the 15-inch guns pointed at the enemy cruisers.

"Never in the whole of my life have I experienced a more thrilling moment than when I heard a calm voice

from the director tower—'Director layer sees the target', a sure sign that the guns were ready and that his finger was itching on the trigger. The enemy was at a range of no more than 3,800 yards (3,475m)—point-blank.

"It must have been the Fleet gunnery officer, Commander Geoffrey Barnard, who gave the final order to open fire. One heard the 'ting-ting-ting' of the firing gongs. Then came the great orange flash and the violent shudder as the six big guns bearing were fired simultaneously.

"At the very same instant the destroyer *Greyhound*, on the screen, switched her searchlight on to one of the enemy cruisers, showing her momentarily up as a silvery-blue shape in the darkness. Our searchlights shone out with the first salvo, and provided full illumination for what was a ghastly sight. Full in the beam I saw our six great projectiles flying through the air. Five out of the six hit a few feet below the level of the cruiser's upper deck and burst with splashes of brilliant flame. The Italians were quite unprepared. Their guns were trained fore and aft. They were helplessly shattered before they could put up any resistance.

"The plight of the Italian cruisers was indescribable. One saw whole turrets and masses of other heavy debris whirling through the air and splashing into the sea, and in a short time the ships themselves were nothing but glowing torches and on fire from stem to stern."

A "MARITIME CAPORETTO"

Fiume was on fire from bow to stern. Her after turret toppled overboard as she began listing heavily to starboard and started to sink. *Zara* was in no better case. She became a pyre of orange fire as her boilers erupted and her forward turret, smashed by a British shell, pirouetted into the sea. *Barham*, joining in the fight, fired a full broadside into the destroyer *Alfieri*, turning her into a smoking hulk. The three destroyers at the end of the Italian line desperately turned and headed for the British in an all-or-nothing torpedo attack. One of them, *Carducci*, was caught by the destroyer *Stuart*, torpedoed and sunk. The other two managed to make their getaway.

Cunningham's destroyers now turned on the inert *Pola*, still wallowing helplessly without power or lights. *Havlock* fired two shells into the ship. Two small fires started but otherwise there was no response. Two other destroyers arrived. Their searchlights revealed 257 of *Pola*'s demoralized crew, many of them drunk on the Chianti they had looted from their officers' cabins, crowded on deck "longing to surrender." Hundreds more had already abandoned ship. The destroyers finished *Pola* off with two torpedoes. It was the end of one of the most one-sided battles in naval history.

▲ Four *Zara*-class heavy cruisers moored in Taranto, *Pola* and *Zara* herself being among their number. At Cape Mataplan, *Pola* was sunk by the destroyers *Jervis* and *Nubian* after being stopped dead in the water by a torpedo hit. *Zara* was scuttled by her own crew after being seriously damaged by British battleship fire while coming to the assistance of her stricken concert. *Fiume*, another *Zara*-class heavy cruiser, met the same fate. She was sunk outright.

HUNTING *BISMARCK*

In April 1941, Grand Admiral Erich Raeder, the commander-in-chief of the Kriegsmarine, was concocting a new battle plan. He and his staff decided to form a powerful new battle group that would be capable of destroying even the most heavily escorted transatlantic convoys.

Raeder's initial idea was to send *Bismarck*, the Kriegsmarine's crack new battleship, and the heavy cruiser *Prinz Eugen* into the Atlantic where they would be joined by *Scharnhorst* and *Gneisenau*, which had already made two successful Atlantic sorties earlier that spring, after which they had made it back to the French port of Brest safely. To take charge of the new sortie, he chose Admiral Günther Lutjens, a highly experienced officer with a proven record as a fleet commander. His most recent success had been as commander of the two battlecruisers during their January 1941 breakout into the Atlantic. Unfortunately for Raeder, the plan had to be changed. *Scharnhorst*'s boilers were giving trouble and she was undergoing repairs that would take weeks to complete. *Gneisenau* had been heavily damaged during a British air raid on Brest on April 6. She would be out of action for at least six months.

Lutjens told Raeder that he favored postponing the sortie until the boiler repairs on *Scharnhorst* had been completed and she was fit for sea again, or until *Tirpitz*, the *Bismarck*'s newly commissioned sister-ship, had completed her sea trials and was ready to take *Scharnhorst*'s place. The Grand Admiral, however, was not willing to wait. He decided that *Bismarck* and *Prinz Eugen* should go it alone. The battleship, though yet to see action, was the pride of the Kriegsmarine. The most advanced warship of her type in the world, the Germans considered her to be practically unsinkable.

BISMARCK AND *PRINZ EUGEN* SAIL
On May 18, 1941, Operation Rheinübung, as the Kriegsmarine's High Command had christened it,

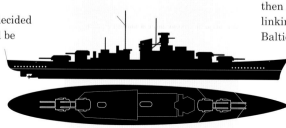

BISMARCK

Class *Bismarck*-class battleship

Displacement 590,900 tons (full load)

Length 794ft (242m)

Beam 118ft (36m)

Draft 33ft (10.1m)

Speed 29 knots

Armament Eight 15-in guns mounted in four turrets, 12 5⅞-in guns mounted in six turrets, 16 4-in anti-aircraft guns, 16 37-mm, and 36 20-mm anti-aircraft cannon

Crew 2,200

Bismarck and her sister-ship *Tirpitz* were the largest German warships of World War II and among the most powerful battleships ever built. Equipped with radar and no fewer than six HA directors, *Bismarck*'s gunnery was astonishingly accurate as she proved in the battle of the Denmark Strait. There—after being intercepted by the battlecruiser *Hood* and the battleship *Prince of Wales*—while trying to break out into the Atlantic with her consort, the heavy cruiser *Prinz Eugen*, she sank *Hood* with only her fifth salvo.

finally started. That afternoon, first *Prinz Eugen* and then *Bismarck* sailed from the Polish port of Gdynia, linking up with their escort and then heading out of the Baltic and up the Norwegian coast toward Bergen, where Gruppe Nord (German Naval High Command North) had advised Lutjens to put into port for refueling before attempting to break out into the North Atlantic via the passage between the Faeroes and Iceland.

Lutjens, however, ignored Gruppe Nord's advice. Instead of stopping at Bergen, he decided to head directly for the Arctic and refuel instead from the tanker *Weissenberg*, stationed near Jan Mayen Island, before trying to break out into the Atlantic via the Denmark Strait. The likely reason for this was that Lutjens had an unfavorable experience using the Iceland/Faeroes route with *Scharnhorst* and *Gneisenau*—the battlecruisers had been spotted there by the cruiser *Naiad* and Lutjens had been forced to reverse course. In addition, the weather there was notoriously foggy and visibility poor in consequence. If it was bad enough, it would help to provide cover for the intended breakout.

Lutjens's intentions were thwarted. As *Bismarck*, *Prinz Eugen*, and their escorts steamed north and west through Scandinavian waters, they were sighted by the Swedish cruiser *Gotland* and some Norwegian fishing boats. Though Sweden was officially neutral, Lutjens was convinced that the Swedes would leak the news of the sighting to the British Embassy in Stockholm. Similarly, the fishermen would pass on the same news to the Norwegian Resistance. He decided to push into Bergen after all, hoping to escape from the port undetected later under the cover of bad weather.

THE BRITISH REACTION
The Germans reached Bergen on May 21, *Bismarck* anchoring in Grimsted Fjord and *Prinz Eugen* in Kalvanes Bay, a little farther to the north. Later the

Bismarck, photographed from *Prinz Eugen*, entering the Korsfjord south of Bergen on the morning of May 21, 1941. She anchored in the neighboring Grimstadfjord. Admiral Günther Lutjens, the squadron's commander, decided to stop in Norway and continue the voyage north under cover of night. *Prinz Eugen* needed to refuel as well. Unfortunately for Lutjens, his ships had been spotted by the Norwegian Resistance, who signaled London with the news of their arrival.

same day, both ships were photographed by an RAF reconnaissance Spitfire. Immediately, they had been positively identified and the news was flashed to Admiral Sir John Tovey, commander-in-chief of the Home Fleet in Scapa Floe, via the Admiralty.

Tovey readied himself for action. *Suffolk* was despatched to join *Norfolk*, its fellow cruiser, which was already patrolling the Denmark Strait with Rear Admiral William Wake-Walker, commander of the 1st Cruiser Squadron, onboard. *Birmingham* and *Manchester*, later joined by *Arethusa,* were to guard over the alternative passage between Iceland and the Faeroes. The battlecruiser *Hood*, the battleship *Prince of Wales*— the latter was so new that she still had civilian workmen onboard when she sailed, sorting out mechanical problems with her gun turrets—and six destroyers were ordered to sail for Hvalfjord, where they would refuel, ready to react immediately if either of the two cruiser squadrons succeed in locating the enemy.

The rest of the Home Fleet, led by Tovey in the battleship *King George V*, would remain at Scapa Flow until the situation became clearer, along with the aircraft carrier *Victorious*, the battlecruiser *Repulse* (actually stationed farther south on the Clyde), four more cruisers, and seven destroyers. *Hood, Prince of Wales* and their escorts left Scapa Floe just before midnight on May 21. Tovey and the rest of the Home Fleet followed at 10:45 p.m. the next evening.

CLASH IN THE DENMARK STRAIT

Meanwhile, *Bismarck* and *Prinz Eugen* were on the move. They both sailed from Bergen in the early evening of May 21, foggy weather cloaking their departure. They made straight northward for the Denmark Strait, turning southwest to enter it just before midnight the following day. Lutjens's hope was that the fog would not lift until his ships had passed through the Strait and entered the North Atlantic, but he was to be disappointed. At around 7:15 p.m. on

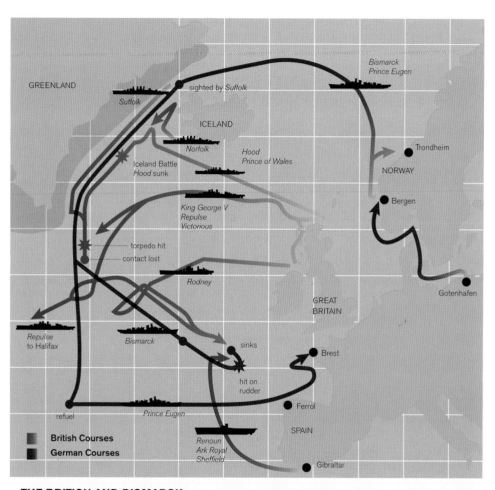

THE BRITISH AND *BISMARCK*

Admiral Sir John Tovey, commander-in-chief of the Home Fleet, was in charge of hunting *Bismarck* down. This map shows the subsequent course of the operation once the fact that the Germans were attempting an Atlantic break out had been confirmed by *Norfolk* and *Suffolk*—the heavy cruisers Tovey despatched to patrol the Denmark Strait. At the same time, the battlecruiser *Hood* and battleship *Prince of Wales*, accompanied by six destroyers, were ordered to Iceland to cover the access points to the Strait south and east of the island. Thick fog aided the Germans as they began their break through, but they had not reckoned with the British ability to detect and track them by radar.

May 27, a lookout onboard *Suffolk* spotted both the German vessels. Joined by *Norfolk*, both the cruisers began to track the enemy squadron with their radar. They also alerted *Hood* and *Prince of Wales* who were some 300 miles (483km) away to the north. Both started steaming at 27 knots toward the enemy, their escorting destroyers struggling to keep up with them.

Onboard *Hood*, Vice Admiral Lancelot Holland, commander of the 1st Battlecruiser Squadron and Deputy Commander of the Home Fleet, expected to make contact with *Bismarck* and *Prinz Eugen* between 1:40 a.m. and 2 a.m. in the morning. Then he received unwelcome news. Shortly after midnight, *Suffolk* signaled that she and *Norfolk* had lost contact with the Germans. It took the cruisers just under three hours to locate *Bismarck* and *Prinz Eugen* again.

THE BATTLE STARTS

Hood and *Prince of Wales* were now approaching *Bismarck* and *Prinz Eugen* head on, the crews on both sides now at action stations ready for immediate combat. Holland's plan was to close the range as fast as he possibly could before turning to bring his full broadside to bear. It was a contentious move, for it meant that, in the opening stages of the battle, Holland would be able to fire only the forward guns of both his ships.

Nevertheless, Holland pressed ahead. He was determined not to give Lutjens the opportunity of using his superior speed to escape. In the light of *Hood*'s known deficiencies in her deck armor, he may also have thought that closing the range in this manner was the best way of ensuring that that his flagship would be less vulnerable to *Bismarck*'s potentially deadly plunging fire.

When the range had closed to about 25,000 yards (2,286m), *Hood* and *Prince of Wales* opened fire. *Bismarck* and *Prinz Eugen* responded within a few minutes. Holland had ordered both his ships to concentrate their fire on the left-hand German vessel,

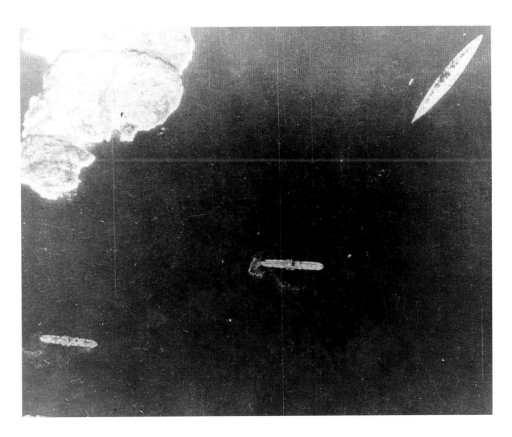

thinking that this was *Bismarck*. In fact, it was *Prinz Eugen*, which had taken over the lead from the German flagship because the latter's radar was temporarily out of action. *Prince of Wales* quickly realized her mistake and corrected her aim; *Hood* continued to fire at *Prinz Eugen* before belatedly switching target.

Either way, *Hood*'s shells were not hitting home. *Bismarck* and *Prinz Eugen*, by contrast, straddled her with only their third salvo. One of the shells from the latter struck *Hood* near the base of her mainmast, starting a fierce fire that quickly spread across her boat deck.

▲ Coastal Command Spitfire photo-reconnaissance pilot Flight Lieutenant Michael Suckling took this celebrated photograph from the air over the Grimstadfjord in the afternoon of May 21, 1941. He had been ordered to patrol the area in an attempt to confirm the initial Norwegian Resistance sighting signal. *Bismarck* can be seen to the right of the picture. She is in company with three merchant ships, the latter acting as a protective shield in the event of a torpedo attack. On receipt of Suckling's report, Tovey immediately ordered his ships into action.

HOOD'S DEATH BLOW

Holland now had the signal "Blue 2" hoisted, ordering a turn to port to let *Hood*'s rear gun turrets come into action. It was while she was executing this turn that she was dealt her death blow.

About eight minutes after the battle had started. *Bismarck*'s fifth broadside straddled *Hood* again. At least one of its shells plunged through the great battle-cruiser's thinly armored deck and exploded in her after magazine. A pillar of flame and then a huge cloud of smoke erupted from her. When the latter cleared, *Hood* had vanished. On *Prince of Wales*, a crewman recorded how he had heard "a great rushing sound which had ominously ceased, and then, as I looked, a great spouting explosion issued from the centre of *Hood*. I just did not believe what I saw—*Hood* literally had been blown to pieces."

Hood was gone. Out of her crew of 1,418 men, only 3, Midshipman William Dundas, Able Seaman Robert Tilburn, and Signalman Ted Briggs managed to survive. Of *Hood* herself, all that remained on the surface was a morass of floating debris and a four-inch-deep oil slick.

Prince of Wales was left to carry on the unequal struggle alone. Severely damaged by the seven hits *Bismarck* had scored on her, she was forced to break off the action. Together with *Norfolk* and *Suffolk*, she continued to trail the Germans from a safe distance.

"SINK THE BISMARCK!"

It was a terrible blow to British naval pride. Author Ludovic Kennedy, then a sub-lieutenant on the British destroyer *Tartar*, wrote: "For most Englishmen the news of the *Hood*'s death was traumatic, as though Buckingham Palace had been laid flat or the Prime Minister assassinated, so integral a part was she of the fabric of Britain and her empire." Churchill immediately ordered Tovey to hunt *Bismarck* down and sink her regardless of cost.

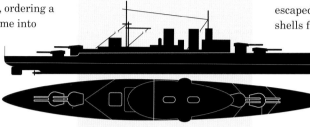

HOOD

Class *Admiral*-class battlecruiser

Displacement 46,200 tons (full load)

Length 810ft (246.9m)

Beam 95ft (29m)

Draft 31ft 6in (9.6m)

Speed 31 knots

Armament Eight 15-in guns in four turrets, 14 4-in anti-aircraft guns, 24 2-pdr anti-aircraft guns, six 20-mm anti-aircraft cannon, five 20-barreled UP rocket projectors

Crew 1,420

During the interwar years, *Hood* was the largest capital ship in the world, but her imposing structure hid a substantial weakness. Designed and built during World War I, her protective deck armor was not thick enough to be up to the demands of modern naval warfare. This left her vulnerable to plunging long-range shellfire. When she went into action against *Bismarck* and *Prinz Eugen*, the German ships (which one is not clear) scored a vital hit on *Hood*, which was suddenly rent by a massive explosion. She sank within minutes, leaving only 3 survivors from her 1,420-strong crew.

As it turned out, the German battleship had not escaped unscathed. She had been hit by two 14-inch shells from *Prince of Wales*, one of which forced her to shut down one of her boilers. The other caused a fuel leak. As a result, Lutjens was forced to abandon his mission. Instead, *Bismarck* turned southeast and headed for Brest, in German-occupied France as night fell. *Prinz Eugen* broke away to the southwest to continue into the North Atlantic. Later, having dodged a torpedo-bomber attack launched by *Victorious*, *Bismarck* managed to give *Suffolk* and *Norfolk* the slip.

For Tovey, many anxious hours now elapsed, particularly as he assumed wrongly that *Bismarck* was retiring to the northeast to make for Germany. All hopes of locating her again rested on the many warships combing the area or in the long-range reconnaissance patrols being mounted by Coastal Command aircraft flying out of Britain and Iceland.

THE FINAL HOURS

At 10:10 a.m. on May 26, Tovey's luck suddenly changed. A Catalina from 209 Squadron spotted *Bismarck* about 670 miles (1,078km) northwest of Brest. The Home Fleet set off in pursuit. The question was whether it could catch up *Bismarck* before it got within range of Luftwaffe air cover. Also, many of Tovey's ships were in imminent danger of running short of fuel. Something had to be done to slow *Bismarck* down.

Fortunately for Tovey, the aircraft carrier *Ark Royal*, who had sailed with Force H from Gibraltar, was southeast of *Bismarck*'s reported location, directly in her path to Brest. The first air strike she launched that afternoon was a failure—the 14 Swordfish *Ark Royal* launched mistook the cruiser *Sheffield*, which had been detached from Force H to shadow *Bismarck*, for the battleship and attacked her unsuccessfully instead.

▲ Salvo after salvo of direct hits blast *Bismarck* shortly before the crippled battleship sank in the Atlantic following a 1,570-mile pursuit by the Home Fleet. She had been on the verge of escaping her pursuers when two torpedoes fired by Swordfish from *Ark Royal* struck her in the stern and jammed her rudders hard to port. The unmaneuverable battleship now steamed directly into the path of *King George V*, *Rodney*, and their supporting cruisers. The unequal battle that followed lasted for 74 minutes until *Bismarck* finally rolled over and sank. For the Kriegsmarine, it was probably the greatest single loss of the war.

The second strike, which took off at 7:10 p.m. that evening, located the right target. The 15 Swordfish taking part in the attack fired 13 torpedoes between them, of which two hit their mark. The first had little obvious effect. The second wrecked *Bismarck*'s steering gear and jammed her rudder. Her speed reduced to a crawl, she was now unmaneuverable. She could no longer escape her converging pursuers.

The final battle started shortly after midnight on May 27, when one Polish and four British destroyers closed in on *Bismarck* to launch multiple torpedo attacks. A few hours after dawn, the British capital ships steamed into view. *King George V* and *Rodney* both engaged *Bismarck* at a range of 16,000 yards (1,463m). After an hour and a half's bombardment,

which went largely unanswered, *Bismarck* was reduced to a blazing shambles. Torpedoed twice more, and eventually scuttled by her surviving crew, the German battleship sank some 300 miles (483km) west of Ushant. Only 110 of her crew of 2,222 survived the sinking. As far as surface attacks were concerned, the balance of power in the North Atlantic had swung back decisively in Britain's favor. The "mighty *Hood*" had been avenged.

GLOBAL WARFARE

In December 1941, total war became global war. The US Navy, its Pacific Fleet decimated by the surprise Japanese onslaught at Pearl Harbor, started off the conflict on the back foot. So, too, did the Royal Navy, after the battleship *Prince of Wales* and the battlecruiser *Repulse*—all that could be scraped together to send east to defend Singapore—were both sunk by the Japanese off Malaya three days later.

From the start, both navies were fighting a two-ocean war, battling against the U-boats in the Atlantic as well as against Japan in the Far East. The British, too, suffered extra losses fulfilling the commitment to run Arctic convoys to Russia. Slowly but surely, the Allies gained the upper hand. After the loss of their crack aircraft carriers at Midway, Japanese naval power started a slow decline, while the U-boats were eventually defeated in the Atlantic. As for the Italian surface fleet, it never emerged from port again except to surrender. The way was set for the great amphibious landings that were to decide the course of the war.

NAVAL STRENGTHS

In 1941, the USA possessed the world's second most powerful navy. Indeed, it might well have supplanted Britain as the world's premier naval power had Congress stuck to the terms of President Woodrow Wilson's 1916 Naval Appropriations Act, which authorized the construction of a fleet that, within five years, would be stronger than any other two navies of the world combined.

As Wilson put it, "this would be a navy fitted to our needs and worthy of our traditions. There is no navy in the world that has so great an area of defense as the American Navy, and it ought to be incomparably the greatest navy in the world." His ambitious target was not to be achieved. As a result of the 1922 International Arms Limitation Agreement signed in Washington between the USA, Britain, Japan, Italy, and France, the participants agreed to establish 5:5:3 ratios in battleships and aircraft carriers between Britain, the USA, and Japan. The ratio for France and Italy was 1.75. The five powers agreed to a ten-year "naval holiday," during which time no new capital ships would be built and to restrict all new battleships laid down after that date to a maximum of 35,000 tons. Following a later international conference, new cruisers were similarly restricted to a weight limitation of 10,000 tons.

The consequences were dramatic. The US Navy had to scrap the three-quarters-completed *Washington*, six partway-built *South Dakota*–class battleships, and the four battlecruisers that were also under construction. Four existing battleships—*Delaware*, *North Dakota*, *Michigan,* and *South Carolina*—were sent to the scrapheap as well. Britain, for its part, scrapped 14 modern battleships and 6 battlecruisers as well as giving up its plans to build four "super-*Hoods*." Japan sacrificed *Tosa*, using her for target practice before sinking her, and scrapped eight of its older battleships. In sum, this left the US fleet with 18 battleships, the British with 16, and the Japanese with 6.

ROOSEVELT REARMS

Over the next decade, US naval strength remained more or less static. Admiral Ernest J. King, who eventually became commander of the US Fleet and Chief of Naval Operations, noted how "except for cruisers, hardly any combatant ships (no battleships or destroyers) were added to our own fleet during that period and few were under construction."

Indeed, there were those—notably Brigadier-General William "Billy" Mitchell—who opined that, like all other navies, the US fleet was obsolete. "The surface ship as a weapon of war is disappearing," Mitchell confidently stated. Even aircraft carriers were "useless instruments of war against first-class powers." According to Mitchell, the money that had been extracted from a reluctant Congress to lay down *Langley*, *Lexington*, and *Saratoga* had been squandered.

Luckily, President Roosevelt did not hold such opinions. As early as June 1933—the year he first came into office—he prodded Congress into authorizing the construction of *Enterprise*, *Yorktown*, the first *Brooklyn*-class cruisers, the *Craven*-class destroyers, and four new fleet submarines. The following year, the first five *New Orleans*–class heavy cruisers joined the fleet.

Between 1935 and 1940, the *Atlanta* class of anti-aircraft cruisers was designed, as were the navy's new *North Carolina*-, *South Dakota*-, and *Iowa*-class battleships. By December 1941, design work on the *Fletcher*-class destroyers, *Cleveland*-class cruisers, *Baltimore*-class heavy cruisers, and *Essex*-class aircraft carriers had all been completed.

THE WAR CLOUDS GATHER

As international tensions mounted, American policy toward the Axis powers was dictated by an overwhelming public desire to stay out of war at almost any cost. Nevertheless, planning for war with Japan following a Japanese invasion of the Philippines got under way. The US Navy's Plan Orange was the result.

One of the three 16-inch gun turrets of the US battleship *Iowa* dominates this dramatic wartime photograph. With her sister-ships *New Jersey*, *Missouri*, and *Wisconsin*, she was one of a new generation of fast super-battleships the US Congress gave the go-ahead to construct in 1938. She was laid down in 1940, launched in 1942, and commissioned on February 22, 1943. *Iowa* spent most of the war in the Pacific as the flagship of Battleship Division 7, taking part in the Marshall Islands campaign, the battle of Leyte Gulf and the liberation of the Philippines, the Okinawa landings, and the bombardment of land targets in Honshu and Hokkaido.

Plan Orange called for the US Army to defend Manila and the Philippines unaided for a minimum of three to four months until the main battle fleet could get across the Pacific to raise the siege. As relations with Japan worsened, this time lag was probably why, in April 1940, the decision was taken to move the fleet from its California bases to Pearl Harbor as a deterrent against possible Japanese aggression. On February 1, 1941, it was renamed the Pacific Fleet—the same day that the Atlantic Fleet was formally reactivated.

The steps had already been taken to ready both fleets for a fight, if push came to shove. On June 14, 1940— the day Hitler's troops marched into Paris—Roosevelt signed the new Naval Expansion Bill Congress had been debating for months. Three days later, it voted the Department of the Navy four billion dollars over and above the amount contained in the Bill to give it the extra resources it said it needed to fight a two-ocean war. The navy got the go-ahead to build six new *Iowa*-class battleships, five even bigger *Montana*-class battleships (though, in the event, these were never constructed), six *Alaska*-class heavy cruisers (only two were built), 11 *Essex*-class aircraft carriers, 40 cruisers, 115 destroyers, and 67 submarines.

JAPAN PREPARES

When completed, this enormous building program would give the Pacific Fleet overwhelming superiority over the Japanese, but in 1941 this was not the case. On December 1, the Americans fielded nine battleships —one more than the Japanese—but only three aircraft carriers as opposed to their ten. Between them, the Pacific and Asian Fleets had 13 heavy and 11 light cruisers, 80 destroyers, and 55 submarines under command. The corresponding figures for the Japanese were 18 heavy and 12 light cruisers, 111 destroyers, and 64 submarines.

Events accelerated the inevitable drift toward war after the Japanese moved into French Indochina that July. The USA, Britain, and the Dutch government-in-exile, responded immediately. They embargoed all oil supplies to Japan. The ban, Roosevelt said, would be lifted only if the Japanese agreed to evacuate French Indochina and withdraw from China itself. Tokyo refused point-blank to yield to the US demands. Instead, the Japanese started to plan for a further military expansion to obtain the oil and other vital raw materials they needed so desperately. Admiral Osami Nagano, the chief of the Naval General Staff, told Emperor Hirohito: "The government has decided that, if there were no war, the fate of the nation was sealed. Even if there is war, the country may be ruined. Nevertheless, a nation which does not fight in this plight has lost its spirit and is already a doomed nation."

Admiral Isoroku Yamamoto, commander-in-chief of Japan's Combined Fleet, had been planning for such an eventuality since the end of 1940. He argued that, in the light of his country's precarious economic situation—it was estimated that the fleet's oil reserves would last for a maximum of only 18 months—a devastating surprise attack on the US Pacific Fleet at its Pearl Harbor base was the best option. He told Koshiro Oikawa, the Navy Minister from September 1940 to October 1941, "we should do our very best to decide the fate of the war on the very first day."

THE TASK FORCE SAILS

Initially, Yamamoto's plan was opposed by many of his fellow admirals and by the Naval General Staff. It was not until September 1941 that he was given a preliminary go-ahead and intensive training for the carrier-borne attack began at Kagoshima Bay. On November 5, 1941, he issued Operation Order 1, in which he outlined details of the audacious scheme to his senior officers. "To the east, the American Fleet will be destroyed," it read. "The American lines of operation and supply to the Far East will be severed. Enemy forces will be intercepted and annihilated. Victories will be exploited to smash the enemy's will to fight."

▲ Admiral Isoroku Yamamoto (center), together with members of his staff, photographed onboard the battleship *Nagato* shortly after his promotion to commander-in-chief of Japan's Combined Fleet in 1939. Yamamoto was opposed to war with the USA, but failed in his attempt to keep his country neutral. When war became inevitable, he planned the surprise attack on the US Pacific Fleet at Pearl Harbor and then sought to destroy remaining US naval power in a single decisive battle. Defeats at Midway and Gaudalcanal forced him onto the defensive.

Yamamoto's intentions were clear. He chose Admiral Chuichi Nagumo, Japan's top carrier commander, to take charge of the Pearl Harbor striking force, though initially at least Nagumo had been vehemently opposed to the planned attack. On November 22, the task force started to assemble at Tankan Bay, in the Kuriles north of Hokkaido. The task force was an imposing one. It included *Akagi*, *Kaga*, *Shokaku*, *Zuikaku*, *Hiryu*, and *Soryu*, the navy's six newest and largest aircraft carriers, carrying 423 combat planes between them. The carriers were screened by nine destroyers plus a light cruiser, supported by the battleships *Hiei* and *Kirishima*, the heavy cruisers *Tone* and *Chikuma*, and three *I*-class submarines. Eight tankers and assorted supply ships made up the fleet train.

The task force sailed on November 26, plowing its way across the stormy North Pacific toward its destination 275 miles (443km) due north of Pearl Harbor. Steaming at 26 knots, it arrived there on schedule early in the morning on December 7. Slowly, the six carriers turned north into the wind to allow the first wave of torpedo bombers, dive bombers, high-level bombers, and escorting Zero fighters to swarm into the air.

The previous evening, Nagumo had ordered all hands on deck throughout his fleet to listen to Yamamoto's final order being read. "The rise or fall of the Empire depends upon this battle," it stated baldly. "Everyone will do his duty to the utmost." It was a reiteration of Admiral Togo's celebrated order delivered before his fleet attacked the Russians in Tsushima Strait in 1905. In an emotional scene, the battle ensign that Togo had raised on his flagship *Mikasa* 36 years earlier was then raised on *Akagi*. Yamamoto, Nagumo, and their subordinate commanders were determined that their victory over the Americans would be just as complete.

One thing, though, did not go according to plan. Yamamoto had stipulated that his planes were not to launch their attack until 30 minutes after Ambassador Kichisaburo Nomura had handed the formal Japanese declaration of war to Secretary of State Cordell Hull in Washington. That way, though Yamamoto would retain the element of surprise, since it would be impossible for the Americans to warn the Pacific Fleet in time, Japan's honor would remain intact.

In the event, Yamamoto's best intentions were thwarted by human miscalculation. The Washington embassy took so long to decode the text of the declaration of war that it was only delivered to Hull several hours after the attack on Pearl Harbor had started. What was to turn into a struggle to the death between the USA and Imperial Japan was already well underway.

SURFACE RAIDERS

Even while the Imperial Japanese navy was starting to ready itself for the possibility of war, the Kriegsmarine was stepping up its surface campaign against Allied merchant shipping in distant waters around the world. It was a hard-fought struggle from first to last in which the Germans scored some notable successes.

From 1940 to 1942, Admiral Raeder's battlecruisers, pocket battleships, and heavy cruisers were joined at various times by 11 other surface raiders. The Germans called these ships *Hilfskreuzer* (armed cruisers)—freighters converted into ghost warships, sailing in disguise to catch their luckless victims unawares. Between them, they accounted for 142 Allies ships captured or sunk, grossing more than 870,000 tons.

VARIED FORTUNES

The first five raiders—*Orion*, *Atlantis*, *Widder*, *Thor*, and *Pinguin*—sailed from their home ports in spring 1940, followed by a further six later in the summer. All carried the same main armament of six 6-inch guns, concealed behind false partitions and dummy deck cargo, two to six deck-level torpedo tubes, four to six dual purpose 37-mm guns, and 20-mm and 92-mm anti-aircraft guns.

The ships themselves varied in size and efficiency. *Atlantis, Pinguin*, and *Thor* were modern diesel-engined converted cargo ships with a range of about 50,000 miles (80,467km) and a cruising speed of ten knots. *Orion* and *Widder* were both former Hamburg-Amerika liners, powered by aging steam turbines, which were prone to breakdowns and uneconomic to operate. Slowness and high fuel consumption made them less well-suited to the demands of sustained raider warfare than their sister-ships.

Widder, for example, was forced to abort her mission and make for the German-occupied port of Brest after

◄ A modern diesel freighter converted into an auxiliary cruiser after the outbreak of war, *Atlantis* sailed on her first cruise as a commerce raider on March 31, 1940. She roamed the South Atlantic, Indian, and Pacific Oceans for 622 days until she was finally trapped south of St. Helena by the British cruiser *Devonshire* on November 22, 1941 while refueling a German U-boat. Totally outranged by *Devonshire*'s guns, Kapitan zur See Bernhard Rogge scuttled his badly damaged ship rather than see her fall into enemy hands. She had sunk 22 ships, totaling 146,000 tons, and captured 6 more during her raiding career.

just six months; the Kriegsmarine had planned for her to be at sea for a full year. Despite frequent breakdowns, *Orion* managed to steam 127,337 miles (204,929km)—the equivalent of more than five times around the world—in a voyage lasting 511 days during which time she accounted for 73,478 tons of Allied shipping.

FATE OF *ATLANTIS*

It was *Atlantis*, however, that won the record for remaining at sea longer than any other commerce raider. She sank 22 ships totaling almost 146,000 tons in the course of an epic 601-day voyage, which took her into the South Atlantic, round the Cape of Good Hope and on into the Indian Ocean, the Pacific and then as far as Australia.

Kapitan zur See Bernard Rogge, *Atlantis*'s commander, showed himself to be a master of deception as well as proving to be an astute naval tactician. At various times, he successfully passed *Atlantis* off as the Norwegian motor ship *Knute Nelson*, the Russian fleet auxiliary *Kim*, the Japanese passenger freighter *Kasii Maru*, and the Dutch motor ship *MV Abbekerk*. Even his fellow raider *Pinguin*—herself disguised as the Greek freighter *Kassos*—was fooled into mistaking *Atlantis* for a British armed merchant cruiser. As month succeeded month, the British doubled and redoubled their efforts to track him and *Atlantis* down as he prowled the shipping lanes stalking his prey.

Atlantis was to meet a sudden and, from the German point of view, unfortunate end. In November 1941, she was about to head for home at last when she was ordered by the Kriegsmarine High Command to rendezvous with U-126 off Ascension Island in the South Atlantic and refuel her. Rogge took advantage of this enforced pause to strip down his port engine to replace a damaged piston. He was unaware that he had been sighted by a scouting British seaplane and that

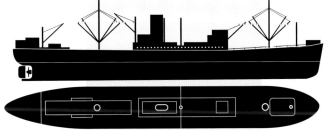

ATLANTIS

Class	Auxiliary cruiser
Displacement	7,862 tons
Length	509ft (155.1m)
Beam	61ft (18.6m)
Draft	29ft (8.8m)
Speed	17.5 knots
Armament	Six 5⅞-in guns, one 75-mm gun, two 37-mm and four 20-mm anti-aircraft cannon
Crew	347

With a range of 60,000 miles cruising at a speed of ten knots, *Atlantis* posed a potent threat to Allied merchant shipping. One of the reasons that she survived for so long was her captain's ability to disguise her true identity. At various times, she posed as a Norwegian motorship, a Russian fleet auxiliary, a Japanese passenger freighter, a Dutch motor vessel, a Norwegian freighter, and even as a British auxiliary cruiser.

Devonshire, a *County*-class heavy cruiser, was hastening toward the scene.

The German lookouts then spotted the rapidly approaching *Devonshire* shortly after 8 p.m. on November 22. There was no way *Atlantis* could outrun the cruiser with only one functioning engine; her 6-inch guns were also completely outranged by *Devonshire*'s 8-inch main armament. Rogge had no alternative but to play for time. He hastily maneuvered his ship to try to hide U-126 from the cruiser's Walrus seaplane, which was now flying overhead. His aim was to try to lure *Devonshire* into gun and torpedo range, or to get her into a position where U-126, which had hastily crash-dived, might get a shot at her.

Captain Robert Oliver, in command of *Devonshire*, did not fall for the ruse. Instead of continuing to close on *Atlantis*, which had signaled she was the Dutch freighter *Polyphemus*, he stood off the raider for about an hour while awaiting confirmation of her identity. Then, having been advised by radio that the mystery ship was not what she claimed to be, he commenced firing, scoring devastating hits on *Atlantis* with his opening salvos.

On fire and almost at a standstill in the water, the raider was obviously doomed. Rogge ordered her crew to prepare her for scuttling and then to abandon ship. Minutes later, *Atlantis*'s magazine exploded. It took her just two minutes to sink. *Devonshire* immediately made off northwest. Only too aware of the danger of U-boat attack, Oliver could not run risk losing his ship in an attempt to rescue any survivors.

BATTLE FOR SURVIVAL

As *Devonshire* steamed into the distance, Rogge and the other survivors made for the lifeboats, cutters, rafts, and floats that had been launched from the sinking *Atlantis*. They were joined by U-126, which now cautiously resurfaced. Taking the survivors in tow, the submarine slowly started to make for the coast of Brazil, more than 900 miles (1,448km) away. It was a daunting prospect, lightened only by a signal from U-boat command, telling U-126 that three other U-boats and the supply ship *Python* had been ordered to the survivors' aid. At first light on November 24, *Python* hove into view.

It seemed as if Rogge's troubles were over, but in fact they were just beginning. With the survivors safely on board, *Python* made for her rendezvous with two more U-boats, which she was scheduled to refuel. Then history began to repeat itself. No sooner had the refueling commenced when *Python*'s lookouts spotted another heavy Cruiser—this time *Dorsetshire*—heading straight for her. The two U-boats crash-dived, but for the unarmed *Python* there was no escape. Forced to heave to, her captain ordered *Python* to be scuttled and all onboard to abandon ship. *Dorsetshire*—like *Devonshire*, unwilling to run the risk of U-boat attack—steamed away southward, leaving crew members and survivors adrift on the high seas.

The U-boats reappeared, each taking 100 survivors onboard and towing the rest in lifeboats behind them. Then, two more submarines joined them. This meant it was just possible to accommodate all the survivors below decks. They got as far as the Cape Verde islands, where they met up with four Italian submarines. Some of the survivors were transferred to them to relieve the pressure on the cramped accommodation.

The submarines, now eight in number, headed for the French port of Saint Nazaire and safety. The first of them made port on December 23. Three more followed on Christmas Day, two more on December 27, one the next day, and finally U-124 on December 29. In addition to the 102,000 miles (164,153km) they had covered on *Atlantis*, Rogge and his surviving crew had traveled 1,000 miles (1,609km) by lifeboat and raft and

KORMORAN

Class	Auxiliary cruiser
Displacement	8,736 tons
Length	515ft (157m)
Beam	66ft (20.1m)
Speed	18 knots
Armament	Six 5⅞-in guns, two 37-mm anti-tank guns, five 20-mm anti-aircraft cannon
Crew	400

With a displacement of 8,736 tons and a top speed of 18 to 19 knots, *Kormoran* was the largest auxiliary cruiser the Kriegsmarine deployed as a commerce raider during World War II. Her most celebrated action was her last. In November 1941, she sank the Australian light cruiser *Sydney* off Western Australia. She, however, was so badly damaged in the battle that she was forced to scuttle herself. *Sydney* went down with all hands.

a further 5,000 miles (8047km) crammed into their rescuing U-boats.

SUCCESS AND FAILURE

It was small wonder that Goebbels and his Propaganda Ministry made the most of Rogge's feat. *Kormoran*, too, received massive media exposure for sinking the Australian cruiser *Sydney* off the country's northwestern coast.

In a bitterly fought battle on November 19, 1941, *Kormoran* inflicted devastating damage on her opponent, repeatedly hitting her bridge and forward gun turrets before finally managing to torpedo her. She blew up, sinking with all hands. *Kormoran*, though, was so badly damaged that she had to be abandoned. Her crew spent the rest of the war in an Australian prisoner-of-war camp. *Thor* was even more successful. During her first voyage, she put two British Armed Merchant Cruisers out of action and sank a third. On her second, she was not as fortunate. On October 10, 1942, she docked in Yokohama harbor, Japan, to refuel and refit. A chance spark set fire to one of the tankers moored beside her. The result was a devastating explosion that destroyed *Thor* and tanker alike.

By this time, the fortunes of war were turning against the raiders. *Stier* was the last one to successfully break out into the Bay of Biscay in March 1942. In December, the conversion of *Coburg* was canceled; the following month *Coronel* was recalled. Only *Michel* was still at sea off Japan, but without a single supply ship to support her. The raider war was effectively over.

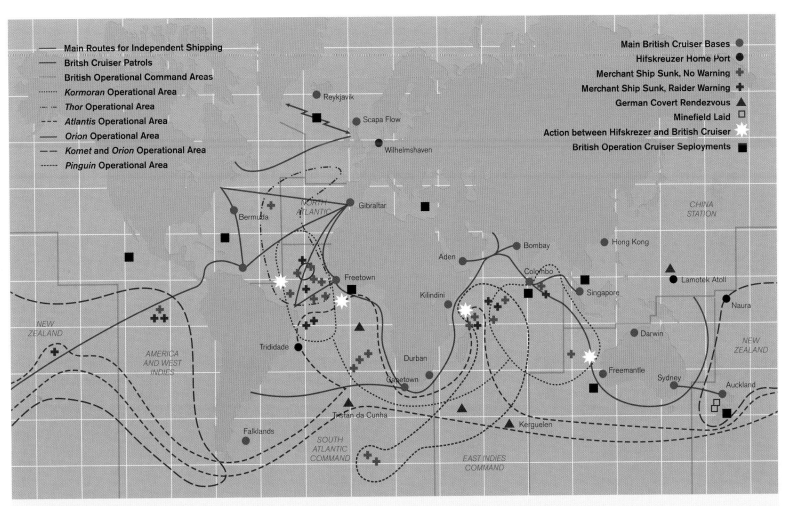

Legend:
- Main Routes for Independent Shipping
- Britsh Cruiser Patrols
- British Operational Command Areas
- *Kormoran* Operational Area
- *Thor* Operational Area
- *Atlantis* Operational Area
- *Orion* Operational Area
- *Komet* and *Orion* Operational Area
- *Pinguin* Operational Area

- Main British Cruiser Bases
- Hifskreuzer Home Port
- Merchant Ship Sunk, No Warning
- Merchant Ship Sunk, Raider Warning
- German Covert Rendezvous
- Minefield Laid
- Action between Hifskrezer and British Cruiser
- British Operation Cruiser Seployments

Map labels: Reykjavik, Scapa Flow, Wilhelmshaven, NORTH ATLANTIC, Gibraltar, Bermuda, CHINA STATION, Hong Kong, Bombay, Aden, Colombo, Singapore, Lamotek Atoll, Freetown, Kilindini, Naura, NEW ZEALAND, Darwin, NEW ZEALAND, AMERICA AND WEST INDIES, Trididade, Durban, Freemantle, Sydney, Auckland, Capetown, Tristan da Cunha, Falklands, Kerguelen, SOUTH ATLANTIC COMMAND, EAST INDIES COMMAND

THE SURFACE RAIDERS AT SEA

The nine auxiliary cruisers the Kriegsmarine deployed as surface raiders during World War II accounted for 142 ships sunk or captured with a gross tonnage of more than 8,700 tons. Between them, they spent a grand total of 3,769 at sea. The map here shows their movements in their vast field of operations and the countermoves that were made to try to track them down and destroy them. The raiders' basic strategy was simple—to stay at sea for as long as possible, disrupt traffic in the sea lanes as much as they could, and to avoid getting into a fight with stronger enemy warships. All their crews were carefully selected volunteers.

PEARL HARBOR

Shortly after sunrise on December 7, 1941, the US Pacific Fleet was settling down to its usual Sunday routine at its anchorage in Pearl Harbor. The forenoon watch was being piped to breakfast, while the men it would relieve were busying themselves concluding their duties on and below decks. Of the 70 warships and 24 auxiliary vessels, a single destroyer was on the move.

As the hour for morning colors to be hoisted approached, the tranquillity of the harbor was suddenly shattered. A horde of unidentified planes suddenly filled the skies as if from nowhere. Hardly anyone recognized them as Japanese; most assumed they were part of some form of mock assault. It took minutes after the attack started in earnest for Rear-Admiral Patrick Bellinger, the senior navy air officer on the scene to send out the first radio alert. It read tersely: "Air raid, Pearl Harbor—this is no drill."

TAKEN BY SURPRISE

The Americans in Hawaii were taken totally unawares, despite the "war warning" Admiral Husband E. Kimmel, commander-in-chief of the Pacific Fleet, received from Admiral Harold R. Stark, the Chief of Naval Operations in Washington, on November 27. The signal told Kimmel to expect "an aggressive move by Japan within the next few days." Stark followed it up with a second dispatch the following day. It warned that "hostile action is possible at any moment." To be fair to Kimmel, Stark did not believe that Pearl Harbor and Hawaii would be the target for Japanese attack. Instead, he expected them to strike "against either the Philippines, Thailand's Kra Peninsula [the narrow isthmus connecting the Malay Peninsula with the Asian mainland], or possibly Borneo." Furthermore, Stark expressly cautioned Kimmel not to "undertake any offensive action until Japan has committed an overt aggressive act." The most he would authorize him to do was to "execute defensive deployment preparatory to carrying out the existing war plan."

The Japanese equivalent was certainly ambitious. It had been resolved in Tokyo that, if no diplomatic agreement could be reached with the USA to lift the American oil embargo on Japan by the end of November, the Japanese would attack the Americans, British, and Dutch, and many points throughout the Far East as soon as possible after December 1.

The US Pacific Fleet at Pearl Harbor would be decimated by a surprise attack by carrier-borne aircraft. Simultaneously, other Japanese planes flying from airfields in Formosa (present-day Taiwan) would strike at US airfields on Luzon as a prelude to a full-scale invasion of the Philippines. Guam, Wake Island, and the Gilbert Islands were also to be attacked and occupied, as was Hong Kong.

◀ Vice Admiral Chuichi Nagumo commanded the carrier strike force that launched the surprise attack on Pearl Harbor in December 1941. Despite not being an expert on naval aviation, the success he scored enhanced his already considerable reputation, which was further bolstered by the raids he and his carriers made across the Pacific and into the Indian Ocean. After his failures at Midway and Guadalcanal, however, he was sidelined, ending up commanding a small naval flotilla in the Marianas. He committed ritual suicide after failing to hold Saipan in the face of US invasion.

Finally, troops would be landed at several places in Thailand and northern Malaya and advance down the Malayan Peninsula to eliminate the British naval and air bases on the island of Singapore. If these initial moves were successful, New Guinea, Borneo, the Dutch East Indies, and Burma would be invaded. The aim was to create what the Japanese grandiloquently christened the "Greater East Asia Co-Prosperity Sphere."

"TORA, TORA, TORA!"

The Pearl Harbor Task Force, consisting of Japan's six crack fleet carriers, escorted by two battleships, two heavy cruisers, a light cruiser, nine destroyers, and three forward-reconnaissance submarines, sailed from Tankan Bay in the Kurile Islands on November 26 with Vice Admiral Chuichi Nagumo in command.

Deliberately choosing to take the longer northern route to Hawaii to lessen the possibility of being spotted by US reconnaissance patrols, the blacked-out fleet maintained strict radio silence as it plowed its way across the stormy ocean. When it got to its launch position around 200 miles (322km) north of Hawaii, it received a single terse radio signal from Tokyo. It read simply *Niitaka yama nobore* ("Climb Mount Niitaka"). It was the signal that the attack was to proceed.

The first wave of Japanese torpedo bombers, dive bombers, high-level bombers, and fighters started to take off at about 6 a.m. on December 7. The second wave followed 70 minutes later. Flying time to Hawaii was around 1 hour 50 minutes, the pilots tuning into Honolulu radio to get a fix on their positions. The first attack began at precisely 7:49 a.m. Four minutes later, as the bombs and torpedoes started to rain down, Lieutenant Commander Mitsuo Fuchida signaled *Tora, Tora, Tora!*—the Japanese code word to signal the start of an attack—to the carriers and the eagerly waiting Commander Minoru Genda, who, with Fuchida, had devised the Japanese plan. It confirmed that complete surprise had been achieved.

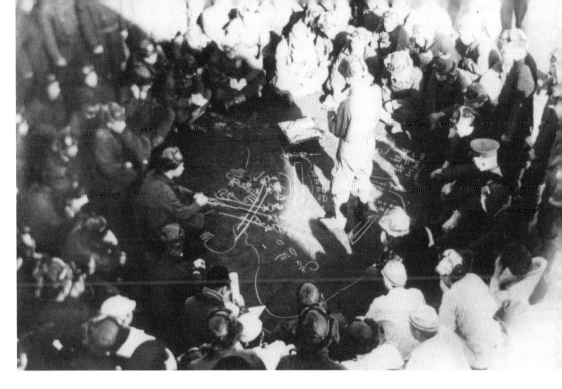

The Americans had their chances. The night before, two patrolling US destroyers attacked and sunk two unidentified midget submarines just outside the harbor, but failed to alert the fleet. Early the next morning, two trainee radar operators manning an army radar station at Opana on the northern point of Oahu detected a swarm of approaching aircraft 130 miles (209km) to the north, but the lieutenant to whom they reported their sighting told them to ignore it. According to him, the planes were US B-17 bombers that were expected to arrive from the mainland that morning. He told them to obey procedure and shut the station down as scheduled. The Japanese were left unchallenged as their planes began their final approach.

SLAUGHTER OF THE BATTLESHIPS

Weeks of rehearsal pouring over mockups and flying at Kagoshima Bay now paid off as the Japanese aviators moved into their attack. While their fighters and high-level bombers peeled away to neutralize Wheeler, Hickam, and Kaneohe air fields, their torpedo planes and dive bombers made for Battleship Row, located along the southeastern shore of Ford Island, a few

▲ Lieutenant Ichiro Kitajima, leader of *Kaga*'s bomber group, briefs his air crews in detail about the Pearl Harbor attack the day before the raid was launched. A diagram of Pearl Harbor and the aircraft attack plan is chalked on the flight deck. The strike force consisted of 353 aircraft. These included 40 torpedo bombers, 103 level bombers, 131 dive-bombers, and 79 fighters. The four Japanese aircraft carriers involved were supported by 2 battleships, 2 heavy cruisers, 35 submarines, 2 light cruisers, 9 oilers, 2 battleships, 11 destroyers, and 9 fleet tankers.

This aerial photograph of Battleship Row, Ford Island, was taken early on during the Pearl Harbor attack from a Japanese bomber. From left to right, the ships shown are *Nevada, Arizona* with *Vestal* moored outboard. *Tennessee* with *West Virginia* outboard, *Maryland*, and *Oklahoma. Neosho* can be partly seen on the far right. *Arizona* has just been hit by a bomb near her stern, while *West Virginia* and *Oklahoma* are gushing oil and listing to port having taken several torpedo hits. *Nevada*, though showing little outward signs of damage, has also been torpedoed.

hundred yards across the main channel from the Navy Yard. Seven battleships were anchored there—some singly, the others in pairs. *Pennsylvania,* the Pacific Fleet's flagship, was close by in No. I Dry Dock.

Arizona was almost torn apart by torpedo and bomb blasts within a minute of the opening attack. One bomb penetrated her forward magazine before it could be flooded, the resulting explosion wrecking half the ship as a fiery column of smoke shot into the sky. *Arizona* settled in the water so quickly that hundreds of sailors were trapped below decks without a chance of escape. Of the 1,400 officers and men on board, 1,103 perished.

Oklahoma, too, never got the chance to make a fight of it. Three torpedoes blasted huge holes in her and she promptly took on a 30-degree list. Two more torpedo hits finished her off. As her crew scrambled over the side to abandon ship, she rolled over and capsized. *Maryland*, moored alongside her, got off more lightly, suffering only moderate damage after being hit by two bombs. *West Virginia* was not as fortunate. She was struck by six or seven torpedoes and two bombs, taking on a 28-degree list as a result. Her crew, however, managed to reduce the list to 15 degrees by counter-flooding their ship. This meant that she ended up settling almost upright on the bottom of the harbor.

Tennessee suffered serious damage aft when the officers' quarters caught fire after being struck by a bomb, but lived to fight another day. *California* was torpedoed twice. It took her about three or four days to sink, coming to rest on the harbor bottom with her mainmasts and the upper part of her main turrets above water. *Nevada* was torpedoed once. She was the only battleship to manage to get underway, eventually running aground off Hospital Point, where she was beached. Probably because she was in dry dock, *Pennsylvania* avoided serious damage, being hit by only one bomb.

The tale of woe did not end here. The rest of the fleet—2 heavy cruisers, 6 light cruisers, 29 destroyers, 3 seaplane tenders, 10 minesweepers, 9 minelayers, 5 submarines, and other auxiliary craft—were also targeted. Three light cruisers were moderately damaged and three destroyers heavily damaged. Aircraft losses were also staggering. In all, 180 planes were destroyed and 159 badly damaged, leaving only 43 operational. Many were lined up wing to wing on their runways and caught helpless on the ground. Japanese losses were minimal. Only 29 planes failed to return.

THE MISSING CARRIERS

So far, everything had gone according to plan—indeed, the attack had succeeded beyond the wildest Japanese expectations. Now, however, things started to go wrong. Fuchida and Genda urged Nagumo to launch a third

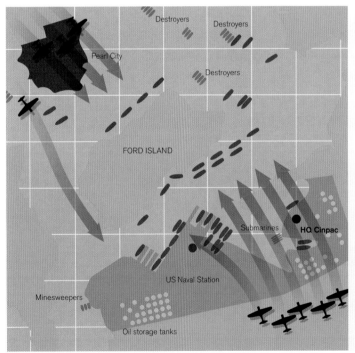

PEARL HARBOR ATTACK

The first wave of 51 dive-bombers, 40 torpedo planes, 50 high-level bombers, and 43 fighters arrived over its target at 7:53 a.m. A second wave took off from Nagumo's carriers an hour-and-a-quarter later. The first wave targeted US airfields and battleships moored in Pearl Harbor, the second other ships and dockyard facilities, though it missed hitting the oil-tank farm that contained the Pacific Fleet's reserve of fuel oil. *Lexington* and *Enterprise*, two of the Pacific Fleet's three aircraft carriers, were at sea and escaped damage. *Saratoga* was at San Diego undergoing repairs. Their absence was one of the reasons Nagumo canceled the planned third strike.

strike just as had been originally intended. The cautious Nagumo, supported by Rear-Admiral Ryunosuke Kusaka, his Chief of Staff who had been opposed to the entire operation right from the start, decided against it.

Genda pleaded with Nagumo in vain. He pointed out that, despite the Japanese success, major targets remained intact. At the least, he argued, the Japanese carriers should remain in the area until *Enterprise* and *Lexington*, the Pacific Fleet's two serviceable aircraft carriers (*Saratoga* was in dock at San Diego undergoing repairs), had been located, attacked, and hopefully sunk. The Japanese had expected them to be in Pearl Harbor with the rest of the fleet, but Kimmel had ordered them to sea to deliver aircraft reinforcements to Wake Island and Midway shortly before the attack. They were heading back toward Pearl Harbor when the Japanese struck.

Nagumo would not change his mind. He had no idea where the American carriers were and feared they might locate him and strike first. He ordered the task force to turn toward home and steam toward the Marshall Islands at top speed. The next day, Nagumo despatched two of his carriers—*Soryu* and *Hiryu*—the heavy cruisers *Tone* and *Chikuma,* and the destroyers *Urakaze* and *Tanikaze* to the support of the Wake Island Invasion Force. The rest of his strike force headed back to its base in Japan's Inland Sea.

LOOKING FOR SCAPEGOATS

Immediately following the attack, the hunt was on for scapegoats. Kimmel and Lieutenant-General Walter Short, in command of Oahu's land defenses, were both unceremoniously relieved of their commands. Neither saw active service again. Admiral William S. Pye, the second most senior officer in the Pacific Fleet, took Kimmel's place until Christmas Eve when he, in his turn, was superseded by Admiral Chester W. Nimitz on the latter's arrival in Hawaii.

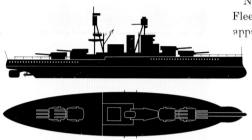

ARIZONA

Class	*Pennsylvania*-class battleship
Displacement	32,567 tons
Length	608ft (185.3m)
Beam	97ft (29.6m)
Draft	28ft (8.5m)
Speed	21 knots
Armament	12 14-in guns mounted in four triple turrets, 18 5-in guns, eight 7-mm anti-aircraft guns
Crew	2,290

Arizona and her sister-ship *Pennsylvania* were among the most powerful battleships in the world when they were launched in 1915. *Arizona* was modernized between the world wars. Both were improved versions of the older *Nevada*-class battleships, notable for being the first US battleships to abandon traditional vertical triple-expansion steam engines for more economical steam turbines. They also adopted a four-engine, four-propeller layout that would become the norm for all future US battleships.

Nimitz proved to be just what the demoralized Pacific Fleet needed. Though he admitted that Japan had apparently scored a great victory, he also held that, in his opinion, the Japanese had made three major mistakes. The first, he opined, was attacking on Sunday morning when nine out of ten crewmen of the fleet were on leave. If the fully crewed fleet had been lured to sea and sunk, the Americans would have lost 38,000 men as opposed to 3,800.

The second was the failure to destroy the dry docks and workshops opposite Battleship Row. If these had been blitzed, every damaged ship would have had to be towed back to California for repair. Thirdly, the Japanese had failed to target Pearl Harbor's fuel-oil tank farm, filled to capacity and situated within easy striking range. Had they done so, the Pacific Fleet would have been immobilized for months.

In time, Nimitz was to be proved right. Though over the next months the Japanese were to go from strength to strength—conquering the Philippines; capturing Hong Kong, Malaya, and Singapore from the British; sweeping through the Dutch East Indies; and raiding deep into the Indian Ocean—they were soon suffering from what military historian Basil Liddell Hart later termed "strategic overstretch" as a result. Unlikely though it seemed at the time, the tide was about to turn against Japan.

Arizona burned for two days as she slowly sank at her moorings following the Japanese attack on her. The second bomb that hit her ignited a fire that detonated her forward magazine. The massive explosion that followed destroyed the forward part of the ship. It also killed Admiral Isaac C. Kidd and Captain Franklin van Valkenburgh, who had rushed to the bridge when the attack began. Lieutenant Commander Samuel G. Fuqua, *Arizona*'s damage control officer, vainly tried to check the fires and rescue survivors. Despite this, 1,177 of the battleship's crew were killed. She herself was a total loss.

THE DESTRUCTION OF FORCE Z

Just after midnight on December 7/8, 1941—some hours before the Japanese struck at Pearl Harbor—Indian troops spotted three large merchant ships anchoring off the beach they were guarding six miles (10km) of Kota Bharu in northeastern Malaya. Just minutes later, they were being shelled; shortly afterward, the veteran troops of the Japanese 56th Infantry Regiment stormed ashore. Japan's invasion of Malaya had begun.

War with Japan had long been feared. In 1938, after years of procrastination, the great British naval base at Singapore, the island at the foot of the Malayan Peninsula, had finally been completed to guard against just such an eventuality. It was certainly an imposing construction. The 1,006-foot (307-m) King George VI Graving Dock and the 858-foot (262-m) No. 9 Floating Dock were both capable of dry-docking the largest battleships and aircraft carriers afloat or under construction, while another floating dock was designed to accommodate cruisers, destroyers, and smaller vessels. With its 22 square miles of anchorages, the base was more than capable of accommodating the naval reinforcements it was intended to send east in the event of war threatening with Japan.

PLANNING FOR WAR

The problem was that there were few reinforcements available. Earlier in 1941, the British Admiralty had decided upon a long-term plan to assemble a force of capital ships in the Indian Ocean, ready for despatch to Singapore as Britain's Eastern Fleet in the event of war looking likely. The force was intended to consist of no fewer than 7 battleships or battlecruisers, an aircraft carrier, 10 cruisers, and 24 destroyers. Together with the US Pacific Fleet, it was reckoned that this force would be a formidable deterrent in the event of further Japanese aggression.

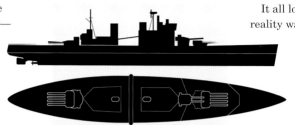

PRINCE OF WALES

Class	King George V–class battleship
Displacement	40,000 tons (full load)
Length	700ft (213.4m)
Beam	103ft (31.4m)
Draft	31ft 6in (9.6m)
Speed	29 knots
Armament	Ten 14-in guns (four in two turrets, two in one turret), 16 5¹/₄-in guns, 32 2-pdr anti-aircraft guns, 16 ¹/₂-in anti-aircraft guns
Crew	1,612

Prince of Wales was the second of five *King George V*–class battleships the British government ordered to be built as part of its emergency naval rearmament program. She joined the Home Fleet in March 1941 and was almost immediately ordered into action against *Bismarck* even though her 14-inch guns were still not fully operational. After *Hood*'s sinking, she was lucky to avoid being sunk herself, but the Germans did not pursue her. Ordered to the Far East with the battlecruiser *Renown* in a vain attempt to deter Japan, she was not as fortunate. That December, she and *Repulse* were sunk from the air off Malaya while returning to Singapore after an abortive mission to attack the Japanese invasion fleet.

It all looked satisfactory—at least on paper. The reality was somewhat different. None of Britain's most modern battleships were to be sent east. Instead, the vessels the Admiralty intended to despatch were *Nelson, Rodney,* and four even older and slower R-class battleships—*Ramillies, Resolution, Revenge,* and *Royal Sovereign. Renown,* the selected battlecruiser, was just as old, though it was faster. Even more crucially, the earliest date by which the Admiralty estimated that this new fleet could be assembled was March 1942.

Subsequent pressure of events forced the watering down of the plan. In August 1941, it was decided that only the old battlecruiser *Repulse* and the four R-class battleships could be spared for detachment. All Britain's more modern battleships were required to protect the Atlantic trade convoys in the event of a breakout by *Tirpitz, Scharnhorst,* and *Gneisenau* and in the Mediterranean to contain the Italian battlefleet.

CHURCHILL INTERVENES

Churchill was far from willing to accept the Admiralty plan. What he wanted was what he termed "a deterrent squadron" sent to the Indian Ocean as fast as possible. "Such a force," he opined, "should consist of the smallest number of the best ships." By "best ships," he meant a *King George V*–class battleship—originally *Duke of York* was his choice, but later *Prince of Wales* was substituted—*Repulse* or *Renown,* and "an aircraft carrier of high speed." His belief was that such a force "would exert a paralysing effect on Japanese naval action."

After much debate and discussion, Admiral Sir Dudley Pound, the First Sea Lord, gave way. On October 20, the War Cabinet agreed that *Prince of Wales* and *Indomitable* should sail for South Africa—the latter from the Caribbean once its sea trials there had been completed—and then on into the Indian Ocean to rendezvous with *Repulse.* The three capital ships and their escorts would then make as quickly as possible for Singapore. Admiral Sir Tom Phillips, the Vice-Chief of the Naval Staff, was to be in command of the squadron.

Churchill had won. He eagerly signaled Stalin as follows. "With the object of keeping Japan quiet, we are sending our latest battleship *Prince of Wales*, which can catch and kill any Japanese ship, into the Indian Ocean and are building up a powerful battle squadron there." Roosevelt was similarly informed. "There is nothing like having something that can catch and kill anything," the premier told him.

FORCE Z ARRIVES

On December 2, *Prince of Wales*, *Repulse*, and their escorts reached Singapore. *Indomitable* was conspicuous by her absence. She had run aground in the Caribbean and, though she managed to make it to the US naval dockyard in Norfolk, Virginia, she was still undergoing repairs. Phillips could have asked for *Hermes*, which had arrived in South Africa at the same time as *Prince of Wales* left for Singapore as replacement, but he failed to do so. Maybe this was because of her slow speed or the fact that she could carry only 16 aircraft. The reason for his decision will never be known.

Nevertheless, morale in Singapore was boosted by the news that the two great capital ships were on their way. Duff Cooper, a cabinet minister who had been sent by Churchill to the Far East three months before to assess the situation, described their arrival. "It was a great moment when they (*Prince of Wales* and *Repulse*) came round the bend into the narrow waters of the straits that divide Singapore from the mainland," he wrote. "We were all at the naval base to meet them and they arrived punctual to the minute with their escort of four destroyers. They conferred a sense of complete security."

There were good reasons for confidence. The 35,000-ton *Prince of Wales* was Britain's newest and most

technologically advanced battleship. Launched as recently as 1939, her main armament consisted of ten 14-inch guns in three turrets with a range of more than 20 miles (32km), backed up by four twin 5.25-inch turrets mounted either side of the main deck—each gun being capable of firing 18 rounds a minute—six batteries of eight-barreled two-pounder pompoms, a 40-mm Bofors gun, and a number of Oerlikon light cannons. No less than 12,500 tons of her total weight was armored plating. The unofficial opinion was that she was unsinkable.

Repulse, displacing 32,000 tons, carried six 15-inch guns mounted in three turrets. Though a much older ship of World War I vintage, she had been completely modernized in the years between 1932 and 1939. Her strength was her speed—she could steam, when new, as fast as 32 knots. Her weakness other than her

▲ A member of *Illustrious*'s crew guides one of its aircraft in to land on its flight deck. *Illustrious* was the aircraft carrier originally chosen to accompany *Prince of Wales* and *Repulse* to Singapore, but she ran aground while completing her working up off Kingston, Jamaica, and had to sail to the USA for repairs. This left Force Z without any independent air cover of its own. For some reason, *Hermes*, which could have replaced *Illustrious*, was not ordered to sail from South Africa to join the British capital ships, but remained behind in the Indian Ocean. By the time *Illustrious* was ready to sail, it was too late.

relatively thin armored protection was the quality and quantity of her anti-aircraft armament. This consisted of just six hand-operated high-angle 4-inch guns and three sets of pompoms.

SAILING INTO THE ATTACK

On the surface at least, Phillips seemed to be in optimistic mood. He even made light of the fact that he had no independent air cover of his own and that it was unlikely that the RAF's land-based aircraft would be able to provide him with meaningful air support. On receiving news of the Japanese landings, he decided to sail north right away, hoping to sink the Japanese transport ships en masse while the troops they carried were still disembarking.

In the early evening of December 8, Phillips and his squadron put to sea, zigzagging north into the night at a speed of 17.5 knots. The weather had broken and the ships were shrouded by low, heavy cloud as they steered through the frequent rain squalls. The conditions could not have suited Phillips better. His intention was to continue steaming northward through the next day and then, if the weather continued to shield him, to turn west and make a dash at high speed into the invasion area in the Gulf of Siam. Having sunk as much Japanese shipping as possible, *Prince of Wales* and *Repulse* would then retire southward at full speed back to Singapore, fighting off any Japanese surface or air attacks along the way.

By 1:30 p.m., the British ships were halfway to their destination. Two hours later, however, they were spotted by a Japanese submarine which, unbeknown to Phillips, surfaced and started to shadow them. At 5 p.m., however, the submarine lost contact. It was restored shortly before sunset, when three Japanese seaplanes struck it lucky. Keeping well out of range of the squadron's anti-aircraft guns, they calmly plotted its speed and course, relaying the information to naval headquarters in Saigon.

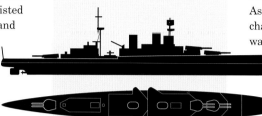

REPULSE

Class *Renown*-class battle cruiser

Displacement 35,200 tons

Length 794ft (242m)

Beam 89ft (27.1m)

Draft 29ft (8.8m)

Speed 31 knots

Armament Six 15-in guns mounted in three turrets, ten 4½-in guns, 24 2-pdr anti-aircraft guns, 16 ½-in anti-aircraft guns

Crew 1, 309

Even while she was being built during World War I, doubts were being expressed about the thickness of the protective armor *Repulse* and her sister-ship *Renown* carried. Though this was strengthened over the years—and other improvements made during *Repulse*'s 1934 to 1936 modernization —she was still not well suited to resist aerial bombardment. When Japanese bombers attacked her off Malaya in December 1941, though she managed to dodge several air strikes, she was eventually hit by no fewer than five torpedoes dropped in rapid succession. Unable to resist such punishment, she took on an immediate list to port and sank within 20 minutes.

ON COURSE FOR DESTRUCTION

As he reached the point where he had intended to change course to head for the invasion beaches, Phillips was faced with a momentous decision. He could continue into the Gulf and run the risk of almost certain attack by Japanese surface ships and aircraft the following morning or abandon the mission. Reluctantly, he chose the second course of action. He signaled *Repulse*: "I have most regretfully cancelled the operation because, having been located by aircraft, surprise was lost and our target would almost certain to be gone by the morning and the enemy fully prepared for us."

Had Phillips held to his course back toward Singapore, he might have made it home safely, but fate said otherwise. Just before midnight, Singapore signaled him that the Japanese had made a fresh landing at Kuantan only 180 miles (290km) north of the island. He decided to investigate, but when the squadron arrived there was nothing to be seen. The destroyer *Express*, despatched close into shore to reconnoiter reported, "All is as quiet as a wet Sunday afternoon." Phillips then lost more time tracking down a small ship and three barges that had been spotted earlier in the area. The delays were probably the final nail in Force Z's coffin. At around 10:15 a.m. it was spotted again by enemy aircraft and, an hour later, Japanese bombers and torpedo planes closed in for the kill. The first wave of high-level bombers made straight for *Repulse*. Just one bomb hit the great battlecruiser, causing minimal damage.

DEAD IN THE WATER

Minutes later, the first torpedo planes arrived on the scene. This time, *Prince of Wales* was the target. Despite her desperate evasive maneuvering, two torpedoes plunged directly into her stern, one irreparably damaging the port-outer propeller shaft and the other tearing a huge hole in the hull.

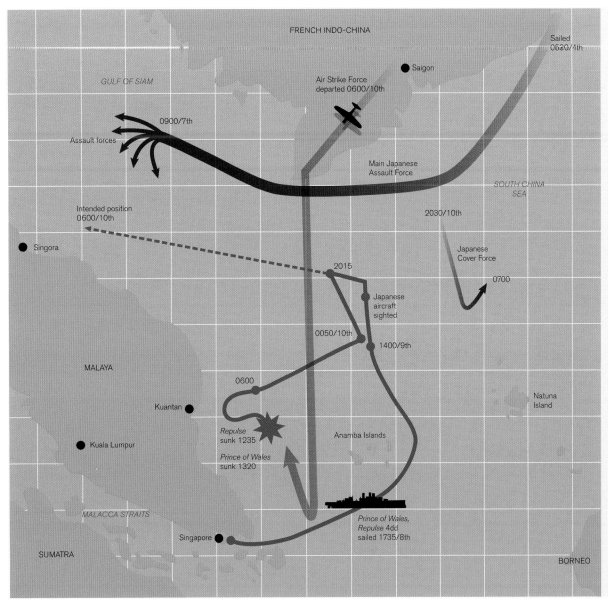

FRENCH INDO-CHINA

GULF OF SIAM

● Saigon

Air Strike Force
departed 0600/10th

Sailed
0630/11th

0900/7th

Assault forces

Main Japanese
Assault Force

SOUTH CHINA
SEA

Intended position
0600/10th

2030/10th

● Singora

Japanese
Cover Force

2015

0700

Japanese
aircraft
sighted

0050/10th

1400/9th

MALAYA

0600

Natuna
Island

Kuantan ●

● Kuala Lumpur

Repulse
sunk 1235

Anamba Islands

Prince of Wales
sunk 1320

MALACCA STRAITS

Prince of Wales,
Repulse 4dd
sailed 1735/8th

Singapore ●

SUMATRA

BORNEO

ATTACKED FROM THE AIR

Force Z, consisting of *Prince of Wales*, *Repulse*, and their escorting destroyers, sailed from Singapore on December 8, 1941. Their mission was to seek out and destroy the Japanese invasion fleet before it could reinforce the initial landings that had already been made in Thailand and Malaya. Believing that he had been spotted by Japanese aircraft and so lost the advantage of surprise, Admiral Sir Tom Phillips, in command of the operation, decided to abandon it and turn back to Singapore. He then lost valuable time altering course to investigate another reported Japanese landing. Without any air cover of his own, he could not resist the Japanese torpedo and high-level bombers that located and attacked him. His ships were sunk in minutes.

This Japanese photograph shows *Prince of Wales* and *Repulse* after they had been blitzed by Japanese high-level and torpedo bombers flying from bases in Thailand to attack them off Malaya. One of the capital ships' escorting destroyers can be seen in the foreground. *Repulse* initially managed to dodge as many as 11 torpedoes before finally being hit; *Prince of Wales* was not as lucky. The first torpedo that hit her near the stern tore open the end of the passage housing the port-outer propeller shaft, allowing a vast amount of water to enter the ship. She never recovered from the blow. Her electrical system failed, leaving every pump in the rear part of the ship without power, while the flooding soon put two engine rooms, a boiler room, an action machinery room, and one of the diesel dynamo rooms out of action.

The results were catastrophic. The battleship slowed down dramatically from 25 to 15 knots and took on a 13-degree list to port. Her stern settled so much that the deck was only two feet (0.6m) above sea level rather than the usual 24 feet (7m). Some 2,400 tons of water had flooded into the ship within four minutes of the two torpedo hits. As a result, five of the ship's eight dynamos failed, leaving the rear half of the ship almost completely without power. *Prince of Wales* wallowed practically helpless in the water. Her steering motors, which relied on electricity to power them, had gone dead.

Repulse, which had emerged from the first phase of the battle almost unscathed, now faced renewed Japanese attack by a combination of high-level bombers and low-level torpedo planes. Remarkably, she still managed to escape damage, dodging the estimated 19 torpedoes the Japanese launched at her. Then her luck ran out. Plane after plane launched what was to prove to be a final, fatal strike. Four torpedoes hit the battlecruiser simultaneously. Mortally wounded, *Repulse* came to a shuddering, shaking halt. Having taken on a 40-degree list, she rolled farther and farther over to sink stern first.

This left *Prince of Wales* on her own and helpless. Just two minutes before *Repulse* went to the bottom, the Japanese torpedoed her again four times—this time along her starboard side. The first torpedo blew a hold straight through the ship, which by now had taken in almost 18,000 tons of water. The high-level bombers then struck for the final time. A single bomb put the last functioning boiler room out of action. *Prince of Wales* came to a dead stop.

The great battleship was settling deeper and deeper in the water by the minute, the sea creeping up along the portside deck from the stern. As her list suddenly started to increase, the order went out from the bridge—"Abandon ship!" Slowly, *Prince of Wales* started to turn turtle, until her bottom lay completely exposed. Her bows reared high in the air as she gave up the unequal struggle and slipped quietly beneath the waves. Phillips went down with his ship.

No one knows what Phillips must have been thinking as Force Z was systematically destroyed. Even after the Japanese attack had begun, he never broke radio silence to advise Singapore that he was under aerial assault. *Repulse* did so on her own initiative. The two signals he sent asked for more destroyers and then "all available tugs" to be sent to his assistance. Quite what he thought either could accomplish remains a mystery to this day.

◀ Members of the *Prince of Wales*'s crew scramble over the side, attempting to escape from the doomed battleship and reach the destroyer *Express*, which was standing off alongside to rescue survivors. "There was no mad rushing," one recalled, "and the evacuation seemed to be absurdly leisurely considering the circumstances."

THE CHANNEL DASH

At 9:45 p.m. in the evening of February 11, 1942, the battlecruisers *Scharnhorst* and *Gneisenau*, together with the heavy cruiser *Prinz Eugen*, raised anchor and started to steam slowly out of the French port of Brest, where the three ships had been holed up since spring 1941. It was the start of what Vice Admiral Otto Ciliax, in overall command, called "a bold and unheard of operation for the German Navy." It was probably the single most daring mission to be mounted by the Kriegsmarine during the whole of World War II.

Operation Cerebus, as the Germans christened it, was certainly daring. The inspiration for it had come from Hitler himself, obsessed with the idea that the British were preparing to invade Norway—a military adventure which, if successful, would deprive the Reich of the Scandinavian iron ore on which its war economy relied, and safeguard the passage of Arctic convoys to Russia. He summoned Grand Admiral Erich Raeder to a conference to discuss future naval plans. It was to be held on September 17, 1941.

HITLER ORDERS THE BREAKOUT

Undeterred by the loss of *Bismarck* earlier in the year, Raeder arrived at the Führer's headquarters expecting to report on his plans for deploying his heavy ships in the Atlantic. That, however, was the last thing on Hitler's mind. He told Raeder that the Atlantic could be left to the U-boats. The Kriegsmarine's major units, he said, had to be stationed along the Norwegian coast, where they could be of "some use in guarding Norway against invasion."

At the time, Raeder managed to appease the Führer by agreeing to send *Tirpitz* to Trondheim, but, on reflection, Hitler decided that this concession was not good enough. On November 29, he demanded that *Scharnhorst* and *Gneisenau* break out of Brest, sail up the English Channel, through the Straits of Dover, and

GNEISENAU

Class *Scharnhorst*-class battlecruiser

Displacement 38,700 tons (full load)

Length 771ft (235m)

Beam 98ft (29.9m)

Draft 32ft (9.8m)

Speed 31 knots

Armament Nine 11-in guns mounted in three turrets, 12 5⅞-in guns, 14 4⅛-in guns, 16 37-mm anti-aircraft cannon, ten (later 16) 20-mm anti-aircraft guns

Crew 1,669

Together with her sister-ship *Scharnhorst*, *Gneisenau* was launched in 1936. She joined the Kriegsmarine three years later. The two ships operated together successfully, but, after the successful homeward dash from Brest in Occupied France up the English Channel to Germany in spring 1942, *Gneisenau*'s luck ran out. She was badly damaged by a magazine explosion triggered by an RAF bomb while she was in dry dock. Though the German Naval Staff started to rebuild her, Hitler vetoed the completion of the project. Her main gun turrets were removed and converted into shore batteries. She was scuttled as a blockship just before the end of the war.

on into the North Sea. Once they had reached Kiel, their home port, they were to be fitted out for Norway's defense. When Raeder protested that the operation was far too risky, an infuriated Hitler dropped a dramatic bombshell. "If the Channel route is impossible," he almost shouted, "the Brest ships must be decommissioned, their guns dismantled and sent with their crews to Norway." He ended with a gratuitous insult. "In any case," he said coldly, "battleships have no place in future wars and I doubt if they are of much use now."

Though Raeder continued to protest, it was in vain. The Führer had made one of his celebrated "unalterable decisions." The Brest ships would sail for home via the English Channel regardless of risk. Strangely enough, Vice Admiral Otto Ciliax, commander of the Brest battle squadron, agreed with the Führer when he summed up why he insisted on pressing ahead with the operation: "The Brest group," he told Raeder, "is like a patient suffering from cancer who is doomed unless he submits to an operation. An operation, on the other hand, even though it might have to be drastic, affords some hope that the patient's life might be saved. The passage up the Channel will be such an operation, therefore the Channel operation has to be attempted."

The Führer went on to explain why he believed Operation Cerebus would be successful. It all depended, he said, on taking the British by surprise. For that reason, the Brest ships would leave port after dark rather than by day, so that they could get a head start up the Channel and hopefully as far as the Straits of Dover before being detected. "You can count on this," he assured the worried Grand Admiral. "From my previous experience I do not believe the British capable of the conception and execution of lightning decisions such as will be required for the transfer of their air and sea forces to meet the boldness of our operation."

THE "CHANNEL DASH" BEGINS

On February 4, after all three ships had completed their sea trials in Iroise Bay, Ciliax reported to Raeder that they were ready to sail. The departure date was set for the night of February 11 to take advantage of the next new moon. Once safely round the Cherbourg Peninsula, *Scharnhorst*, *Gneisenau*, *Prinz Eugen*, and their six escorting destroyers were joined by two E-boat flotillas numbering ten boats each. Off Cape Gris Nez, the squadron would be joined by 24 more E-boats, plus gunboats and minesweepers from Western and Northern Naval Commands, making a grand total of 63 ships.

It was a formidable armada. By dawn, it had steamed more than 250 miles (402km), having successfully bypassed the various precautions the British had put in place to provide early warning in case of an attempted German breakout. *Sealion*, the duty submarine the Admiralty had stationed just off Brest, was forced to withdraw to recharge its batteries just before Ciliax's ships emerged. The Coastal Command aircraft patrolling between Brest and the tip of the Breton Peninsula developed a radar fault and had to return to base. It took two hours to get a replacement into the air. The same thing happened to the plane patrolling along what the British called Line S-E, while the patrol covering the area between Le Havre and Boulogne was brought to end an hour early because of the fear of fog.

These were not the only British countermeasures. At 4 a.m., a signal from Dover brought the naval forces assigned to guard the Channel to a state of immediate readiness. The Swordfish torpedo bombers stationed at Manston were manned ready to take to the air, while, at Harwich, six destroyers raised steam, ready to get underway at 15 minutes' notice. This was a routine alert called every morning on the assumption that the Germans, if they sailed, would reach the Straits of Dover before dawn. After that, the Swordfish and destroyers would stand down and revert to their normal routines.

THE BATTLE OF THE NARROW SEAS

Thanks to German jamming, even the British long-range radar stations failed to detect Ciliax's progress. The circling blips their operators started to see were put down to atmospheric interference or taken as a sign that some sort of air–sea rescue operation was in progress. In fact, it was the Luftwaffe fighter umbrella Ciliax had been promised starting to assemble. It was not until 10:33 a.m. that two Spitfires, hunting for German aircraft to attack over the Channel, made the first visual sighting. They immediately turned for home to report what they had seen orally. More valuable time was lost. Standing orders forbade the use of radio to transmit an instant warning. Not until 11:25 a.m. was Dover was finally alerted to what was going on in the

▲ *Gneisenau* pictured steaming at speed. She and *Scharnhorst* were among the most graceful ships of their day—even though the RAF bomber crews who had been pounding unsuccessfully at them in Brest for months had derisively christened them "the ugly sisters."

Channel and the imminent approach of what looked like a major part of the German fleet.

At noon, the Germans started to steam through the Straits of Dover. There was still no sign of any British opposition. At 12:18 p.m., however, they came under desultory fire at extreme range from the coastal artillery batteries stationed at Dover. No shells fell anywhere near the armada. Five MTBs (Motor Torpedo Boats) from Dover now finally arrived on the scene and moved into the attack, trying to break through Ciliax's screening E-boats, gunboats, and destroyers and get a clear torpedo shot at the two battlecruisers and *Prinz Eugen*. They were up against impossible odds. Confronted by a wall of enemy shellfire, they were forced to withdraw. The torpedoes they gallantly managed to launch all missed their targets.

It was now the turn of the six Fleet Air Arm Swordfish from Manston to show what they could do. They had been promised a protective escort of five squadrons of Spitfires, but only ten planes turned up at the rendezvous. Lieutenant Commander Eugene Esmonde, in command of 825 Squadron, decided to continue with the attack. Despite being swamped by hordes of Luftwaffe fighters—the air umbrella was now at its maximum strength—and facing the massive anti-aircraft barrage put up by Ciliax's ships, he and his fellow pilots dropped to wave-top height and made for their targets. All six Swordfish released their torpedoes before being shot down, though no hits were scored. Five aircrew were rescued from the sea by the patrolling MTBs. The other 13 perished. Esmonde was one of them. He was awarded a posthumous Victoria Cross.

STRUCK BY MINES

The Germans had been at sea for more than 15 hours and so far had remained unscathed. The MTB and Swordfish attacks had failed: Coastal and Bomber Commands were desperately endeavoring to bring organized confusion to unorganized chaos. Then, at 2:20 p.m., *Scharnhorst* was forced to a wallowing standstill. She had struck a British mine. Ciliax was forced to transfer his flag to the destroyer *Z-29*, which hustled off to catch up with the rest of the fleet. The wounded battlecruiser was left behind while her crew struggled to repair her propeller shafts, which had been damaged in the massive explosion.

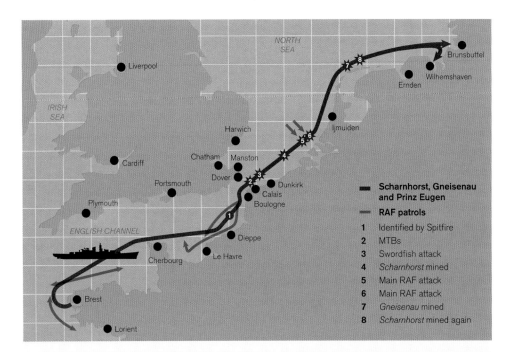

■	Scharnhorst, Gneisenau and Prinz Eugen
▬	RAF patrols
1	Identified by Spitfire
2	MTBs
3	Swordfish attack
4	*Scharnhorst* mined
5	Main RAF attack
6	Main RAF attack
7	*Gneisenau* mined
8	*Scharnhorst* mined again

STEAMING UP THE CHANNEL

Vice Admiral Otto Ciliax took his ships out of Brest late in the evening of February 11, 1942. By 1:30 a.m., they were steaming at 30 knots off Ushant and preparing to steam up the English Channel. The British were convinced that no such passage would be attempted at night. The Germans, they argued, would sail in daylight, aiming to reach the Straits of Dover—the narrowest part of the Channel—as night fell and take advantage of darkness to steam through them safely. They were to be proved hopelessly wrong. Nor were their torpedo bombers and their fighter escort concentrated ready to attack. They were dispersed around various airfields. By contrast, Ciliax could count on a constant aerial umbrella of 250 of the Luftwaffe's crack fighters overhead once dawn had broken.

British torpedo attacks—launched this time by Coastal Command Beauforts—continued sporadically during the long afternoon. They were all total failures. Some of the Beaufort pilots had not even been told what they were supposed to be attacking. Others were given map reference locations that were hours out of date. In all, 15 Coastal Command aircraft attacked. Two of them failed to drop their torpedoes and four were shot down. Bomber Command, attacking later, was as unsuccessful. The 240 bombers it committed to the assault attacked in dribs and drabs. Many got lost and returned to base.

The Harwich destroyers were the last show left in the navy's locker. Like Esmonde, they had been expecting to strike under cover of darkness. Like him, they were now faced with making a daylight attack. Captain Mark Pizey in *Campbell* led the way, attacking *Gneisenau* accompanied by *Vivacious* and *Worcester*. Steaming out of the afternoon mist at maximum speed toward their target, they took the battlecruiser by surprise, though her gun crews were quick to react to the oncoming threat. *Worcester* was so badly damaged that it was thought she was certain to sink. Rather than abandoning ship, her crew battled to get her back to port under her own steam. The other destroyers had to face air assault. British bombers attacked them by mistake. It was an ignominious end to an embarrassing day.

HOME AT LAST

The Germans by now were running up the Dutch coast, heading for the Friesian Islands and the approach to home waters. *Scharnhorst* had been temporarily repaired and was steaming at full speed again in an attempt to catch up with the rest of the fleet. As darkness fell, the scattered remains of the Luftwaffe umbrella returned to its home airfields. Ciliax could now rely on the weather and nightfall for aerial protection.

It looked like a triumph for the Kriegsmarine, but then fate took another unexpected turn. *Gneisenau*,

making a good 27 knots in waters where regulations said she should be steaming at no more than ten, struck a mine. The explosion made a gaping rent in her bottom near her stern. It took 30 minutes to patch over her wound with a steel collision mat, put her pumps to work, and get her moving again. She dropped anchor off the Elbe at 7 a.m., the first of Ciliax's armada to make it home.

Prinz Eugen followed shortly before dawn. This left only *Scharnhorst* unaccounted for. She was doubly unlucky. Just passed the Friesians, she struck a second mine. This time, the damage she suffered was more severe and it was only at midnight that she managed to get underway again. Limping along at 12 knots, she managed to make Wilhelmshaven around dawn the following day. The great Channel Dash was over.

▲ *Gneisenau*, photographed from the heavy cruiser *Prinz Eugen*, steams up the English Channel. *Scharnhorst* is in the distance behind her. Operation Cerebus, as the Germans termed their bold Channel dash, was carried out at Hitler's personal insistence. The ships in Brest, he told his doubting naval commanders, were "like a man with cancer." The only hope for them as well as the cancer sufferer was "a bold operation." Therefore, "the operation was to be attempted." The Führer gambled on the fact that the British would not be able to react quickly enough to counter the daring move.

CORAL SEA

By May 1942, Japan's drive through the Pacific was reaching its apogee. Its blitzkrieg attack on the Philippines was followed by the capture of Wake, Guam, Hong Kong, Thailand, northern Borneo, the Malayan Peninsula, and Singapore. After a last-ditch stand by the four Allied navies in the Java Sea, the entire Dutch East Indies was forced to surrender. Burma, too, was on the brink of falling. At much the same time, Admiral Nagumo's crack carrier force was raiding deep into the Indian Ocean. Between March 25 and April 8, planes from his carriers bombed Colombo and Trincomalee, sank the British aircraft carrier *Hermes* and two heavy cruisers, and about 136,000 tons of merchant shipping.

In the four months before it retired to home waters, Nagumo's task force sailed the equivalent of one third of the way around the world. During that time, he launched devastating air strikes against ships and shore installations as far apart as Pearl Harbor, Rabaul, Ambon, Darwin, Java, and Ceylon. He sank five battleships, an aircraft carrier, two cruisers, and seven destroyers, damaged several more capital ships, and sent a total of some 200,000 tons of fleet auxiliaries and merchant shipping to the bottom. His aircrews shot down hundreds of Allied planes into the bargain. Not a single one of his ships was damaged by enemy action.

US RETALIATION

Admiral Nimitz, the newly appointed commander-in-chief of the US Pacific Fleet, was fully aware that the perilous situation demanded retaliatory action. Relying on the aircraft carriers that fortuitously had been at sea when the Japanese struck Pearl Harbor, he launched a series of hit-and-run air strikes, hoping to catch the Japanese off guard. On February 1, *Enterprise* raided Kwajalein in the Marshall Islands. Next, *Lexington* struck at Rabaul before, joined by *Yorktown*, she blitzed the Japanese at Lae and Salamaua on the northern coast of Papua.

HORNET

Class	*Yorktown*-class aircraft carrier
Displacement	29,282 tons (full load)
Length	827ft 5in (252m)
Beam	114ft (252.2m)
Draft	28ft (8.5m)
Speed	22 knots
Aircraft carried	90
Armament	Eight 5-in dual-purpose guns, 16 28-mm anti-aircraft guns, 30 20-mm anti-aircraft cannon
Crew	2,919

Hornet, *Enterprise*, and *Yorktown* were the three carriers making up the US Navy's *Yorktown* class. Of them, *Hornet* was the last to be built, being launched in December 1940. She was slightly bigger than the others of her class, with a larger flight deck. This probably was one of the reasons why she was chosen to launch the celebrated Doolittle bombing raid on Tokyo in April 1942. She fought at Midway the following month and also in the Solomons campaign before being sunk by multiple torpedo hits off Santa Cruz on October 27, 1942.

The three raids did much to raise the Pacific Fleet's morale, even though they were no more than pinpricks. The bombing strike *Hornet* launched against Tokyo on April 18, 1942 was another matter. As the US Navy then had no aircraft with the range to reach the Japanese capital, 16 US Army Air Force B-25 bombers, commanded by Lieutenant-Colonel James Doolittle, were flown off *Hornet* instead. Reaching Tokyo by noon, their strike, though inflicting only superficial damage, took the Japanese completely by surprise. It demonstrated that the USA was not down and out. In fact, it was ready and willing to strike back.

JAPANESE REACTION

The Japanese High Command was divided as to its best course of action. Admiral Yamamoto and the Naval War Staff argued that all the navy's efforts should be directed at wiping out the US Pacific Fleet once and for all. Achieving this would win Japan the time it needed to make its outer defense zone impregnable. The belief was that, if this could be accomplished, the USA would eventually tire of waging a futile war and would negotiate a peace that would leave the Japanese masters of the Pacific.

Japan's generals thought differently. They urged the navy to divert some of its forces to support their land operations in the southwestern Pacific, where the army's two immediate aims were to capture Port Moresby, on the southeastern coast of New Guinea, and occupy Tulagi in the southern Solomon Islands. Taking control of Port Moresby, the army believed,

Looking aft from *Hornet*'s central island, eight of the 16 B-25B bombers chosen to fly the Doolittle Raid can be seen lining the carrier's flight deck. *Nashville*, one of her escorts, is visible to port in the distance. The bomber on the left is warming up its engines, as was done periodically during the voyage. Despite gale-force winds, driving rain, and lashing waves strong enough to make her flight deck heave violently, *Hornet* launched all Mitchell's bombers successfully.

was particularly important. It would put the Japanese within aircraft range of northern Australia. Eventually, it would be the springboard for the invasion of Australia itself.

Initially, Yamamoto resisted the army's demands in favor of striking what he confidently expected would prove to be a knockout blow against the US Pacific Fleet in the central Pacific. The battle was to be triggered by attacking Midway, along with the launching of diversionary raids on Dutch Harbor and the occupation of Kiska and Attu in the southern Aleutians. The army countered by arguing that, should

their amphibious and land operations look successful, the Americans would be bound to order their fleet into the area to try to intervene. Yamamoto's decisive action could be fought there just as well as at Midway. The Japanese admiral temporized. Then, he decided to go ahead with both plans.

BATTLE IN THE CORAL SEA

Yamamoto ordered three separate task forces into the Coral Sea to carry out his plan. The first, commanded by Rear Admiral Kiyohide Shima, headed for Tulagi in the Solomon Islands, while the second sailed south for

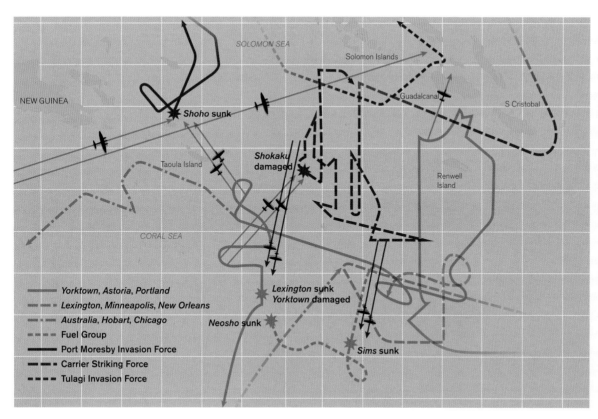

Yorktown, Astoria, Portland
Lexington, Minneapolis, New Orleans
Australia, Hobart, Chicago
Fuel Group
Port Moresby Invasion Force
Carrier Striking Force
Tulagi Invasion Force

SOLOMON SEA
Solomon Islands
NEW GUINEA
Guadalcanal
S Cristobal
Shoho sunk
Shokaku damaged
Taoula Island
Renwell Island
CORAL SEA
Lexington sunk
Yorktown damaged
Neosho sunk
Sims sunk

AIR–SEA COMBAT

Four days of battle between Japanese and US aircraft carriers in the Coral Sea ended in a tactical stalemate but a strategic victory for the USA. This map charts the course of the air–sea confrontation (the battle was fought entire by the aircraft carriers and there was no ship-to-ship action). By the time the clash was over, the Americans had lost the carrier *Lexington* and *Yorktown* had been damaged. The Japanese light carrier *Shoho* had been sunk and the fleet carrier *Shokaku* badly hit. Aircraft losses were 66 American planes to the Japanese 70. This meant that the Japanese could no longer provide air cover for the forces they intended to land at Port Moresby in New Guinea and the operation had to be abandoned.

Port Moresby. Vice Admiral Takeo Takagi's Carrier Strike Force—consisting of the aircraft carriers *Shokaku* and *Zuikaku* fresh from their triumphs at Pearl Harbor, two heavy cruisers, and six destroyers—was ordered to force any American warships that might intervene to come to battle.

In all probability, the plan would have worked, but for one crucial factor of which Yamamoto and his fellow admirals were totally unaware. US Navy cryptologists in Pearl Harbor had succeeded in cracking the Japanese naval code. Alerted to Japanese intentions by decoded radio intercepts, Nimitz was able to despatch the carriers *Yorktown* and *Lexington* to the Coral Sea in time to protect Port Moresby.

The Japanese won the first trick when they occupied Tulagi unopposed on May 1. The Americans responded the next day when *Yorktown* launched three strikes against the island, sinking a destroyer and five merchant ships. She then steamed south to rendezvous with *Lexington*. For the next two days, the Japanese and American carriers searched for each other without success, though at one time they were only 70 miles (113km) apart. However, aircraft from both sides did manage to locate some secondary units. The Japanese crippled the American fleet tanker *Neosho* and sank *Sims*, its escorting destroyer. US planes found the light carrier *Shoho*, which was providing cover for the Port Moresby task force, and sank it. Only 255 men out of a crew of around 800 were saved.

Both carrier task forces finally located each other early in the morning of May 8. Yorktown's planes struck first at *Shokaku*. *Zuikaku*, concealed by a sudden rain squall, escaped unscathed. Then aircraft from *Lexington* arrived on the scene and bombed *Shokaku* as well. She was forced to make for home for repairs. In the meantime, the Japanese attacked both American carriers. *Yorktown* was hit by a single 750-lb (340-kg) bomb on her flight deck but managed to dodge the three torpedoes that were aimed at her. *Lexington*

was not as lucky. She took two torpedo hits on her starboard side, and two bomb hits. As she started listing, her crew fought to bring the onboard fires under control. Suddenly, she was racked by two massive internal explosions caused by sparks that had ignited the fumes from her ruptured aviation fuel tanks. The crew was forced to abandon ship. Torpedoed by *Phelps*, one of her escorting destroyers, to avoid the wreck falling into enemy hands, *Lexington* sank later that evening.

In terms of the number of ships sunk, the Japanese won a tactical victory. Strategically, they suffered their first defeat. Vice Admiral Shigeyoshi Inoue, in overall command of the operation, decided that, without clear air superiority, he could not run the risk of proceeding with the Port Moresby landings. He ordered the invasion task force back to Rabaul. The battle also impacted on Yamamoto's preparations for the attack on Midway. The damage to *Shokaku* took two months to repair while *Zuikaku* had lost many of its planes in combat. As a result, both missed taking part in the battle there in early June.

▲ *Lexington* burning during the battle of the Coral Sea after being crippled by Japanese carrier-borne bombers. Highly flammable aviation gasoline vapor leaking from her ruptured fuel storage tanks triggered a series of massive internal explosions, which sparked fires that eventually proved uncontrollable. Abandoned by her crew, "Lady Lex," as she was nicknamed, had to be torpedoed and sunk by one of her escorting destroyers in order to avoid capture.

MIDWAY

Even before the battle of the Coral Sea began, Yamamoto was preparing to launch what he thought would be a decisive strike against the Americans at Midway in the central Pacific. He confidently believed the battle there would end with the annihilation of what remained of the US Pacific Fleet and consequent Japanese victory in the Pacific war.

Practically the entire Japanese navy would be involved in the action. Vice Admiral Moshito Hosogaya's Northern Area Force, consisting of the light aircraft carriers *Ryujo* and *Junyo*, two heavy cruisers, a screen of destroyers, and four troop transports, would start the ball rolling by mounting a diversionary attack on the Aleutians. Admiral Nobutake Kondo's Midway Occupation Force, consisting of 15 troopships escorted by the light carrier *Zuiho*, 2 battleships, 8 heavy cruisers, 9 destroyers, and a number of minesweepers, would sail from the Marianas to Midway, where it would rendezvous with the main battle fleet under Yamamoto himself. Vice Admiral Chuichi Nagumo's First Carrier Striking Force would sail for Midway, ahead of Yamamoto, to provide air support. It consisted of the fleet carriers *Akagi, Hiryu, Soryu,* and *Kaga,* the battleships *Kiriskima* and *Maruna,* 3 cruisers, and 12 destroyers. Finally, 16 submarines were to be deployed at intervals between Pearl Harbor and Midway to scout for and attack any US naval force putting to sea.

It was a formidably strong armada. All in all, Yamamoto fielded 200 ships, including 11 battleships, 8 carriers, 22 cruisers, 65 destroyers, and 20 submarines. Two of his battleships, *Yamato* and *Musashi,* were especially noteworthy. Each displaced 72,908 tons when fully laden. With a main armament of nine 18-inch guns with a maximum range of 22.5 miles (936km) and capable of steaming at 27.5 knots, they were the biggest, most modern battleships in the world.

YORKTOWN

Class	*Yorktown*-class aircraft carrier
Displacement	25,000 tons (full load)
Length	761ft (232m)
Beam	83ft (25.3m)
Draft	28ft (25.2m)
Speed	33 knots
Aircraft carried	81–90
Armament	Eight 5-in anti-aircraft guns, 16 28-mm anti-aircraft cannon, 16 5-in anti-aircraft guns
Crew	2,919

Yorktown played a vital role in the battle of the Coral Sea, her first Pacific action. Though damaged, a Herculean effort by the Pearl Harbor Navy Yard got her repaired in time to take part in the battle of Midway. During this, her planes sank the Japanese carrier *Soryu* before *Yorktown* herself was hit by Japanese dive-bombers. A bomb knocked out her boilers and she stopped dead in the water. Though power was eventually restored, a second attack—this time by torpedo planes from *Hiryu*—forced her crew to abandon her. She finally sank after being torpedoed yet again by a Japanese submarine while a salvage crew was attempting to repair her enough to be taken in tow back to Pearl Harbor.

NIMITZ FOREWARNED

Nimitz could only field his two carrier task forces. Task Force 17, commanded by Rear Admiral Frank Fletcher, consisted of *Yorktown*, the bomb damage she had sustained in the Coral Sea having been repaired in world record time at Pearl Harbor, two heavy cruisers, and six destroyers. Rear Admiral Raymond Fletcher, who had just taken over Task Force 16 from the hospitalized Admiral William "Bull" Halsey, had *Enterprise, Hornet,* 6 cruisers, and 11 destroyers under his command.

Nimitz knew that Yamamoto was about to strike again but where and when remained a mystery. The commander-in-chief was desperately trying to anticipate Japan's next move. There was no room for error. If Nimitz miscalculated, the results might well be disastrous. Fortunately, he had another string to his bow. Commander Joseph Rochefort and his code-breaking experts at Pearl Harbor had been working patiently for months attempting to crack the Japanese Navy's primary operational code. By June 1942, they had finally succeeded. Even more importantly, they had positively identified Midway as Yamamoto's next target. This gave Nimitz the invaluable time he needed to get his two carrier task forces into position northeast of Midway ready to ambush the unsuspecting Japanese carriers when they arrived on the scene.

FIRST STRIKE AT MIDWAY

The Northern Force and the Second Carrier Strike Force were the first into action, bombing Dutch Harbor in the eastern Aleutians on June 3 and attacking Attu and Kiska in the western Aleutians. Yamamoto had hoped that Nimitz would be fooled into thinking this was the main attack, but the American commander-in-chief was not deceived. Leaving Rear Admiral Robert A. Theobald to cope on his own, the American carrier groups, rather than changing course to head into the northern Pacific, continued steaming toward Midway.

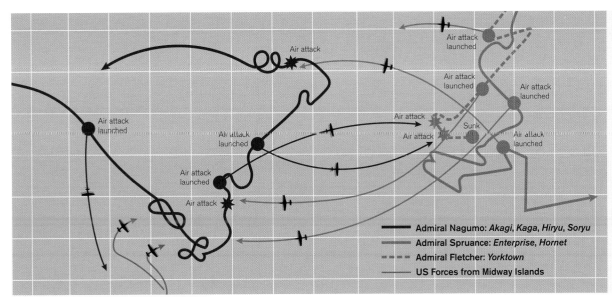

MANEUVERS AT MIDWAY

Thanks to his codebreakers, Admiral Nimitz was able to ensure that his three aircraft carriers—*Enterprise*, *Hornet*, and *Yorktown*—were in the right place at the right time to successfully deal with the four Japanese carriers that Admiral Yamamoto had ordered to attack the island of Midway. The US carriers' presence took Admiral Nagumo, the task force commander, totally by surprise. Though an initial low-level torpedo bomber attack failed, US dive-bombers put *Kaga*, *Akagi*, and *Soryu* out of action within minutes. They had to be abandoned as they sunk. *Hiryu* managed to launch a counterstrike that badly damaged *Yorktown*, but she, too, went to the bottom late in the afternoon. Yamamoto abandoned the entire operation.

Shortly after 6 a.m. on June 4, a Catalina flying boat scouting from Midway reported sighting two of Nagumo's carriers and their escort steaming southeast toward the island. Fletcher, who had made his rendezvous with Spruance two days previously, acted right away, ordering *Enterprise* and *Hornet* to "proceed southwesterly and attack enemy carriers when definitely located." *Yorktown* would follow them as soon as the search planes she had launched were recovered.

Two and a half hours earlier, Nagumo had launched his first strike against Midway and at 6:30 a.m., ten minutes after Fletcher had issued his pregnant order to Spruance, the bombing of the island began. It continued for some 20 minutes. Nagumo believed that one attack would be enough to knock out Midway's defenses, but he was soon disillusioned. The attacking force was spotted by American radar 93 miles (150km) out from shore. As the Japanese fighters, dive-bombers, and torpedo bombers powered toward their target, every fighter on the island was scrambled to intercept them, while four waves of Midway-based land bombers, consisting of 6 Avenger torpedo planes, 16 Dauntless dive-bombers, 16 B-17s, and 4 B-26s, took off to counterattack Nagumo's carriers.

Though the bombers were all driven off or shot down by Nagumo's fighter umbrella, 67 out of the 108 aircraft attacking the island were destroyed or badly damaged by Midway's anti-aircraft defenses. Lieutenant Takeichi Tomonoga, the air group commander of *Hiryu* who was leading the first strike, signaled to Nagumo that a second one would be needed.

FATAL INDECISION

Nagumo was caught on the horns of a dilemma. He had 93 planes sitting waiting on the flight decks of *Akagi* and *Kaga*, armed with torpedoes and armor-piercing bombs in case his scout planes sighted any US warships in the vicinity. No such reports had been received, so he decided to take a calculated risk. He ordered the planes to be taken down to the hanger decks to be rearmed with incendiary and fragmentation bombs. The flight decks were to be left clear for the surviving first-strike planes to land to be refueled and similarly armed.

At the time, it seemed a reasonable enough decision, but it soon proved to be a terrible mistake. Though Nagumo's scout planes now reported that they had sighted some American ships 200 miles (322km) or so away to the northeast, he was still unaware that the US carriers were approaching. It was not until 8:20 a.m. that he finally received accurate intelligence. The terse message read: "Enemy force is accompanied by what appears to be a carrier." It was Spruance's task force closing for action.

Nagumo hesitated. The second wave's rearming for land attack was nearing completion. Now it would have to be rearmed again. Also, his fighter umbrella was running low on fuel, while he still had to recover the last planes of his first wave. As he changed course eastward to meet the new threat, the flight decks of his carriers were crowded with planes—some rearming, others refueling, and more waiting for the chance to land. The result was complete confusion.

At 9:30 a.m., *Hornet*'s torpedo bombers located Nagumo's carriers. Fifteen of them attacked without fighter cover, having lost contact with their escort en route. All of them were shot down by Nagumo's protective screen of Zero fighters and by anti-aircraft fire. *Enterprise*'s planes attacked next. Ten out of 14 were lost. Then it was *Yorktown*'s turn. Of the 12 torpedo bombers she launched, all but four were shot down. Not a single torpedo hit was scored.

Nagumo believed victory was within his grasp. He was mistaken. No sooner had he dealt with the torpedo bombers than the US dive-bombers arrived on the scene. *Enterprise*'s 37 planes were the first to attack, targeting *Kaga* and Nagumo's flagship *Akagi*. *Yorktown*'s attacked *Soryu* just as she was turning into the wind to launch her own aircraft.

THE DIVE-BOMBERS STRIKE

The Japanese, who had been concentrating on fighting off the torpedo bombers, were totally unready to meet this new threat. *Akagi* was hit twice—first by a bomb that penetrated via the flight deck's elevator shaft to the hanger deck, detonating the torpedoes and bombs that were lying around there. The second

ENTERPRISE

Type *Yorktown*-class aircraft carrier

Displacement 25,000 tons (full load)

Length 809ft 6in (246.7m)

Beam 83ft 2in (25.3m)

Draft 27ft 11in (8.5m)

Speed 33 knots

Aircraft carried 80–96

Armament Eight 5-in dual-purpose guns, 24 0.5-caliber machine guns, four 75-mm Quad cannon, 32 20-mm machine guns, four 40-mm Quad cannon

Crew 2,919

Out of more than 20 major actions the US Navy fought in the Pacific during World War II, Enterprise, or the "Big E" as she was known throughout the US Navy, was involved in all but two of them. Her planes and guns downed 911 enemy aircraft; her dive- and torpedo bombers sank 71 ships and damaged or destroyed 192 more. She fought her last battle on May 14, 1945, when a kamikaze strike off Kyushu left a gaping hole in her flight deck, which forced her out of the war.

bomb exploded among the helpless planes that were scattered around her flight deck, which had been switching over from bombs to torpedoes just minutes before.

Almost instantly, *Akagi* was ablaze and being ripped apart by massive internal explosions. Her starboard engine went dead and her speed dropped to 12 knots. Then, as she turned to avoid another attack, the rudder jammed and her remaining engines also ground to an immediate halt. Nagumo realized reluctantly that he had no alternative but to shift his flag—first to a screening destroyer and then to the light cruiser *Nagara*. Captain Taijiro Aoki, *Akagi*'s commander, fought stubbornly until 7:25 p.m. that evening when he finally ordered his remaining crew to abandon ship. *Akagi* finally went to the bottom at 5 a.m., sunk by the Japanese themselves on *Yamato*'s personal order by torpedoes fired by her four escorting destroyers.

Aoki survived to fight another day. Captain Ryusaku Yanagimoto, commander of *Soryu*, went down with his ship. She sank at 7:13 p.m. *Kaga*'s commander, Captain Jistaku Okada, was killed with most of his senior officers by the third of four bombs. It hit *Kaga* just forward of her bridge, shattering the planes on her flight deck and destroying the flight deck itself. She sank at 7:25 p.m. after two massive internal explosions ablaze from stem to stern.

HIRYU AND YORKTOWN

Only *Hiryu*, which was steaming somewhat to the north of the three stricken carriers and so escaped attack, was left to carry on what had now become a totally unequal fight. Still believing that he was facing only a single US carrier, Nagumo ordered her aircraft to attack *Yorktown*. Her 18 remaining torpedo bombers, 10 dive-bombers, and 12 escorting fighters took off in two waves to carry out the mission.

The first wave scored three direct hits on the American carrier, damaging her boilers, starting a fire that was eventually put out by flooding, and putting a large hole straight through her flight deck. The damage was so severe that Fletcher was forced to transfer his flag to the heavy cruiser *Astoria*, leaving Captain Elliott Buckmaster, *Yorktown*'s commander, fighting to save his ship. He managed to get her underway again, working her up to a speed of around 20 knots. Then *Hiryu*'s second wave arrived. *Yorktown* was hit by four torpedoes and the carrier again lurched to a halt. Her rudder jammed and she took on a list to port. When this reached 26 degrees, Buckmaster decided to abandon ship.

It was not over yet. The battered carrier stubbornly refused to sink. While Buckmaster and a salvage party returned to the stricken vessel, the minesweeper *Vireo* took her in tow. Then the Japanese struck what proved to be the fatal blow. As *Yorktown* was inched slowly toward home, she was torpedoed twice by one of their submarines. Soon after 5 a.m. on June 7, she finally rolled over gently in the water and sank.

Hiryu had not escaped. About an hour after her planes had begun their first attack on *Yorktown*, the Japanese carrier was located by dive-bombers from *Enterprise* and *Hornet*, who scored four direct hits on her. Fierce fires broke out at once. Though for a time it looked as if they might be brought under control, at 8:58 p.m. on the evening of June 4, they were rekindled by a tremendous internal explosion. At 1:05 a.m., the order was given to abandon ship. Just over an hour later, she sank, torpedoed by the Japanese themselves.

The defeat was as total as it was devastating. In one day, the Japanese had lost their entire fleet carrier force. Yamamoto was forced to cancel the Midway operation and order his fleet back to Japan. Only six months after its triumphant victory at Pearl Harbor, the Japanese Navy was forced onto the defensive. It was to remain on it for the rest of the war.

B-17 strategic bombers from Midway attacked but missed, *Hiryu* (top); the strike took place early in the battle between 8 a.m. and 8:30 a.m. The dive-bombers from *Enterprise* and *Yorktown* were more fortunate when they located the Japanese task force. All three dive-bomber squadrons arrived at the perfect time to strike at Nagumo's other carriers, which were in the process of refueling and rearming their planes. They were thus extraordinarily open to attack. *Kaga* was the first to be bombed by *Enterprise*'s aircraft, closely followed by *Akagi*. *Yorktown*'s planes went for *Soryu*, scoring at least three direct hits and setting her ablaze.

ARCTIC CONVOYS

The first Arctic convoy carrying vital war supplies to the Soviet Union sailed from Reykjavik in Iceland bound for Archangel in the far north of Russia in late August 1941, two months after Hitler's surprise attack on his ally had brought the Soviets into the war. Many others followed regularly throughout the course of the war, the last one sailing shortly before the Third Reich's unconditional surrender in May 1945. By that time, the convoys had transported over four million tonnes of cargo to the USSR, including tanks, fighter planes, ammunition, raw materials, fuel, and food.

The 2,500-mile (4,023-km) odyssey was perilous. It took the convoys to within 750 miles (1,207km) of the North Pole, where temperatures in winter could fall as low as 50 degrees below freezing. Such were the rigors of Arctic conditions that seamen were compelled to undergo special medical examinations before being allowed to sail. If passed fit, they were then kitted out with extra-thick clothing to help them to withstand the cold. Duffle coats were lined with lambswool. They also were fitted with special hoods which covered the face, leaving only slits for the mouth and eyes.

The weather was frequently so harsh that the salt spray froze as it fell. Ships and seamen had to contend with fierce storms, thick freezing fogs, and ice floes, as well as the freezing cold. It was little wonder that the sailors christened the route the "gateway to Hell." Winston Churchill agreed with them. It was, he said, "the worst journey in the world."

UNDER CONSTANT THREAT

As if the weather was not enough, the convoys had to contend with the Luftwaffe's bombers and the Kriegsmarine's U-boats and surface ships operating from their secure bases in northern Norway. Between September 1941 and May 1945, one in every 20 Allied ships sailing in convoy to or from northern Russia were sunk by enemy action—a total of 104 vessels in all. The

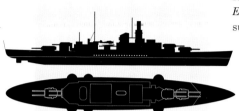

ADMIRAL HIPPER

Class *Hipper*-class heavy cruiser

Displacement 18,600 tons (full load)

Length 640ft (195m)

Beam 70ft (21.3m)

Draft 25ft (7.6m)

Speed 32 knots

Armament Eight 8-in guns in four turrets, 12 4⅛-in anti-aircraft guns, 12 37-mm and four 20-mm anti-aircraft cannons

Crew 1,600

Admiral Hipper and *Blücher* were the first heavy cruisers to be laid down by the Kriegsmarine in 1936; *Prinz Eugen*, *Seydlitz*, and *Lutzow* followed in 1938 and 1939. *Blücher* was an early war casualty, being sunk by a shore battery while conveying troops up the fjord to land in Oslo at the start of the 1940 Norwegian invasion. *Hipper* took part in the same campaign. Between November 1940 and February 1941, she made two Atlantic cruises, attacking convoys and sinking several merchant ships. She then served in the Arctic, where, in December 1942, she was severely damaged in the battle of the Barents Sea. A furious Hitler ordered her to be decommissioned. She never saw action again.

Royal Navy lost 22 escort vessels, including the cruisers *Edinburgh* and *Trinidad*. Kriegsmarine losses were 4 surface warships and 31 submarines.

The convoys—identified by the code letters PQ when outward bound and QP on their return voyage—were routed as far north as possible to avoid enemy bases. In winter, most of the passage was by night, but in summer it was daylight all the way. Once a convoy had been located, it came under almost continuous attack by bombs and torpedoes from the air as well as by U-boats and surface vessels. The point of greatest danger was the narrow passage between north Norway and the Great Ice Barrier, which is where the majority of Allied losses were incurred.

The early convoys encountered little German opposition. By the end of 1941, seven of them had delivered 750 tanks, 800 planes, 2,300 vehicles, and more than 100,000 tons of other cargo to the Soviet Union. By early February 1942, 12 convoys totalling 93 ships had made the northbound journey with the loss of only one vessel, the destroyer *Matabele*, to U-boat attack.

This relative immunity did not last. Hitler, whose celebrated intuition had warned him—falsely as it turned out—that the British were planning to invade Norway, decided to strengthen his naval and air forces stationed in the north of the country. On January 16, 1942, *Tirpitz*, *Bismarck*'s sister-battleship, arrived at Trondheim. She was soon to be joined by the pocket battleships *Admiral Scheer* and *Lützow*, the heavy cruiser *Admiral Hipper*, and several flotillas of the Kriegsmarine's most modern destroyers. The Luftwaffe, too, was substantially reinforced with more dive-bombers, torpedo planes, and long-range reconnaissance planes. Its commanders in northern Norway now had more than 250 aircraft at their disposal.

THE SHIP THAT TORPEDOED ITSELF

From March 1942, every Allied convoy sailing to and from the USSR faced almost constant attack as they

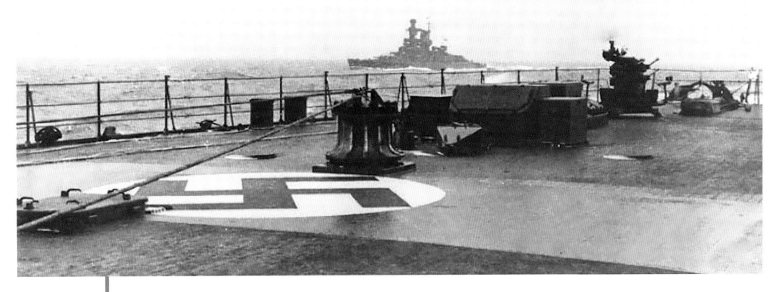

The pocket battleship *Admiral Scheer*, photographed from the heavy cruiser *Prinz Eugen*, as both ships sail for northern Norway in 1942. Hitler demanded that the majority of the Kriegsmarine's surface fleet was transferred to Norway to counter any British landings. Raeder and his fellow naval chiefs protested, but the Führer was not in the mood to change his mind. The increased German naval presence, however, meant that Britain's Arctic convoys to Soviet Russia were at even greater risk of attack.

fought their way through to their destinations. PQ-13, sailing for Murmansk on March 20, was the first to suffer substantial casualties. It consisted of 10 merchantmen, heavily laden down with tanks, guns, planes, trucks, and ammunition, escorted by the brand-new cruiser *Trinidad*, and her two attendant destroyers. By the time it arrived at its destination, it had lost five ships to Luftwaffe dive-bombers, two to U-boats, and one to a flotilla of three marauding Kriegsmarine destroyers.

Trinidad, too, was seriously damaged—not by enemy action, but by one of her own torpedoes, which had malfunctioned when it was fired at a German destroyer, turned full circle, and hit *Trinidad* herself. With hundreds of gallons of seawater pouring into the stricken cruiser through the gaping hole the rogue torpedo had made on her port side, she was lucky to manage to limp into port.

Her good fortune was not to last. Having been hurriedly patched up in the Murmansk dockyard, she was soon at sea again, escorting QP-11 home to Govan in Scotland. A few days out from the Russian port, she fell victim to a bomb dropped by a Junkers Ju88, which exploded on one of her mess decks to devastating effect. The patch that had been fitted over the damage to her port side started an uncontrollable fire. The order was given to abandon ship, after which one of *Trinidad*'s own escorting destroyers torpedoed her twice and she sank "slowly and gracefully," bow first.

ARCTIC DISASTER

Churchill told Roosevelt and Stalin that he was deeply concerned about the mounting Arctic losses, saying that they were rapidly becoming unsustainable. The President was not impressed. "Every promise the English have made to the Russians they have fallen down on," he told Henry Morgenthau, his Secretary of the Treasury. "Nothing would be worse than to have the Russians collapse."

Stalin was even more dissatisfied. The premier cabled the Soviet leader personally to warn him that, if the shipping losses continued to mount, "then the only thing we can do will be to hold up the further sailings of convoys until we have greater sea space when the ice recedes northward in July." Stalin replied bluntly that the convoys must continue sailing whatever the cost.

Churchill gave way. On April 18, PQ-14, escorted by the heavy cruiser *Edinburgh*, six destroyers, four corvettes, four minesweepers, and two antisubmarine and rescue trawlers set off from Iceland for Murmansk. Four days out from Hvalfjord, misfortune struck. The convoy ran into a thick blanket of fog and then into a floating ice field. By the time the weather cleared, only eight out of the 23 merchant ships that had started the voyage remained. The others, badly damaged while trying to fight their way through the ice, had turned back. The survivors now had to contend with a U-boat attack. *Empire Howard*, hit by three torpedoes fired by U-403, sank almost instantly.

The return voyage was equally eventful. This time *Edinburgh* herself was the chief victim. While steaming unescorted on patrol around 20 miles (32km) from the convoy, U-456 hit her with two torpedoes, one striking her squarely amidships and the other further after. The badly wounded cruiser drifted to a stop, listing heavily to starboard. Though she managed to get underway again, she could only make two knots as she started to struggle back toward Murmansk and safety. She never made port. She sank after being hit by two more torpedoes—one fired by a German destroyer and the other by one of her escorts, which had arrived to rescue the crew after they had been ordered to abandon ship.

THE TRAGEDY OF PQ-17

The sailings went on. PQ-16, the biggest convoy yet, set out as scheduled from Iceland for Archangel on May 21. By the time it made port, seven of its 36 ships had been lost, all but one sunk by the Luftwaffe's Heinkel and

The light cruiser *Trinidad* met with a singular fate while escorting convoy PQ-13 to Murmansk in March 1942. With the convoy scattered by a devastating Arctic gale, the light cruiser fought off a flotilla of German Narvik-class destroyers before falling victim to a totally unexpected accident. A torpedo she fired at point-blank range at the leading enemy destroyer malfunctioned. As it streaked toward the destroyer's stern, it suddenly turned, headed back toward *Trinidad*, and plunged into her port side. With her forward boiler room flooded and mess deck on fire, she limped southeast, making no more than four knots, toward safety.

Junkers bombers. PQ-17, which was the next to brave the passage, was as big. Its 35 merchantmen sailed from Iceland on June 27. They carried $700 million worth of armaments (in 1942 prices)—297 aircraft, 594 tanks, 4,246 army trucks and troop carriers, and more than 156,000 tons of general cargo.

Leaving port, PQ-17 made an impressive sight. Escorted by 2 destroyers and 15 other armed ships, 22 American, 8 British, 2 Russian, 2 Panamanian, and a single Dutch cargo vessel made for the open sea. About 40 miles (64km) north, the British cruisers *London* and *Norfolk*, the US cruisers *Wichita* and *Tuscaloosa*, and three US destroyers gathered to give the convoy close cover, while, in Scapa Flow, the Home Fleet prepared to sail to trail PQ-17 at a distance of 200 miles (322km) to provide it with distant support. It included the battleship *Duke of York*, the aircraft carrier *Victorious*, 2 cruisers and 14 destroyers, reinforced by the US battleship *Washington*.

All in all, it was an imposing display of naval force, which the Admiralty believed would be sufficient to deter the Germans from attacking the convoy. What it did not realize was that German naval intelligence had foreknowledge of the size and importance of PQ-17 and that Admiral Erich Raeder, commander-in-chief of the Kriegsmarine, had laid his plans accordingly. Nor did it know that U-456 had spotted it as soon as it had reached open water.

Early on July 1, a Focke-Wulf Kondor long-range reconnaissance aircraft confirmed the submarine's sighting. Two more U-boats—U-235 and U-408—were despatched to shadow the convoy. Though they lost contact with it when it entered a massive fog bank, contact was re-established by another Kondor when the weather cleared. PO-17 braced itself for the inevitable attack.

The Luftwaffe was the first to strike, but its Heinkel He 115 torpedo bombers were driven off by determined anti-aircraft fire. When the air force returned over the next couple of days, however, its planes were more successful. They sank the US Liberty ship *Christopher Newport* and the merchantmen *Navarino* and *William Hooper*. The Soviet tanker *Azerbaijan* was badly damaged but managed to limp on and eventually make it to port.

THE ORDER TO SCATTER

Despite the losses, PQ-17 was defending itself brilliantly, but then the Admiralty intervened. Admiral Sir Dudley Pound, the First Sea Lord, received the erroneous intelligence that *Tirpitz* and its supporting consorts were on the move and heading to intercept the convoy. He ordered the cruiser force to withdraw and,

SUPPLIES FOR RUSSIA

Running Arctic convoys to and from Murmansk and Archangel in Soviet Russia was fraught with difficulty almost from the start. Both summer and winter routes (shown here) were well within the range of U-boats, Luftwaffe aircraft, and surface ships operating from bases on and along the Norwegian coast. During the winter months, there were fierce storms and intense cold to contend with; in the summer, perpetual daylight made the convoys an easy target for scouting U-boats and Luftwaffe reconnaissance aircraft to find and track. The first convoy sailed from Iceland in August 1941, the last after the German surrender in May 1945.

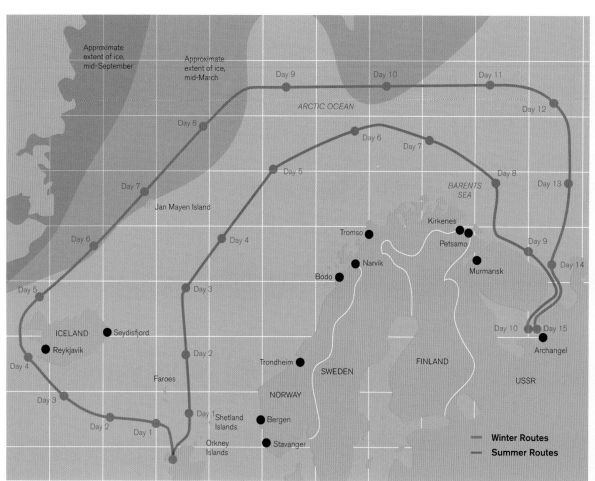

The *Colorado*-class battleship *Washington* was detached from the US Atlantic Fleet to become the flagship of Task Force 39—assigned to serve with the British Home Fleet in the North Atlantic and charged with escorting the Allied convoys supplying Soviet Russia via Murmansk and Archangel. *Washington* served with the task force for four months before returning to the USA. Her main task was to deal with *Tirpitz*, should the giant German battleship emerge from her Norwegian lair to raid the Arctic convoys.

believing the merchant ships would stand a better chance of avoiding attack by scattering, signaled them to disperse.

Bereft of its escort, PQ-17 was now at the mercy of the enemy. Soon, its slaughter commenced. *Empire Byron* was among the first victims, torpedoed by a U-boat. Carlton and *Honomu* followed her to the bottom. Luftwaffe dive-bombers put an end to *Daniel Morgan* and *Washington*. By the time nightfall put a temporary end to the attack, *Bolton Castle, Paulus Potter, Earlston, Pankraft, River Afton, Aldersdale, Zaafaran, Fairfield City,* and *Peter Kerr* had all been sunk.

It was by no means over yet. For the next three days, attacks continued without respite. The Luftwaffe sank *Hoosier* and *El Capitan*, while U-boats accounted for *John Witherspoon, Alcoa Ranger, Olopana,* and *Hartlebury*. Only 11 of the 35 merchantmen that had sailed from Iceland made it to Archangel. It was the highest loss rate yet.

Churchill was appalled. On July 18, he cabled Stalin, telling him that Britain was temporarily suspending sailing more convoys to the USSR. German naval and air strength in the most exposed parts of the Arctic was simply too great. "It is therefore with the greatest regret that we have reached the conclusion," the premier wrote, "that to attempt to run the next convoy, PQ-18, would bring no benefit to you and would involve a dead loss to the common cause."

It was September before PQ-18 was allowed to sail. The Luftwaffe sank ten out of its 45 ships, while another five were torpedoed by U-boats. Convoys to the USSR were suspended again until winter. By that time, defensive tactics had improved and more escort vessels were assigned to guard each convoy. Though later convoys were still subject to attack, the loss rate dropped dramatically. The Germans had finally lost the battle to dominate the northern seas.

GUADALCANAL

What makes the battle of Gaudalcanal, an island in the Solomon chain strategically situated in the southwest Pacific, so interesting is the sheer number of naval actions fought between the US and Japanese fleets there. Over the space of six months from August 1942 to February 1943, seven major engagements took place in the waters around the island—more than the Royal Navy and Germany's Imperial High Seas Fleet fought in the whole of World War I. Unusually, most of these battles were fought ship-to-ship at night.

The Americans were determined to recapture Guadalcanal for one simple reason. Shortly after their invasion of the island, the Japanese started to build an airfield there. Admiral Ernest J. King, the commander-in-chief of US naval forces and chief of naval operations, ordered prompt action to be taken to drive the garrison back into the sea. Otherwise, when the airfield was completed, the bomber flotillas that the Japanese planned to station there would menace the entire American position in the southern Pacific. This had to be avoided at all costs.

On July 2, the Joint Chiefs of Staff decided to deploy the 1st Marine Division, already en route to Noumea, to recapture Guadalcanal as well as Tulagi and two more islands on the other side of the New Georgia Sound. D-Day was set for August 7. The Marines were loaded on 15 transports, escorted by 8 cruisers plus a screen of destroyers. A carrier group, made up of *Saratoga*, *Enterprise*, and *Wasp*, plus the battleship *North Carolina*, 5 heavy cruisers, 1 light cruiser, 16 destroyers, and 3 tankers, provided further support.

The landings on Guadalcanal met with only slight resistance. By midnight on August 9, the beachheads and the incomplete airfield had been secured. For the first time, the Americans had succeeded in wresting some territory from the Japanese. Things, however, soon started to go wrong. Rear Admiral Frank Fletcher, in command of the carrier group, said originally he would stay in the vicinity of Guadalcanal for 48 hours to provide the Marines with air cover against the inevitable Japanese air counterattacks while their supplies were unloaded. His ships remained on station about 120 miles (193km) from the island for just 36 hours before withdrawing to the southeast. The Japanese launched their first air strikes on August 7, using all their available land-based bombers against the invaders and their transports. By August 9, there were no US planes available to oppose them.

BATTLE OF SAVO ISLAND

Savo Island was the first naval battle of the Guadalcanal campaign. In it, the Americans undoubtedly came off worst. They lost four heavy cruisers; *Chicago* and three destroyers were heavily damaged. Not a single Japanese ship was sunk, though three of their heavy cruisers were slightly damaged. Such was the extent of the defeat that the censorship covered it up for two months until the US victory at Cape Esperance could be announced at the same time.

It was Vice Admiral Gunichi Mikawa, commander of the newly formed Japanese Eighth Fleet, who precipitated the battle. He sailed southeast from Rabaul on August 7, planning to attack the Allied warships covering the landings and destroy as many transport ships as he could. Flying his flag from the heavy cruiser *Chokai*, he left his base with the light cruisers *Tenryu* and *Yubari* and the destroyer *Yunagi* to rendezvous with Rear Admiral Aritomo Goto and his heavy cruisers *Aoba*, *Furutaka*, *Kako*, and *Kinugasa*. The combined force would then steam along the east coast of Bougainville before advancing down the "Slot"—the name the US Navy had given to the area between Choiseul, New Georgia, and Santa Isabel—to Guadalcanal. Mikawa's intention was to sail south of Savo Island, launch a devastating night attack, and then withdraw north.

US invasion forces gather off Guadalcanal in July 1942. Major General Alexander A. Vandegrift was in command of the initial landing force. It consisted of some 19,000 Marines from the 1st Marine Division embarked in 19 troop transports. Operation Watchtower, as it was code-named, was the brainchild of Admiral Ernest J. King, the commander-in-chief of the US Fleet. It was the first amphibious operation to be launched by the USA since 1898. Preparations for it were so hasty, and the military and naval resources available so stretched, that the officers chiefly involved nicknamed the invasion plan Operation Shoestring.

The *Takao*-class heavy cruiser *Chokai* (top left) was Vice Admiral Mikawa's flagship during the battle of Savo Island, fought on August 9, 1942. As well as *Chokai*, Mikawa had *Aoba*, *Kako*, *Kinugasa* (bottom), and *Furutaka* under his command, plus the light cruisers *Tenryu* and *Yubari* and the destroyer *Yunagi*. The American ships patrolling the area were taken by surprise. The cruisers *Astoria*, *Quincy*, and *Vincennes* and a destroyer were sunk. The Australian cruiser *Canberra* had to be scuttled. *Chicago*, though heavily damaged, survived to fight another day. *Chokai* eventually suffered the same fate as *Canberra*. She had to be torpedoed by one of her own escorts after being stopped dead in the water during the battle of Leyte Gulf in 1944. *Kinugasa* capsized and sank off Guadalcanal on November 14, 1942 after being hit by US carrier-borne planes.

ALLIED DISPOSITIONS

Rear Admiral Richmond Kelly Turner was in overall command of the South Pacific Amphibious Force, which was charged with defending the landings against Japanese naval attack. It consisted of 4 US heavy cruisers and 19 destroyers, supported by 2 Australian heavy cruisers and 1 light cruiser. Rear Admiral Norman Scott, with two light cruisers and two destroyers, patrolled the area between Tulagi and Guadalcanal.

Rear Admiral Victor Crutchley, a British officer attached to the Australian Navy, guarded the two channels north and south of Savo Island. The southern approach was covered by the US heavy cruiser *Chicago* and the Australian heavy cruiser *Australia* and her sister-ship *Canberra*, along with the destroyers *Bagley* and *Patterson*. The northern channel was defended by the heavy cruisers *Vincennes*, *Quincy*, and *Astoria,* plus the destroyers *Helm* and *Wilson*. The radar-equipped destroyers *Ralph Talbot* and *Blue* were positioned to the west of the island to provide early warning of any Japanese approach. It was Crutchley's ships that were to bear the brunt of the battle when the Japanese struck. Crutchley was not even present. Before the attack began, he had been summoned by Turner to a conference onboard his flagship some 20 miles (32km) away in Lunga Roads. This left the Support Force without its tactical commander.

UNREADY FOR ACTION

None of Crutchley's crews were at battle stations—half of them were resting, while several cruiser captains were actually asleep in their cabins—as Mikawa's ships steamed undetected in-line ahead between *Blue* and *Ralph Talbot*. When the Japanese admiral ordered his ships to open fire on the southern force, it took *Patterson*, the first ship to spot the enemy, five minutes to raise the alarm. As she did so, two torpedoes ripped into *Canberra*'s starboard side, followed almost

instantaneously by salvo after salvo of heavy shells striking the ship. The stricken cruiser stopped dead in the water. As fire broke out and she started to list alarmingly, her crew struggled vainly to keep her afloat. Eventually, she had to be abandoned and scuttled.

Chicago was the sole surviving heavy cruiser. It took vital minutes to wake up Captain Howard D. Bode, her commander, and by the time he got to the bridge it was too late. A torpedo severed part of the bow, while a lucky shell-hit shell toppled *Chicago*'s foremast. The totally confused Bode then miscalculated the position of Mikawa's ships, which were now turning hard to port, and, instead of engaging them, steered west instead, away from the battle. *Bagley* never managed to get into action at all. The entire Southern Force had been eliminated as a fighting force in six minutes.

Mikawa now split his ships' force into two columns to tackle the equally unready Northern Force. *Astoria* was the first ship to be engaged. Repeated salvos of shells turned her into a blazing shambles. She sank the next day. *Quincy* was caught in the crossfire between the two Japanese columns. Though her crew tried to beach her on Savo Island, she capsized and sank at 2:35 a.m. *Vincennes* sank 15 minutes later after taking three torpedo hits.

▲ The *Northampton*-class heavy cruiser *Chicago* was one of the US ships to be taken by surprise by Mikawa's task force during the battle of Savo Island. It took the sound of gunfire to awaken Captain Howard D. Bode, her commander, out of a sound sleep and when he eventually reached the bridge, he made all the wrong decisions. Rather than getting his ship into the fight against the Japanese heavy cruisers, he steamed westward in pursuit of *Yunagi*, Mikawa's sole destroyer, and away from the main action. Captain Bode also failed to warn the northern part of the US task force that it faced imminent attack. Following a subsequent Court of Inquiry, he committed suicide on hearing that its findings censured him for his conduct during the battle.

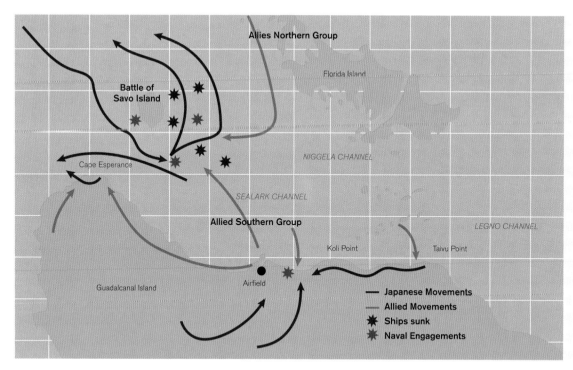

Battle of Savo Island

Allies Northern Group

Florida Island

Cape Esperance

NIGGELA CHANNEL

SEALARK CHANNEL

Allied Southern Group

LEGNO CHANNEL

Koli Point

Taivu Point

Guadalcanal Island

Airfield

— Japanese Movements
— Allied Movements
✳ Ships sunk
✳ Naval Engagements

THE NAVAL BATTLES

The initial landings on Guadalcanal met only slight and scattered opposition. The airfield the Japanese had been building there was secured by 4 p.m. Tulagi put up more resistance, but it, too, was occupied by the morning of August 8. The next day, the first major naval clash of the campaign took place at Savo Island. Further battles followed off the eastern Solomons, Cape Esperance, the Santa Cruz Islands, Guadalcanal itself, Tassafaranda, and Rendell Island. In the last of these battles, the luckless US heavy cruiser *Chicago* was finally torpedoed and sunk.

The Japanese admiral was now faced with an important decision. Should he continue his attack and turn on the US transports, which were now lying totally exposed in the Guadalcanal anchorage? Continuing the action might leave him exposed to Allied air attack so he decided not to run the risk. As his ships were scattered and also low on ammunition, he ordered them to withdraw back to Rabaul at their utmost speed.

VICTORY AT CAPE ESPERANCE

Mikawa was not finished yet. In early October, he sent a convoy carrying much needed reinforcements to the island. Led by Rear Admiral Takatsugu Jojima, the force consisted of six destroyers and two seaplane tenders. In addition, Mikawa ordered Rear Admiral Aritomo Goto to lead three cruisers and two destroyers to shell Henderson Field while Jojima's ships landed the troops they were transporting. Sailing from the Shortlands early on October 11, both forces proceeded down the "Slot" toward Guadalcanal.

NEW US TACTICS

The Americans were also making plans to reinforce the Marines on Guadalcanal. Sailing from New Caledonia on October 8, transports carrying the 164th Infantry Regiment steamed steadily north toward the island. Vice Admiral Robert Ghormley assigned Task Force 64, commanded by Rear Admiral Norman Hall, to operate nearby to screen the convoy. As well as the heavy cruisers *San Francisco* and *Salt Lake City* plus the light cruisers *Boise* and *Helena*, Hall's task force included the destroyers *Farenholt*, *Duncan*, *Buchanan*, *McCalla*, and *Laffey*. Initially taking station off Rennell Island, he moved north on October 11 after receiving reports that the Japanese had been sighted in the Slot.

Aware that the Americans had fared badly in previous night encounters with the Japanese, Hall changed tactics. Ordering his ships into a column with destroyers at its head and rear, he instructed them to light up any potential targets with their searchlights so that the cruisers could fire accurately. Hall also told his ships that they were to open fire independently as soon as the enemy was sighted rather than waiting for the order to do so.

BATTLE IS JOINED

Approaching Cape Hunter on the northwest corner of Guadalcanal, Hall ordered his cruisers to launch their scouting seaplanes at 10 p.m. An hour later, one of them spotted Jojima's ships. Expecting more Japanese ships to be sighted, Hall maintained his course northeast, passing to the west of Savo Island. Reversing course at 11:30 p.m. some confusion led to the three leading destroyers (*Farenholt*, *Duncan*, and *Laffey*) getting out of position. About this time, Goto's ships were spotted by American radar.

Initially thinking that the contacts were from the out-of-position destroyers, Hall took no action. As *Farenholt* and *Laffey* sped up to reassume their original stations, *Duncan* moved to attack the approaching Japanese vessels. At 11:45 p.m., Goto's ships were visible to the American lookouts and *Helena* radioed for permission to fire. Hall responded in the affirmative. Somewhat to his surprise, the entire American battle line opened fire simultaneously.

During the next few minutes, the Japanese flagship *Aoba* was hit more than 40 times by *Helena*, *Salt Lake City*, *San Francisco*, *Farenholt*, and *Laffey*. On fire with many of its guns out of action and Goto dead, *Aoba* turned away in an attempt to disengage. The Americans next turned on *Furutaka*. Set ablaze by a hit on its torpedo tubes, she lost power after taking a torpedo from *Buchanan*. She sank later that night. The Americans then shifted their fire to the destroyer *Fubuki* and sank it. As the battle continued to rage, *Kinugasa* and *Hatsuyuki* turned away, with *Boise* and *Salt Lake City* in pursuit.

At 12:20 a.m., with the Japanese in full retreat, Hall broke off the action. He had lost only one destroyer, though *Boise* and *Farenholt* were both badly damaged.

The Japanese lost a cruiser and three destroyers. *Aoba* was put out of action until the following February

GAINING THE INITIATIVE

Though a much-needed victory for the Americans, Cape Esperance was a tactical rather than a strategic one. They did not achieve the latter until November. In the first naval battle of Guadalcanal, fought between November 13 and 15, Allied success ensured that the Japanese fleet was now unable to reinforce or adequately supply the troops on the island. During the battle, they lost 2 battleships, a heavy cruiser, 3 destroyers, and 11 transports. On December 12, the navy recommended that Guadalcanal be abandoned.

Though General Tojo, the Japanese premier, and the army opposed it right up to the last minute, on December 31, Imperial General Headquarters reluctantly agreed to the evacuation. It began on February 2 and was over by February 8. The defeat spelled the beginning of the end. The subsequent retreat culminated in Japan's unconditional surrender.

▼ The Japanese heavy cruiser *Aoba* suffered a shell hit during the battle of Savo Island, but managed to withdraw otherwise undamaged toward Kavieng. Serving as Admiral Aritoma Goto's flagship at the battle of Cape Esperance, she was hit by up to 40 six- and eight-inch shells, which wrecked her bridge, knocked out her number two eight-inch gun turret, destroyed her third, and put four of her boilers out of action. Goto was mortally wounded and died two days after the battle. *Aoba* was subsequently repaired and survived to fight another day.

MEDITERRANEAN CONVOYS

If, as Churchill himself proclaimed in 1940, the Mediterranean was "the carotid artery of the empire," then Malta and Gibraltar were the keys to its control. The former sat firmly astride the main sea route from Italy to North Africa. Whoever held it could dominate the central Mediterranean. The latter stood guard over the only channel into the western Mediterranean from the Atlantic.

Churchill was keenly aware of Malta's strategic significance. It had been christened the "Lock of the Mediterranean" in 1530, when the Holy Roman Emperor Charles V ordered the Order of the Knights of St. John of Jerusalem to garrison it after they had been ejected from Rhodes by the Ottoman Turks, and had been in British hands ever since the Napoleonic Wars. Its loss, Churchill opined, would be "a disaster of the first magnitude … and would probably be fatal in the long run to the defence of the Nile Valley." It was vital, therefore, for it to hold out in the face of Axis attack, even if the Mediterranean Fleet had shifted its main base from Valletta to Alexandria just before the war to avoid the risk of Italian air attack. The island was only 20 minutes' flying time from Sicily.

Securing the British hold on Gibraltar was considered to be equally important. They did everything they could to make it impregnable. Some 25 miles (40km) of tunnels were bored deep into the rock to store ammunition and house workshops, while the airstrip was extended out into the sea. Eventually, it could accommodate 600 planes.

No matter how well defended Gibraltar was, however, ultimately its survival depended on the goodwill of neutral Spain. The constant fear was that General Francisco Franco, the Spanish Nationalist dictator who had defeated the Republicans in the Spanish Civil War with Italian and German assistance, would be persuaded to enter the war on the Axis side. If he did so, the obvious course for him was to allow the Wehrmacht to attack Gibraltar from the rear.

ITALIAN FAILURES

The day after Mussolini declared war on Britain and France, the Regia Aeronautica launched its first bombing strikes on Malta. Despite the promises of its commanders that they would "sterilize" the island, the Regia Aeronautica proved to be not as powerful as some had feared. Consequently, RAF fighter aircraft—first of all a handful of Gloucester Gladiators and then a larger force of Hurricanes—were able to mitigate the effect of subsequent Italian air attacks, at least until the Luftwaffe arrived on the scene.

Similarly, the Regia Marina was unable to put a stop to British convoy movements in the central Mediterranean. Its admirals were reluctant to risk being defeated. This reluctance, combined with a growing shortage of fuel, ensured that the bulk of the fleet spent much of its time sheltering at Taranto and La Spezia. Its few aggressive commanders found themselves hamstrung at every term by this overall timidity. Admiral Alberto Da Zara, for instance, who attacked a British convoy off Pantelleria in June 1942, was promptly ordered by his combat-shy superiors to break off the action and return to port.

The Italians seemed to suffer from an acute inferiority complex as far as the Royal Navy was concerned. The first big naval action of the war they fought at Punta Stilo, off the coast of Calabria in July 1940, ended in anticlimax. As soon as *Giulio Cesare*, one of the two Italian battleships present, took a hit from the British battleship *Warspite*, the Italians hastily threw up a smokescreen and the entire force scuttled for home. Ten days later, off Cape Spada in northern Crete, two patrolling cruisers threw away their advantages of speed, range, and firepower when they went into action against an inferior force of British destroyers. In theory, the cruisers should have made short work of their opponents. In practice, one was sunk and the other heavily damaged.

AXIS CONVOYS

Organizing supply convoys to North Africa was another Regia Marina responsibility. One problem was the limited capacity of the Libyan ports the Italians controlled. Tripoli could only unload five freighters and four troopships at a time, and Tobruk, while it was in Italian hands, could take three freighters and two troopships. Benghazi started off by accommodating two troopships and three freighters, but RAF air raids forced the Italians to abandon unloading operations in the harbor. This meant that the port's capacity was reduced to just three ships. By 1941, continuous pounding from the air had also cut Tripoli's capacity by half.

This shortfall meant that it would have been useless organizing big convoys consisting of ten or more ships at a time as the British did to supply Malta. Instead, Italian convoys were frequently very small, more often than not consisting of just a single merchantman escorted by two or three warships. Though this reduced the chances of enemy attack, it hardly was a recipe for efficiency. Another handicap was that supplies frequently had to be redistributed after they arrived to Derna, Bardia, Ain el Gazala, and Mersa Matruh in smaller coastal vessels. The overstretched Italian navy had to find escorts for these as well.

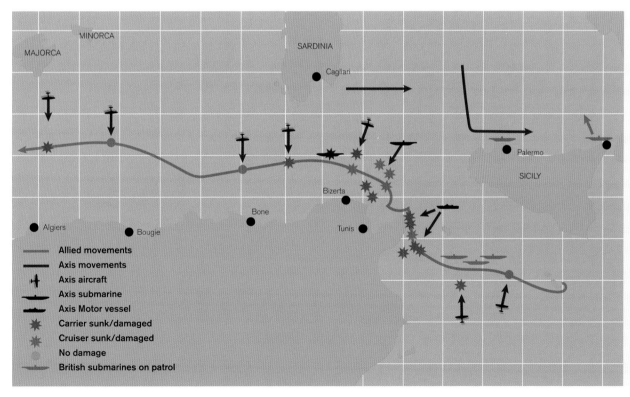

Allied movements
Axis movements
Axis aircraft
Axis submarine
Axis Motor vessel
Carrier sunk/damaged
Cruiser sunk/damaged
No damage
British submarines on patrol

MINORCA
MAJORCA
SARDINIA
Cagliari
Palermo
SICILY
Bizerta
Bone
Algiers
Bougie
Tunis

OPERATION PEDESTAL

The ships making up Operation Pedestal, a last-ditch attempt to resupply Malta, sailed from Gibraltar on August 10, 1942. They were escorted by 2 battleships, 4 aircraft carriers, 7 cruisers, 33 destroyers, and 24 submarines and mine-sweepers, while 200 planes provided air cover. Over the next four days, the convoy endured a massive aerial and submarine attack by German and Italian forces alerted to its approach by Axis intelligence. Out of the 14 supply ships involved, three battered freighters reached the island on August 13; the tanker *Ohio* arrived the following day. Their arrival saved Malta from starvation and enforced surrender.

FORCE K STRIKES

Initially, Britain relied mainly on aircraft and submarines in its efforts to interdict the Axis supply line. The protection the Regia Aeronautica could offer the ships sailing it was minimal. Italian pilots were not trained to fly over the open sea and were only able to operate in daylight. They often found it difficult to locate the convoys they had been assigned to protect. The Regia Marina had no underwater Sonar to help its ships to detect submarines, while its depth charges were unreliable and its anti-aircraft armament inadequate.

The British success rate—helped by the fact that Royal Navy cryptologists had cracked the Italian naval code—was high enough to worry General Erwin Rommel, commander of the Afrika Korps Hitler had reluctantly despatched to prop up his faltering ally. He bombarded his superiors with complaints about the Regia Marina's incompetence. Nevertheless, aircraft and submarines alone were not enough on their own. As Churchill quickly recognized, surface ships were needed as well. Force H, based at Gibraltar and commanded by Admiral Sir John Somerville, was already fully occupied in the western Mediterranean and escorting convoys to Malta. Force K, based there and commanded by Captain William Agnew, was now tasked with attacking Axis North African convoys and their escorts sailing through the central Mediterranean passing from Italy.

Consisting of two cruisers, *Aurora* and *Penelope*, and the destroyers *Lance* and *Lively*, Force K arrived at Malta on October 21, 1941. The date had been aptly chosen—it was Trafalgar Day—and it was not long before Force K was in action. On November 9, Agnew and his squadron successfully ambushed its first convoy, sailing south in the Ionian Sea. It consisted of nine merchantmen and a 10,000-ton oil tanker, escorted by two Italian cruisers and ten destroyers. Two of the latter were sunk in a few minutes and a third was badly damaged—it later sank after being torpedoed by

the British submarine *Upholder,* which also hit another of the Italian escorts. Then Agnew turned on the merchantmen. All nine of them were sunk outright. The tanker was set on fire and so badly damaged that it had to be written off as a total loss.

On November 24, Agnew struck again—this time intercepting a convoy sailing from Greece to Benghazi, west of Crete. He sank the merchant ships *Marotza* and *Procido* and damaged *Lupo* and *Cassiopeia,* two escorting torpedo boats. The Italians reacted by suspending all convoy sailings. They told their German allies that Tripoli was "practically blockaded." For his part, Churchill prodded Cunningham into reinforcing Force K. Force B—the light cruisers *Ajax* and *Neptune* and the destroyers *Kimberley* and *Kingston*—were promptly despatched from Alexandria to Malta to join Agnew.

Force K's luck was not to last. Under German pressure, the Italians were press-ganged into resuming convoys, in the main using cruisers as an expedient to ferry enough fuel to keep Rommel's Luftwaffe support

in the air and his panzers on the move. Though Force K had one more success, sinking a tanker and its escorting destroyer off Tripoli, it ran into a minefield on November 23 while attempting to hunt down another convoy. The cruiser *Neptune* and the destroyer *Kandahar* were sunk; *Aurora* was heavily damaged.

MALTA BESIEGED

These were not the only British naval losses. German U-boats sank the battleship *Barham* in the east and the carrier *Ark Royal*, which had helped keep Malta supplied with aircraft, in the west on November 14 and November 25 respectively. To cap it all, Italian human torpedoes made their way stealthily into Alexandria harbor, where they succeeded in temporally disabling *Queen Elizabeth* and *Valiant,* the Mediterranean Fleet's last two remaining battleships.

The balance of power in the Mediterranean seemed to be swinging in favor of the Axis. In January 1942, Hitler ordered Fliegerkorps II and X to Sicily. Combined into a new air command—Luftflotte 2—their task was to win aerial supremacy over the central and eastern Mediterranean, put an end to all British efforts to convoy supplies to Malta, and to bomb the island into submission.

The Luftwaffe's arrival in force soon told. Axis aircraft devastated the next attempt to run a major convoy to Malta from the east. When the next convoy was run in March 1942, though its escorting cruisers succeeded in holding off a vastly superior Italian surface force in a brilliantly fought action off Sirte, Luftwaffe and Regia Aeronautica bombers still prevented anything more than 7,500 of the 26,000 tons of supplies embarked at Alexandria from being landed at their destination. One ship was sunk just 20 miles (32km) from Valletta. The remaining two ships were sunk in the harbor.

That June, two major efforts to resupply the island also ended in failure. Two convoys—one, code-named

Vigorous, sailing west from Alexandria, and another, code-named Harpoon, east from Gibraltar, failed to get through. Of the 17 merchant ships involved, only two reached Malta. Six had been sunk and the rest damaged enough to force them to turn for home. The efforts cost the British five cruisers and one destroyer damaged, and four destroyers sunk.

OPERATION PEDESTAL

No fuel was getting through to Malta. This was potentially disastrous. Though the British aircraft carriers *Argus* and *Eagle* and the US carrier *Wasp* succeeded in getting Spitfires into the island in March, May, and June, they could not fly without fuel. Air Vice Marshal Sir Keith Park, now in command of Malta's air defense, warned in July that he had only seven weeks of aviation spirit in reserve. Without resupply, Malta would be forced to surrender.

Operation Pedestal, the largest convoy yet, was Britain's last throw. Fourteen merchant ships sailed from Gibraltar on August 10 in a last-ditch effort to get supplies to the island. They were escorted partway by 2 battleships, *Nelson* and *Rodney*, 4 aircraft carriers, *Victorious*, *Indomitable*, *Eagle*, and *Furious*, 7 cruisers, and 33 destroyers. The Luftwaffe and Regia Aeronautica threw in every plane they could muster against them. As well as 784 aircraft, 18 Italian submarines, 3 German U-boats, and 23 Axis torpedo boats were waiting to strike.

A U-boat claimed the first victim. On August 11, U-73 scored four torpedo hits on *Eagle*. The carrier capsized and sank within minutes. The next day, *Indomitable* was hit three times by Luftwaffe dive-bombers, while the destroyers *Deucalion* and *Foresight* were torpedoed from the air. Three cruisers, *Cairo*, *Kenya*, and *Nigeria*, were torpedoed by Italian submarines. *Cairo* had to be abandoned, while *Nigeria* turned back to Gibraltar. Of the merchantmen, *Ohio*, the only tanker in the convoy, was also torpedoed

by the Italians and set on fire. After emergency repairs, she nevertheless managed to steam on, though at a reduced speed of only 13 knots. The abandoned *Empire Hope* had to be sunk by an escort; *Clan Ferguson* exploded and sank; *Brisbane Star* was crippled by a torpedo bomber.

SAVING *OHIO*

On August 15, the story was much the same. The battle, if anything, intensified with 15 Regia Marina torpedo boats making a total of 15 attacks on the convoy. They torpedoed the cruiser *Manchester* and the merchantmen *Santa Elisa*, *Almeria Lykes*, *Wairangi*, and *Glenorchy*, all of which sank. Luftwaffe Junkers 88 bombers sank *Waimarana*. The Stukas targeted the crippled *Ohio*. As a result of several near misses, which buckled her plates, the forward part of the tanker flooded. Then a Stuka bounced off the water and onto her. After a Junkers 88 attack, the stricken tanker almost split in two. Her crew abandoned ship.

A destroyer tried to take *Ohio* in tow, but the sheer weight of the tanker repeatedly broke the tow lines. She was now under constant air attack, but the combined efforts of Luftwaffe and Regia Aeronautica aircraft still failed to sink her. Two volunteer survivors from *Santa Elisa* went back onboard to man her guns to provide a semblance of anti-aircraft protection. Nevertheless, one bomb smashed her rudder to smithereens, while another made a huge hole in her stern. Taken in tow again by a minesweeper and sandwiched between two destroyers to keep her afloat, *Ohio* finally made harbor on August 15 to be greeted by cheering crowds. *Rochester Castle*, *Port Castle*, *Melbourne Star*, and *Brisbane Star* had arrived in Valletta before her.

Though the convoy had suffered heavy casualties, Operation Pedestal was the strategic success the British needed. Malta was saved. The island never again came near capitulation.

The American fast tanker *Ohio* was specially loaned by the USA to Britain to make the Malta run. She is seen here after her arrival in Valletta harbor. She survived being torpedoed and set on fire by an Italian submarine and then being blasted from the air by Stuka and Junkers 88 bombers. Finally, her engines silenced, decks awash, and lashed between the destroyers *Penn* and *Ledbury* to prevent her from sinking, she arrived under tow at her destination. Thousands of Maltese lined the dockside to cheer her to the echo as she made port.

An Italian Savoia-Marchetti tS79-II trimotor bomber circles high in the sky above a Mediterranean convoy (left) before descending to deliver a low-level torpedo attack. The S79s aircrews nicknamed the plane *Gobbo Maledetto* (damned hunchback) because of the distinctive hump on its upper forward fuselage. Some 74 of them were among the Regia Aeronautic aircraft despatched to attack the ships taking part in Operation Pedestal, but, despite the best efforts of the Regia Aeronautica and the Luftwaffe, Malta's lifeline was never completely severed. Marshal Ugo Cavallero, head of the Italian High Command, and Field Marshal Albert Kesselring, Rommel's immediate superior, urged the launching of Operation Herkules, the projected invasion of the island by a mixed force of German and Italian paratroops supported by five Italian divisions landing on its south coast. Rommel, however, persuaded Hitler to turn down the plan. The only time the Italian battlefleet got near to the island (right) was when it sailed there to be interned by the Allies after Italy's unconditional surrender in September 1943.

OPERATION TORCH

Torch, the amphibious invasion of French North Africa by the Allies, was, said Henry Stimson, Roosevelt's Secretary of War, the President's "secret baby." General Sir Alan Brooke, Chief of the Imperial General Staff, noted in his diary: "If Torch succeeds, we are beginning to stop losing this war." General Dwight D. Eisenhower, the newly appointed supreme commander of the Allied Expeditionary Force tasked with implementing Torch, was less sanguine. He considered the operation to be "an undertaking of a quite desperate nature." Indeed, at one time he considered petitioning Roosevelt to call it off completely.

It was hardly surprising that Eisenhower had his doubts. He had never commanded an army in the field before and, apart from the obvious hazards of battle, he also had other worries. Would the Vichy French, whose North African territories the Allies were invading, cooperate with the invaders or resist the invasion? What would happen if Axis intelligence got advance wind of the plan? Would the Spanish stay neutral or would they finally side with the Axis and launch the 130,000 troops they had stationed in Spanish Morocco against the invaders? Or, even if he stayed officially neutral, would Franco provide the Luftwaffe with air bases from which it could blitz Gibraltar's exposed air strip and crowded anchorage? These and other uncertainties were constantly in the back of Eisenhower's mind.

ALLIED DISAGREEMENTS

The operation had been controversial from its inception. While Churchill and his generals were united in their backing for Torch, General George Marshall, Chief of Staff of the US Army, and Admiral Ernest King, head of the US Navy, were opposed to it, favoring the invasion of northern France instead. The two Americans visited London in July 1942 to argue the question out. "We found both of them still hankering after an attack across the Channel this year to take pressure off Russia," Brooke recorded irritably. "They

fail to realize that such an action could only lead to the loss of some six divisions without achieving any results."

Roosevelt wavered between the two sides. Initially, it looked as if he was coming down in favor of launching the long-awaited Second Front. On June 1, he cabled Churchill that he was "more than ever anxious that Bolero (the code name for the cross-Channel attack) proceeds to definite action beginning in August." Then he changed his mind. On August 1, the news came through from Washington. Torch was to go ahead later in the fall. The attack on mainland France was postponed for at least a year. Instead, the British and Americans would combine to drive the Axis powers out of North Africa for good. "I am directing all preparations to proceed," Roosevelt cabled Churchill. "We should settle this whole thing with finality at once."

PLANNING TORCH

Admiral Sir Andrew Cunningham, formerly in command of the Mediterranean Fleet and now appointed naval commander-in-chief, Allied Expedition force, was in charge of the naval side of the planning. With the exception of a brief visit to London, he did not return from Washington until mid-October, so Vice Admiral Sir Bertram Ramsey, his deputy, did the lion's share of the work.

After much debate, it was decided on September 5 that there would be three landings—at Casablanca to the west, Algiers in the center, and Oran in the east. The convoys for Casablanca would sail direct from the USA. The others would start from Scotland. Major General George S. Patton, with 35,000 US troops, would be put ashore at Casablanca. Major General Lloyd R. Fredendall, with 18,500 troops building up to 39,000, was given Oran as his objective. Lieutenant General Kenneth Anderson would land his 20,000 strong Anglo-American forces at Algiers.

The naval task forces were similarly divided.

US troops meet little resistance as they go ashore at Sidi Ferruch, west of Algiers on November 8, 1942. They made up the eastern wing of the Anglo-American invasion of North Africa. The Central Task Force landed around Oran and the Western Task Force on the Atlantic coast of French Morocco. Like the Germans, the Vichy government was taken totally by surprise by the landings. Admiral Jean-François Darlan, commander-in-chief of the French Navy, had assured his colleagues in Algiers that the Allies would be incapable of mustering a sufficiently strong invasion fleet before 1944.

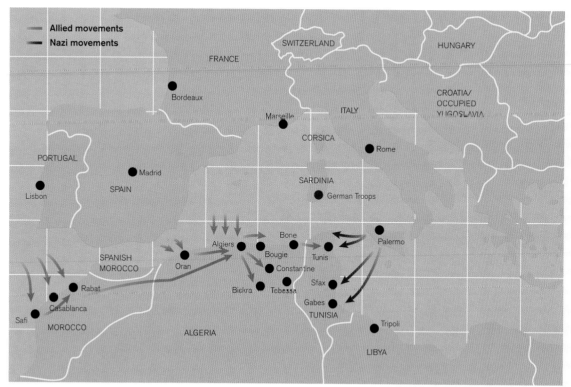

Allied movements
Nazi movements

In the final version of Torch, 65,000 troops divided into three Assault Forces sailed from the USA and Britain in 370 merchant ships escorted by 300 warships. The Eastern Assault Force, commanded by Lieutenant General Kenneth A. N. Anderson would move eastward as soon as Algiers was secured to pre-empt the inevitable Axis counter thrust—as troops were rushed from Sicily to Tunisia. The Central Assault Force consisted of 19,000 US troops, commanded by Major General Lloyd Fredendall and sailed from Britain to secure Oran. The 25,000-strong Western Assault Force, led by General George S. Patton, sailed directly from the USA to its Moroccan destination.

The Western Naval Task Force, commanded by Rear Admiral H. Kent Hewitt, was an all-American effort. Hewitt had 3 battleships, 5 aircraft carriers, 7 cruisers, 38 destroyers, 8 minesweepers, and 5 tankers at his disposal, together with an accompanying assault force of 91 vessels. The Central Naval Task Force, commanded by Commodore Thomas Troubridge, consisted of the headquarters ship *Largs*, as well as 2 aircraft carriers, 2 cruisers, 2 anti-aircraft ships, 13 destroyers, 6 corvettes, 8 minesweepers, and various ancillary craft.

Finally there was the Eastern Naval Task Force. Vice Admiral Sir Harold Burrough had *Bulolo* (the other headquarters ship), two aircraft carriers, three cruisers, three anti-aircraft ships, a gun monitor, three sloops, seven minesweepers, and seven corvettes under his command. All in all, the three task forces were an imposing collection of naval might.

SECRET NEGOTIATIONS

All the preparations were nearing completion. The first troop convoys left the Clyde on October 22 with more following four days later and on November 1. The *Casablanca* sailed from Chesapeake Bay on the eastern coast of the USA on October 24. The covering warships departed from their various bases. As some 340 Allied vessels converged on the Straits of Gibraltar, the date of the landings was set for November 8.

Much to Eisenhower's relief, it seemed that Italian and German Intelligence had both failed to deduce what might be in the wind. Though they had noted the arrival of some of the convoys at Gibraltar, they had assured their respective High Commands that these were heading for Malta, not North Africa, or that they would attempt to force the passage of the Mediterranean to supply General Bernard Montgomery's advancing 8th Army directly by sea.

Admirals Raeder and Dönitz had already violently disagreed as to whether the Atlantic or the Mediterranean should take priority for U-boat reinforcement; by the time Dönitz decided to despatch 25 more U-boats from the former to the latter, it was too late.

How the French would react to the invasion still worried the American supreme commander. The North African garrison was an estimated 20,000-strong; Eisenhower could field only 112,000 troops in the initial assault. Robert Murphy, the US Minister in Algiers, assured him that the French would not oppose the landing as long as it was US-led. To make doubly certain, General Mark Clark was ferried secretly by submarine to Algiers to confer with Major General Charles Mast, Chief of Staff of the French 19th Corps. Mast assured Clark that, given four days' warning, he could practically guarantee that there would be little if any armed resistance.

According to Murphy, General Alphonse Juin, the garrison's commander-in-chief, also made no secret of his pro-Allied sympathies. Both men, however, warned that they could not answer for Admiral François Darlan, who Petain had despatched from Vichy to Algiers, where his son was gravely ill, as acting High Commissioner in North Africa. The Allies decided to counter this by importing an even more prestigious French military figure. The obvious choice was General de Gaulle, the leader of the Free French in London, but Roosevelt, who cordially disliked him, vetoed the suggestion. Instead, the Americans turned to General Henri Giraud, who, after his capture by the Germans in 1940, had managed to make a dramatic escape from his prison camp and flee to safety in the unoccupied zone of France. He was flown to Gibraltar to broadcast an appeal to his North African compatriots to rally to the Allies.

The scheme backfired. Giraud proved just as difficult to handle as de Gaulle would have been. He insisted that, in return for his help, the Americans would make him commander-in-chief of all the invasion forces after they had gone ashore. It was an impossible request and the landings went ahead without him. Roosevelt broadcast an appeal to the French to come over to the Allies instead.

ATTACKING CASABLANCA

As the Allies landed, Marshal Petain, the head of the Vichy regime, ordered all French forces in North Africa to resist them. Though the order was not universally obeyed, some fierce fighting ensued before Darlan decided to come to terms with the invaders.

At Casablanca, General Charles Nogues, who had survived a Free French attempt to launch a coup against him the night before the invasion, and Vice Admiral Felix Michelier put up a spirited, though short-lived, resistance. To defend the port, Michelier had the incomplete battleship *Jean Bart*, which, though immobile, had one of its 15-inch gun turrets operational, a light cruiser, 2 flotilla leaders, 7 destroyers, 8 sloops, and 11 submarines available. Coastal defense batteries on El Hank at the western end of the harbor provided further protection.

In fact, the Americans elected to land at Fedala, a little further up the coast from the city. At midnight on November 7, Patton's ten troopships anchored eight miles (13km) offshore; at 6 a.m., their heavily loaded landing craft started making their way toward the beach. The coastal defense batteries there promptly opened fire, though they caused little damage at first. As dawn broke and the sun rose, their fire became more intense. Hewitt ordered four of his destroyers to steam closer inshore to shorten the range and silence the batteries. In the meantime, five of Michelier's submarines were ordered to sortie against the invaders, while French fighters took to the air to intercept the carrier-borne bombers the Americans had launched to strafe the harbor. The fighters ran into escorting F4F Wildcats from the aircraft carrier *Ranger* and a fierce dogfight ensued. The French lost seven aircraft and the Americans five planes.

Other US aircraft now began blitzing targets in the harbor itself. They sunk four French submarines and numerous merchant vessels. A little later, the battleship *Massachusetts*, the heavy cruisers *Wichita* and *Tuscaloosa*, and four destroyers began shelling the El Hank batteries and *Jean Bart*. Quickly putting the French battleship out of action, the Americans then concentrated their fire on El Hank.

THE FRENCH SORTIES

Michelier was quick to respond. At around 9 a.m., the destroyers *Malin*, *Fougueux*, and *Boulonnais* left harbor and began steaming at full speed straight for the American transports. Strafed by aircraft from *Ranger*, they succeeded in sinking a landing craft before gunfire from Hewitt's ships forced *Malin* and *Fougueux* ashore. Two hours later, the light cruiser *Primauguet*, the flotilla leader *Albatros*, and the destroyers *Brestois* and *Frondeur* intervened. Encountering *Massachusetts*, the heavy cruiser *Augusta*, and the light cruiser *Brooklyn*, the French found themselves outgunned. Turning and running for home, all got back to Casablanca, except for *Albatros* which had to be beached to prevent her from sinking. *Primauguet* caught fire and beached herself in the harbor, while the two surviving destroyers capsized at their moorings. *Boulonnais* was also not to escape. At around noon, *Augusta* ran her down and sank her.

A lull followed, which gave the French the opportunity to make temporary repairs to *Jean Bart* and get her gun turret back into action. The fighting resumed when two minesweepers emerged from Casablanca to shell Patton's troops, which were now closing in on the city. *Augusta* and two destroyers forced them back into port. Hewitt's ships then retired in their turn after they came under fire from *Jean Bart*. In response, Douglas SBD Dauntless dive-bombers from *Ranger* struck at the battleship. The two hits they scored with their 1,000-lb (454-kg) bombs were enough

JEAN BART

Class	*Richelieu*-class battleship
Displacement	48,950 tons (full load)
Length	813ft (248m)
Beam	108ft (33m)
Draft	31ft (9.4m)
Speed	32 knots
Armament	Eight 15-in guns in two main turrets, nine 152-mm anti-aircraft guns in three triple turrets, eight 40-mm and 20 20-mm anti-aircraft cannons
Crew	911

Jean Bart was still only 75 percent complete as the Germans neared St. Nazaire in June 1940. Her captain was given two stark choices—to try to reach safety at Casablanca in French North Africa or to scuttle his ship. He chose the former alternative. Lack of dockside facilities, however, meant that work on *Jean Bart* proceeded at a snail's pace; by November 1942, when the Allies landed, she still had only one of her 15-inch turrets operational. Nevertheless, she opened fire on the US ships covering the landing until the battleship *Massachusetts* and dive-bombers from the aircraft carrier *Ranger* put her out of action.

to sink her. Offshore, three French submarines attempted to launch their torpedoes against the US ships, but with no success.

THE FRENCH SURRENDER

Oran, too, put up a fight. An attempt to land troops right on the jetties of the crescent-shaped harbor was repulsed with heavy casualties by several French destroyers, two of which were sunk as they attempted to sail out past the breakwater to strike at the landing fleet. Landings to the east and west went unopposed. The city fell to the Allies the day before Casablanca.

By that time, the order for capitulation had come through from Darlan in Algiers, which had been swiftly and easily occupied by the Allies. The French admiral played what cards he had well, managing to get the Americans to let him retain his position at the price of agreeing to the ceasefire and allowing him to continue ruling French North Africa "in the name of the Marshal"—that is, in the name of Petain. Vichy itself was not to survive. Hitler's response to the Allied invasion was to order the immediate occupation of the unoccupied zone of metropolitan France. The French fleet at Toulon, obeying Darlan's secret orders to the letter, scuttled itself to avoid falling into German hands.

The *South Dakota*–class battleship *Massachusetts* enters Boston harbor after leaving the Fore River Shipyard at Quincy on May 12, 1942. As part of the Allies' invasion fleet, she engaged French warships in and off Casablanca in November 1942, silencing the incomplete battleship *Jean Bart*'s main armament and sinking two French destroyers as they attempted to leave harbor. She was probably the last US battleship to fire her giant 16-inch guns in actual ship-to-ship combat.

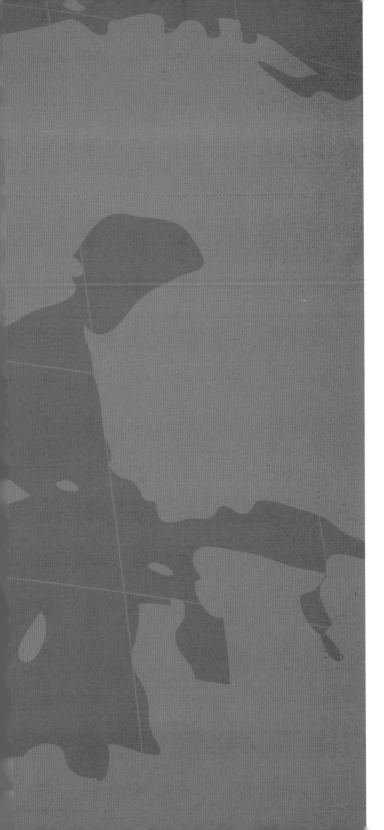

THE TURNING OF THE TIDE

As the tide of war turned inexorably against the Axis powers, the Allies won command of the sea in practically every ocean of the world. Though at times it looked likely that the Kriegsmarine's U-boats would win the Battle of the Atlantic, they failed to halt the flow of supplies from the USA to Britain. The climax of the battle came in May 1943, after which U-boat losses rose to the point when Admiral Dönitz was forced to withdraw them to safer waters. In the Far East, the Americans started leapfrogging their way across the Central Pacific, each step bringing them nearer and nearer to Japan itself. Back in Europe, the Allies launched the invasion of Sicily—as the preliminary to landing in Italy. In June 1944 came the Normandy landings—the greatest amphibious operation of all time.

BATTLE OF THE ATLANTIC

It was a drawn-out battle of attrition that lasted for more than four years. In its early stages, Germany's U-boats came close to gaining the upper hand Between June and October 1940, they sank 247 merchant ships—a total tonnage of 1,400,000 tons.

By the end of the year, the figure had risen to 1,281. Most of them were British, the majority being sunk by U-boats and the rest by surface raiders, mines, and attacks from the air. This was the equivalent to more than one fifth of Britain's prewar merchant fleet. The Germans lost only six U-boats—and only two of those had been sunk by convoy escorts. The escorts would sink only two more over the next four months.

It was small wonder that the U-boat crews christened this period the "happy time." It was not to last. As the number of escort vessels increased, so did the amount of protection the Royal Navy and Royal Canadian Navy could provide. The Canadians gradually extended their convoy cover eastward, while the Royal Navy did the same westward. In May 1941, the first eastward convoy to be escorted all the way across the North Atlantic sailed successfully; in July, the first westbound convoy received the same protection. The so-called "escort gap," which had given the U-boats the chance to strike at convoys in the mid-Atlantic, where they had been virtually defenseless, was closed.

The British also managed to partially counter the wolf-pack tactics the U-boats had been employing so successfully. They abandoned the aggressive anti-submarine sweeps they had been mounting in favor of defensively screening convoys more closely. To deal with night attacks on the surface, new types of radar were developed to enable the escorts to pick up the U-boats in the dark; star shells and "snowflake" flares could then be fired to illuminate them successfully. The consequence was that, for the first time, the escorts started to sink U-boats in appreciable numbers.

TYPE XXI U-BOAT

Class Long-range attack submarine

Displacement 1,621 tons (surfaced), 1,819 tons (submerged)

Length 251ft 7in (76.7m)

Beam 21ft 7in (6.6m)

Draft 20ft 8in (6.3m)

Speed 15.7 knots (surfaced), 17.2 knots (submerged)

Armament Six 21-in bow torpedo tubes, 2 x 20 twin flak cannon

Crew 57

The revolutionary Type XXI U-boat would probably have revolutionized submarine warfare had it come into service early enough, but production delays meant that it never got into action. Older submarines were slow and unmaneuverable underwater; they could also stay submerged for only limited periods of time. The Type XXI was faster submerged than on the surface and could remain underwater for up to 11 days. She could run practically silently underwater too, thanks to her new "creep" motor, while her pressure hull, fabricated from 1mm-thick steel aluminum alloy, allowed her to dive to 919ft before imploding. Firepower was also increased. A Type XXI could load and launch six salvos of torpedoes in just under 20 minutes, as opposed to the ten minutes it took to reload just one torpedo tube on a conventional submarine.

By the end of 1941, although 432 merchant ships had still been sunk, 35 U-boats had been destroyed, 27 of them by escort vessels of the Royal Navy.

OPERATION DRUM ROLL

It seemed as if the Atlantic battle might be nearing stalemate. Then, on December 7, 1941, something happened that took Hitler, as much as the USA, completely by surprise. The Japanese blitzed the US Pacific Fleet at Pearl Harbor, at the same time attacking British-held Malaya, Singapore, and Hong Kong.

Dönitz was as surprised as the Führer by this unexpected turn of events, but was quick to respond when Germany, a few days later, declared war on the USA. Shipping along the whole of the American east coast was now wide open to attack. Despite opposition from the Naval Staff in Berlin, he resolved to strike hard and fast with the few long-range Type IX U-boats he had immediately available. On December 18, the first of them—U-125 commanded by Ulrich Folkers—sailed from Lorient for US coastal waters. U-123, skippered by Reinhard Hardegen, left port five days later. Richard Zapp's U-66 sailed on Christmas Day, followed by Heinrich Bleichrodt's U-109 and Ernst Kals' U-130 on December 27.

Operation Drum Roll, as Dönitz christened it, was underway. Folkers was to operate off New Jersey, while Hardegen was to make for New York harbor, after which he was to search for targets down the coast as far as Cape Hafferas in North Carolina. Zapp, too, was to operate off the Cape, while Bleichrodt and Kals were to patrol off Halifax in Nova Scotia and the mouth of the Gulf of St. Lawrence.

Hardegen was the first into action. On January 12, 1942, he torpedoed *Cyclops*, a British steamer en route from the Panama Canal to Halifax to join a homebound convoy there. The incident occurred about 500 miles (805km) east of Cape Cod. Hardegen fired two torpedoes in all, the first striking *Cyclops* on her

The 88-mm deck gun crew on U-123 prepare for action. This was the first German submarine to go hunting for prey in American waters. Her first sinking was the freighter *Cyclops*, which she torpedoed 200 miles (322km) east of Cape Cod on January 12, 1942, the day before Dönitz had set for the launch of the campaign. She went on to sink two tankers—*Norness* and *Coimbra*—and the freighters *San Jose*, *City of Atlanta*, and *Ciltvaira* with her torpedoes before severely damaging *Malay* and sinking two more ships with her deck gun.

starboard side and the second, fired at close range into the already sinking vessel, on her port. The following day, Kals was the next to strike, sinking two small freighters off Newfoundland.

In the meantime, Hardegen headed south. On the night of January 14, he reached Rhode Island Sound, where he was immediately amazed by the sight that confronted him. The shore was a fairyland of glowing lights and street signs. The Americans were making no attempt to enforce a dim-out, let alone a blackout. Headlights could be clearly seen as automobiles drove up and down the coast, which itself was clearly marked by dozens of flashing light buoys. Suddenly, Hardegen was alerted to the presence of an approaching ship. It was the Norwegian tanker *Norness*, steaming a straight course at ten knots, totally unaware that she was in any danger. Hardegen fired five torpedoes at her in quick succession, three of which hit home to sink her.

Hardegen was not finished yet. He spent much of the next day laying submerged on the seabed off Long Island, surfacing at nightfall to head for the Ambrose Light and the shipping channel. Cautiously probing along the shoreline, he gradually closed on Rockaway Beach and Coney Island. Sandy Hook lay to port, while ahead of him the lights of Brooklyn and Manhattan lit up the night sky. He waited patiently below the narrows, hoping that a ship would emerge. When nothing appeared, he was steering back toward the open sea when a lookout reported that a vessel was following him. It was the 6,700-ton British tanker *Coimbra*, clearly silhouetted by the lights of the city beyond. Hardegen maneuvered to intercept her. One of the two torpedoes he fired struck *Coimbra* below her bridge. The second broke her back. Of her crew of 36, only six survived.

"TORPEDO JUNCTION"

Hardegen resumed his southward course for Cape Hatteras to join Zapp's U-66, which was already in

action there. Hardegen arrived in time to catch sight of the brilliant flash as Zapp's first victim, the US tanker *Allan Jackson* exploded. Zapp had stalked her for four days before firing two torpedoes into her. His next victim was the Canadian passenger liner *Lady Hawkins*, which sank so quickly that her crew managed to launch only three of her lifeboats. Of these, just one, with 71 survivors on board, was located by the rescue ships. The other two vanished without trace.

U-123 was soon at work as well. On January 19, Hardegen sank the US freighter *City of Atlanta*, followed later the same day by *Ciltvaira,* a small Latvian cargo ship on her way to Savannah. Now running short of torpedoes, he then attacked the tanker *Malay* with his deck gun. Though he inflicted heavy damage on her, even a torpedo failed to sink her. She managed to limp into Norfolk, Virginia. With all his torpedoes spent, Hardegen made for home via Bermuda, on the way sinking the Royal Mail steamer *Culebra* and another Norwegian tanker. He arrived back at Lorient on February 7 to be greeted on the quayside by Dönitz himself.

Zapp was the next to return home. Before he did so, he sunk another four ships off Cape Hatteras between January 22 and 24. It was now Kals's turn to steer south for the killing field. Starting on January 21, he sank five ships off the east coast between Nantucket and Hatteras. After sinking a freighter off Nova Scotia, Bleichrodt in U-109 also headed south, sinking four vessels between the US east coast and Bermuda.

It was scarcely surprising that the hapless tanker and freighter crews started calling the area around Hatteras "Torpedo Junction." The U-boat crews nicknamed it "the American shooting gallery." Some 150 million gallons of vitally needed oil was spilled into the sea and onto the beaches. "We had to almost give up swimming in the ocean," one civilian resident recalled. "It was just so full of oil you'd get it all over you."

THE ATLANTIC BATTLEGROUND

The battle of the Atlantic was World War II's longest continuous maritime campaign. The fight between the Allied and Axis powers for control of the Atlantic shipping lanes was unremitting, involving thousands of ships and stretching across thousands of square miles of perilous ocean. The map here charts the key moments and turning points of this great battle. The most vulnerable part of the crossing was the so-called Atlantic Gap in the mid-Atlantic; it was not until mid-1943, by which time U-boat sinkings of Allied merchant ships had reached an all-time high, that the tide turned in favor of the Allies when escort carriers and long-range aircraft provided the convoys with continuous air cover. From May onward, U-boat losses became unsustainable.

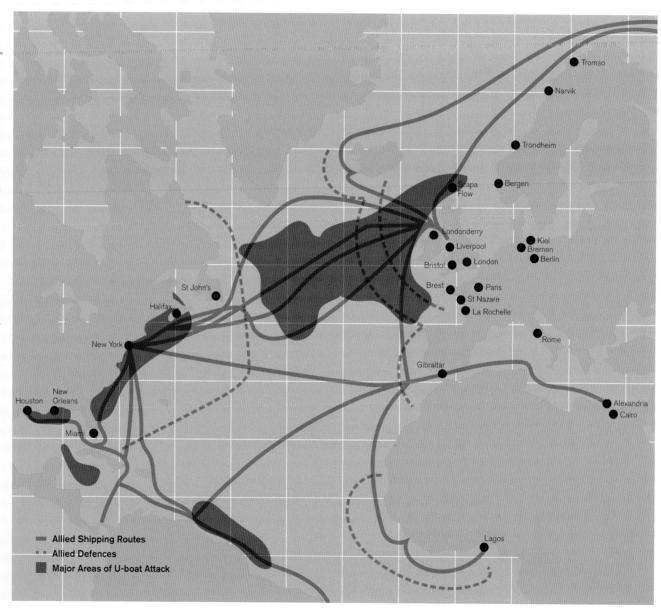

Allied Shipping Routes
Allied Defences
Major Areas of U-boat Attack

THE ATTACK INTENSIFIES

Dönitz was delighted by his success. The U-boats taking part in Drum Roll between them sank 27 ships with a gross tonnage of 165,267 tons. Not a single U-boat had been lost. In his war diary, Dönitz noted that the US Navy seemed totally unready for war. "The expectation of finding much single-ship traffic, unskilled ship-handling and little sea and air anti-submarine protection,' he wrote, "had been fulfilled." The Americans were certainly slow in taking the most elementary precautions. Even after Dönitz's crews started their attack, coastal convoys were not organized until mid-May—and even then the system only extended as far south as the Florida Keys. Nor was it until late April that a partial coastal dim-out was imposed.

Dönitz was quick to build on what Drum Roll had accomplished. A second wave of five Type IX U-boats was already in action off the east coast. A third one of another five Type IXs was on its way south to the oil ports of Aruba and Curacao in the Dutch East Indies, while a further two were making for the coast of Florida. In May alone, the Type IXs in the Caribbean sank 48 ships with an aggregate tonnage of more than 200,000 tons. A large proportion of them were tankers. A further 26 ships were sunk in the Gulf of Mexico. It seemed that, wherever the U-boats struck—whether it was along the US coast, in the Gulf of Mexico, or in the Caribbean—there was no effective defense.

BACK TO THE NORTH ATLANTIC

Dönitz, however, realized that the decisive battle still had to be fought. He decided to renew the offensive against the main Allied convoy routes across the North Atlantic, alerting Hitler to the "vast possibilities" he foresaw arising, thanks to "the rapid increase in the number of U-boats and the use of supply submarines." By October 1942, there were no fewer than 196 front-line U-boats available for action, compared to less

than 100 at the start of the year. German shipyards were churning out new U-boats at the rate of 20 per month, while U-boat losses from all causes were averaging only 11. The long winter nights ahead were ideally suited to wolf-pack tactics, while there was still a gap in the North Atlantic that was not covered by Allied air patrols. Dönitz took the risk and went ahead.

The first phase of the renewed offensive began in August with a convoy battle so fierce that the crews of three merchantmen took to the lifeboats even though their ships had not been torpedoed. As the attacks continued through the fall and on into the winter, the sinkings mounted. By the end of the year, the U-boats had sunk in total 1,160 ships of over 6,000,000 tons in weight; a further 1,500,000 tons had been sunk by the Luftwaffe and surface ships. This was more than had been sunk in the years 1939, 1940, and 1941 combined.

THE TIDE TURNS

It was not, however, a totally one-sided battle. In the last six months of 1942, Dönitz lost 66 U-boats. This increase was due to an increase in the number of escorts and also to the technologically advanced equipment they now possessed. High-frequency direction-finders, known as Huff-Duff, which could pinpoint a U-boat's position by tracking its radio signals, meant that shadowing submarines ran a constant risk of detection while the wolf packs were assembling. Type 271 centimetric radar made it easier to locate U-boats on the surface at night. Aircraft fitted with ASVII radar and Leigh Lights were also starting to become effective U-boat killers, particularly in the Bay of Biscay. Dönitz was forced to order his U-boats to cross the Bay submerged at night as well as by day.

As early as August 21, Dönitz was beginning to show the first signs of doubt. "The numerical strengthening of enemy flights, the appearance of a wide variety of aircraft types, the fitting of the aircraft with an

excellent location device against U-boats, have rendered U-boat operations in the eastern Atlantic very much more difficult," he wrote in his war diary. "This increasing difficulty of operations must lead, with corresponding further development, to high, insupportable losses, a decline in success and this to a decline in the prospects of success for the U-boat war as a whole." He told Albert Speer, Hitler's Minister of Armaments, as he pleaded with him to examine ways of improving U-boat armament: "If all resources are not deployed in the first line to maintain the battle strength of the U-boats at the highest level, the danger must be recognized that one day the U-boat will be crushed by the Allied defense and eliminated."

Nevertheless, Dönitz was determined to continue the offensive. "Despite the heaviest depth-charging attacks and little success," he opined, "a resolute confident mood persists, unbroken through unshakeable faith in victory." The sinkings in November 1942 certainly served to rekindle his optimism. The Allies suffered the highest shipping losses of any month of the war. One hundred and thirty-four ships, totalling 807,754 tons, were sunk, the U-boats accounting for 730,000 tons of the total. Hitler recognized the extent of this

achievement. In January 1943, he forced Raeder to resign and appointed Dönitz as commander-in-chief of the Kriegsmarine in the older admiral's place.

CRISIS POINT

In March 1943, the battle reached crisis point. Dönitz had 178 U-boats in the Atlantic, the majority stationed in two large groups either side of the North Atlantic air gap. He deployed 42 of them to attack two convoys, SC122 and HX229, sailing from New York to Britain. In the ensuing four-day battle, which the Germans called "the greatest convoy battle of all time," 21 merchant ships were sunk. The losses finally forced the Allies to take drastic action to close the air gap. Long-range Liberator bombers were finally deployed, while the number of escorts—including new escort carriers—was substantially increased.

The effects were immediate. In April, the sinking rate dropped to little more than half the March total. By the end of May, the U-boat loss rate was becoming insupportable. Dönitz lost 41 submarines to Allied attack. He managed to sink only 50 Allied merchantmen in return. As a result, he was forced to withdraw his U-boats to the relative safety of the area west of the Azores. The day of mass wolf-pack attacks was over. It was never to return.

BOGUE

Class	*Bogue*-type escort carrier
Displacement	15,400 tons (full load)
Length	465 ft (141.7 m)
Beam	69 ft 6 in (21.2 m)
Draft	36 ft (11 m)
Speed	18 knots
Aircraft carried	28
Armament	Two 5-in anti-aircraft guns, eight 40-mm and 12 20-mm anti-aircraft cannon
Crew	890

Twenty-one *Bogue*–class escort carriers were constructed in 1941–42, and 24 of the *Prince William*–class in 1942–43. The latter had better anti-aircraft armament than the former. The US equivalent was the *Casablanca*–class escort carrier, of which no fewer than 50 were built in the 12 months from mid-1943 onward. *Bogue* herself joined a submarine hunter-killer group in the Atlantic in February 1943; by the time she sank her last U-boat in April 1945, her planes had accounted for ten U-boats and a single Japanese submarine.

OPPOSITE An eastbound transatlantic convoy (top left) assembles in the Bedford Basin, Halifax, Nova Scotia, in April 1942. Such convoys were constantly vulnerable to U-boat attack, particularly in the mid-Atlantic, where Grand Admiral Dönitz had marshaled the bulk of his wolf packs to strike in force. Crewmen (top right) perched on a U-boat's coning tower are scanning the horizon for potential targets, ready to radio their position and course to the other submarines in the pack. Dönitz himself had been a U-boat captain during World War I. As commander-in-chief of the U-boat arm of the Kriegsmarine (bottom left), he welcomes the crewmen of U-94 home, having just awarded their commander the Knight's Cross. The picture (bottom right) shows submerged U-boats in the midst of a convoy being depth-charged by an American escort vessel.

MAIALE, X-CRAFT, AND KAITEN

During World War II, at least four of the navies engaged in the fighting experimented with underwater and surface assault craft. It was Italy's Regia Marina that led the way.

Italian interest in such unconventional vessels dated back to World War I. First came the MAS (Motoscascafi Anti-Sommergibile) motor-torpedo boats—MAS was later was to become the chosen soubriquet for Italian Underwater Special Forces). Two of them managed to sink the Austro-Hungarian battleship *Szent Istvan* off the island of Bermuda in the Adriatic in June 1918. This was followed by the Mignatta (leech). Devised by Captain Raffaele Rossetti and Lieutenant Raffaele Paolucci, it was the world's first human torpedo. The forward section consisted of two cylindrical explosive charges, which the two-man crew could detach and secure to the bilge keel of a target or drop onto the sea bottom immediately under a target's hull. Rossetti and Paolucci used a Mignatta to sink the battleship *Viribus Unitis* and the coastal defense ship *Wien* while both vessels were at anchor in the Pola naval base that November.

FROM MIGNATTA TO MAIALE

The Mignatta's mid-1930s successor was the Silura a Lente Corsa, human torpedoes labeled Maiale (pigs) by their crews because they were cumbersome to maneuver. Developed by Captains Teseo Tesei and Elios Toschi, both Regia Marina engineering officers, the SLC was somewhat faster and had a longer range than a Mignatta. Even more importantly, it could submerge to penetrate enemy naval bases—its underwater speed was around three knots. The leading member of its two-man crew, both of whom were clad in wet suits and wearing scuba-diving gear, steered it much as if riding a horse. Trials started off the northern coast of Tuscany in 1938, a specially adapted submarine being used to get the first SLCs near to their targets.

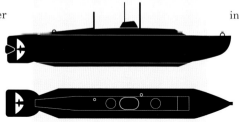

X-CRAFT

Class X-craft miniature submarine

Displacement 27 tons surfaced, 30 tons submerged

Length 51ft 3in (15.6m)

Beam 5ft 9in (1.8m)

Draft 5ft 4in (1.6m)

Speed 6.5 knots (surfaced), 5.5 knots (submerged)

Armament Two 4,000-lb (1814-kg) detachable explosive side charges

Crew 3–4

X-craft were miniature submarines primarily devised by the British to attack the remaining German capital ships at their Norwegian moorings. The vessels were towed to their intended area of operation by mother submarines with passage crews onboard. Operational crews were transferred from the mother submarines to their X-craft by dinghy once the operational area was reached. After their attacks were over, the X-craft rendezvoused with their mother submarines to be towed home again.

Tesei and Toschi advocated mass deployment of their invention, but, when war came, only a small number of SLCs were ready for action. Tesei himself perished in July 1941 when he deliberately blew himself up in an attempt to break through the boom and anti-torpedo nets protecting shipping in Valletta's Grand Harbour in Malta. The mission he was leading turned into a disaster. The British had been tracking the assault force by radar and the SLCs were blown out of the water by gunfire from the harbor forts.

Two months later, the SLCs had better luck. Three of them were launched from the submarine *Scire* off Algeciras in Spain and then made their way east across the bay toward Gibraltar. Two of them dived under two of the tankers anchored in the bay and attached magnetic charges with delayed-action fuses to them. The third dived under the boom protecting the inner anchorage, eased its way through some antitorpedo netting and steered for another tanker moored alongside the harbor's mole. After attaching a 660-lb (229-kg) charge to the bilge keel, the crew took the same route back into the bay.

All three crews then scuttled their craft before swimming ashore at Algeciras to take refuge on board *Olterra*, an interned Italian tanker that had been secretly converted into an SLC base. Three thunderous explosions signaled that the operation had been a complete success.

IN ALEXANDRIA HARBOR

The SLCs' next operation was even more ambitious. Late in the evening of December 18, *Scire* launched another three SLCs less than a mile from the approach to Alexandria harbor, the main base of Britain's Mediterranean Fleet. The three pilots submerged their craft and set off for the boom protecting the harbor entrance. They had luck on their side. As they neared the boom, it was raised to allow three British destroyers to pass through it. The Italians sneaked into the harbor behind them before the boom was lowered again.

Once inside the harbor, Commander Count Luigi de la Penne made for the battleship *Valiant*, while the other two SLCs took the flagship *Queen Elizabeth* and the tanker *Sagona,* which was moored close by, as their targets. Both planted their charges successfully; de la Penne dropped his on the shallow seabed just a few feet under *Valiant*'s keel. He then scuttled his boat and together with his fellow crewman swam to a nearby buoy, where they were spotted, captured, and sent for interrogation. The other Italians reached the shore, where they were taken prisoner later.

De la Penne and his fellow crewman refused to talk. Sir Andrew Cunningham, commander-in-chief of the Mediterranean Fleet onboard *Queen Elizabeth*, ordered both of them to be locked up below decks on *Valiant* well below her waterline. Five minutes before his charge was due to exploded, de la Penne sent a message to Captain Charles Morgan, *Valiant*'s commander, warning him of the imminent explosion. The Italians were brought back on deck just before all three charges exploded.

The first charge sank *Sagona* and badly damaged the destroyer *Jervis* lying alongside her. The two battleships settled to rest on an even keel on the bottom of the harbor. Three of *Queen Elizabeth*'s boiler rooms were flooded and several thousand square feet of her double-bottom destroyed. *Valiant* had a huge hole blown through the protective anti-torpedo bulge under one of her main gun turrets. Her forward magazines were flooded.

Cunningham was appalled. "We are having shock after shock out here," he recorded, "the damage to the battleships at this time is a disaster." Repairs took six months. Nevertheless, the Admiral paid de la Penne and his compatriots a handsome tribute. "One cannot help but admire," he noted, "the cold-blooded bravery and enterprise of these Italians." The navy paid the SLCs the ultimate compliment. It copied their design for its own human torpedo, the so-called *Chariot*.

X-CRAFT

As well as Chariots, the British deployed midget submarines of their own. X-craft, as they were termed, were designed in 1942 for one specific purpose—to sink the German battleship *Tirpitz*. The abiding British fear was that *Tirpitz* might emerge from her bolthole in a Norwegian fjord and either break out into the Atlantic or steam north into the Arctic to inflict disastrous damage on the convoys Britain was despatching to get aid to Soviet Russia.

X-craft were small and cramped. Their 50-foot-long (15-m) hulls were divided internally into four compartments—the battery compartment forward, the wet-and-dry chamber or diving lock also containing a toilet, the control room, and, right aft, the propulsion unit. Overall headroom was no more than six feet (1.8m). Each X-craft had two crews—the passage crew, responsible for the submarine while it was being towed submerged toward its target—and the operations crew, which took over once the target was in sight.

ATTACKING *TIRPITZ*

Code-named Operation Source, the attack on *Tirpitz* took place on September 22, 1943. Six X-craft set out on the operation, sailing from their base in Scotland on September 11. X-8 and X-9 were lost on passage as they

▲ An X-craft on a training exercise at the ultra secret base the British established at Loch Erisort on the Isle of Lewis in Scotland. Their first war mission began on September 11, 1943, when six X-craft were towed from Scotland into the North Sea and on toward Norway, where they were to target *Lutzow*, *Scharnhorst*, and *Tirpitz*. However, the attacks on the first two warships had to be aborted. X-8 was badly damaged when her leaking side charges exploded while being jettisoned. She was scuttled by her own crew. X-9 sank with all hands when her towing cable parted in the North Sea, while X-10 found that *Scharnhorst* had put to sea for gunnery practice.

Tirpitz at anchor in Kafjord. On September 20, X-5, X-6, and X-7 moved into the fjord to attack her. X-7 successfully released her two side charges directly under the battleship's hull. When they detonated an hour later, they inflicted substantial damage on her. Tirpitz took on an estimated 14,000 tons of water. Her electrical and fire control systems were badly damaged and one of her 15-inch gun turrets was thrown off its bearings by the force of the explosions. She was put out of action for six months until April 1944 before she was ready to sail again.

were being towed across the North Sea. X-9 sank after its tow rope broke, while X-8 developed major technical problems. So, too, did X-10, which meant it had to be abandoned in the outer fjord.

This left three remaining X-craft to make the attack. Of these, X-5 disappeared somewhere in the inner fjord. It was presumed that she must have been sighted and sunk. Both X-6 and X-7 found it extremely difficult to penetrate the formidable antisubmarine and anti-torpedo nets that protected the battleship. However, the X-craft managed to get to within striking distance of their target.

Lieutenant Donald Cameron in X-6 was fortunate. Rather than having to order his diver into the water to cut a way through the antisubmarine nets, he managed to follow a German tug through an opened boom, reach Tirpitz, and release his two saddle charges, each containing two tons of high explosive. Then his luck ran out. As he tried to make his way out of the fjord, X-6 struck an uncharted rock. The damage was so great that Cameron was forced to surface. He had to scuttle his boat and surrender. X-7, commanded by Lieutenant Godfrey Place, also jettisoned its charges successfully, but did not manage to get far enough from Tirpitz before they exploded. The resulting damage forced Place and his crew to flood the craft and try to

escape through the diving lock. Two did not survive the attempt. The others were captured by the Germans and taken onboard Tirpitz.

Although Tirpitz was not sunk, she was seriously damaged. Both Cameron and Place were awarded the Victoria Cross. Subsequently in January 1944, X-20 landed hydrographical experts to examine conditions on the Normandy beaches; on D-day itself, she, together with X-23, acted as navigational beacons to guide in the first wave of assault craft. Prior to this, in April 1944, X-24 attacked and then in September sank a floating dock being used to repair U-boats in Bergen harbor. In the Far East, XE-1 and XE-3 penetrated the Singapore naval base to sink the Japanese cruiser Takao on July 31, 1945, while XE-4 and XE-5 severed the underwater telephone cables linking Saigon, Hong Kong, and Singapore.

SUICIDE WEAPONS

In Germany, human torpedo and midget submarine development lagged behind that of other naval powers. The human torpedoes Neger and Marder made their combat debuts attempting to attack Allied supply ships after the Normandy landings in 1944, while Seehund, a two-man midget submarine never got into action at all. Though Negers sank three minesweepers and damaged a destroyer beyond repair, they proved extremely vulnerable. Out of 21 Negers launched from Trouville at the mouth of the Seine on July 9, none returned. The Marder track record was equally bad. When they went into action by night against Allied shipping in August, out of the 58 only 12 survived. Both were little better than suicide weapons, even though they were not deliberately intended as such.

The Japanese thought differently. Two young naval officers, Lieutenants Sekio Nishina and Hiroshi Kuroki, devised a piloted version of the standard Type 93 torpedo as a suicide weapon to be transported into action by Japan's giant I-class submarines. The new weapons were christened "kaitens." They first went into battle on November 19, 1944, led by Nishina himself. Kuroki had been drowned in an accident during training.

Only five kaitens managed to launch successfully when they reached their destination off Ulithi. Only one of them succeeded in hitting a target. The others were sunk—one by ramming and the rest by depth charges and gunfire. The same thing happened to the kaitens launched off Hollandia and New Guinea, in Kossol Passage in the Paulus, and off Apra in Guam. Not one of them claimed a victim, despite Japanese boasts of the damage the kaitens were inflicting.

Kaiten operations off Iwo Jima in February and March 1945, and Okinawa the following month, were just as unsuccessful. Nevertheless, hundreds more kaitens were built right up to the end of the war and Japan's unconditional surrender. Nor was there any shortage of young volunteers ready to crew them. They were all more than willing to die for their country and their Emperor.

ATTACKING *TIRPITZ*

The maps here show how X-5, X-6, and X-7 set about attacking *Tirpitz*. X-6 successfully penetrated the fjord, but struck a submerged rock near where the battleship was berthed and was forced to surface before she could drop her side charges. She was spotted by the German deck watch, and her crew forced to surrender. X-7 released her charges under *Tirpitz*'s hull, where they exploded. As she started to make her getaway back down the fjord, however, she became entangled in the battleship's protective torpedo netting. X-7 was now half-submerged and taking in water fast, so her crew decided they had to abandon her. Only two of them made it through her escape hatch; the other two drowned. X-5 never got near *Tirpitz* at all, seemingly vanishing somewhere in the fjord. Some believe that she may have been sunk by the battleship's secondary armament as she attempted a surface approach, but this has never been confirmed. The Admiralty listed her officially as missing and presumed sunk with all hands.

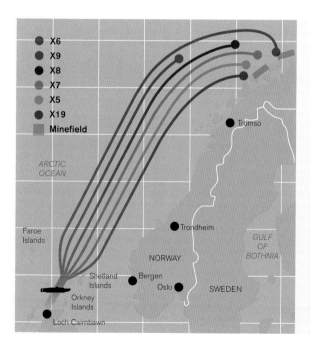

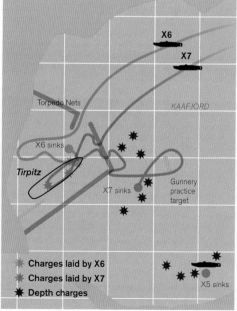

ISLAND HOPPING

Island hopping, or leapfrogging as it was later termed as the strategy was refined, was like a gigantic game of checkers. The vastness of the Pacific Ocean was the checkerboard, with the Japanese Home Islands as the ultimate prize.

What made the adoption of this bold strategy possible was the US naval victory at Midway in May 1942. This was the key to the establishment of US naval superiority over the Japanese in the Pacific theater of war. Even before the battle, however, Admiral Chester W. Nimitz, commander-in-chief of the revitalized US Pacific Fleet, and General Douglas MacArthur, commander of Allied land forces in the region, had already started working out the best way of regaining the military initiative as soon as the time was ripe.

ALLIED PLANNING

While the Japanese were busy consolidating what they termed their outer defensive perimeter to secure their conquests, the Allied planners were also hard at work. As a preliminary to the main campaign, the USA was to launch Operation Cartwheel, which was designed to isolate the Japanese stronghold at Rabaul on New Britain. The subsequent strategy was to capture strategically situated islands in the Pacific one by one, bypassing and isolating strongly held ones that were centers of Japanese resistance. These, said MacArthur, could be left "to wither on the vine."

There were to be two prongs to the Allied attack. MacArthur was to push northward along the coast of New Guinea and on into the Bismarck Archipelago, with the liberation of the Philippines as his ultimate goal. Nimitz was to island-hop his way across the Central Pacific, starting from the Aleutians and continuing via the Gilberts, the Marshalls, and the Carolinas, ending up in the Marianas. If the plan worked, Japan would be brought well within range of the new generation of US strategic bombers, which would blitz the country remorselessly until it was ripe for invasion.

It all sounded fine on paper, but there was a substantial delay before the plan could be put into action. Roosevelt, Churchill, and Stalin had all agreed that the defeat of Germany was their top priority. Japan would have to wait until the Third Reich had been crushed. This meant that the Pacific was starved of naval reinforcements—most notably of aircraft carriers and landing craft. Though MacArthur and Admiral William "Bull" Halsey had started moving forward in New Guinea and the Solomons, progress was slow. At the rate they were going, it was estimated that it would taken them ten years to reach Japan

FROM ISLAND HOPPING TO LEAPFROGGING

Leapfrogging began almost inadvertently in May 1943. Nimitz started the process in the Aleutians when he decided to leapfrog over Kiska, which the Japanese had occupied in June 1942, and instead take Attu, around 200 miles (322km) away and the less defended of the two islands. When finally the Americans did land on Kiska in August, they found that the Japanese had abandoned it, taking advantage of heavy fog to evacuate its garrison undetected. Nimitz suggested to Halsey that he should employ the same tactic. Ignoring Kolombangara, with its 10,000-strong garrison—though, unbeknown to him, the Japanese had already decided to evacuate it—Halsey instead landed his marines on Vella Lavella to the northwest.

The marines went ashore on August 15 on Barakoma Bay at the eastern foot of the island. The landing was uncontested, the Japanese having withdrawn into the interior. The marines pushed forward methodically but slowly until, on September 18, they were relieved by Major General Harold Barrowclough's New Zealanders. Launching a pincer movement up both the island's coasts, the New Zealanders cornered about 600 Japanese on the northwest of the island by October 1.

US Marine Corps Chance-Vought F4U-1 Corsairs, Grumman F6F-3 Hellcats, a Douglas SBD Dauntless, and a Royal New Zealand Air Force Curtiss P46-F Kittyhawk Mark IV on the airstrip at Barakoma airfield on Kella Lavella in the Solomons in December 1943. The US 35th Infantry Regiment and some New Zealand troops landed on the island on August 15, 1943; the 58th Naval Construction Battalion completed work on the airfield the following month. Barakoma remained operational until June 15, 1944. When the battle passed it by, it was decided to abandon it.

These were the men the Japanese High Command had sent to Vella Lavella to operate the Horaniu barge base.

BATTLE OF VELLA LAVELLA

Rear Admiral Matsinji Ijuin, the senior Japanese naval commander in the area, was determined to rescue his stranded compatriots. To this end, he marshaled some 20 barges plus some smaller craft, escorted by the destroyers *Fumizuki, Matsukaze,* and *Yunagi* with six more destroyers—*Akigumo, Isokaze, Kazagunmo, Samidare, Shigure,* and *Yugumo*—in support. To counter the threat, the Americans had only six destroyers available, split into two groups of three destroyers each. Captain Frank R. Walker commanded *Selfridge, Chevalier,* and *O'Bannon*; Commander Harold B. Larson *Ralph Talbot, Taylor* and *La Vallette.* Walker was about 20 miles (32km) in advance of Larson, his destroyers steaming in column ahead.

The clash between the two sides began shortly before 11 p.m. on October 6. *Yugumo* was the first ship to score a hit. She torpedoed *Chevalier* on her port bow, the torpedo's warhead detonating in the forward magazine. The resulting explosion tore off *Chevalier*'s bow up to the bridge. The doomed destroyer promptly collided with *O'Bannon*, which was next in line behind her. *O'Bannon* sheered away out of the battle. Meanwhile, *Selfridge* had succeeded in torpedoing *Yugumo.* She sank within minutes.

Rather than wait for Larson to catch him up, Walker chased after the other two destroyers *Selfridge*'s radar had spotted on his own. This brought her into a fight with *Shigure* and *Samidare. Selfridge*'s guns repeatedly straddled her opponents, but they, in their turn, fired 16 torpedoes at her. One hit her forward on her port side and brought her to a shuddering stop.

Ijuin ordered all his destroyers to retire, fearing that a larger US force was on its way north. *Selfridge* and *O'Bannon* made it safely back to Tulagi; *Chevalier* was torpedoed and sunk by *La Vallette*, after Larson had

succeeded in rescuing 250 of her 301-man crew. Ijuin's barges succeeded in rescuing the trapped Japanese.

THE BOUGAINVILLE BATTLES

Bougainville, the largest of the Solomon Islands, was the next US target. If it could be taken, Rabaul, only 170 miles (274km) from its northern tip, would be open to attack by American air power and the Japanese position there would eventually become indefensible. Allied control of the island would also neutralize many of the Japanese airfields in the area.

To defend Bougainville, the Japanese had more than 50,000 men on the island, but the chosen landing spot, Empress Augusta Bay, was separated from the main garrisons by many miles of dense tropical rainforest.

▶ The Buka Passage, a narrow strait between Bougainville and Buka Islands, photographed by a US reconnaissance plane in 1943. Bougainville was the last Japanese stronghold in the Solomons to be recaptured. The Japanese finally capitulated on September 3, 1945, when what remained of the garrison surrendered to the Australians.

BELOW The US destroyers *Chevalier, O'Bannon,* and *Selfridge* on patrol off Kella Lavella. On the night of October 6, 1943, they ran into a superior Japanese destroyer force, which was escorting some 20 barges in an attempt to evacuate the island. Hit by a Japanese torpedo, *Chevalier*'s stern swung round and rammed *O'Bannon*, which stopped dead in the water as *Chevalier* began to flounder. *Selfridge*, too, was badly damaged in the action.

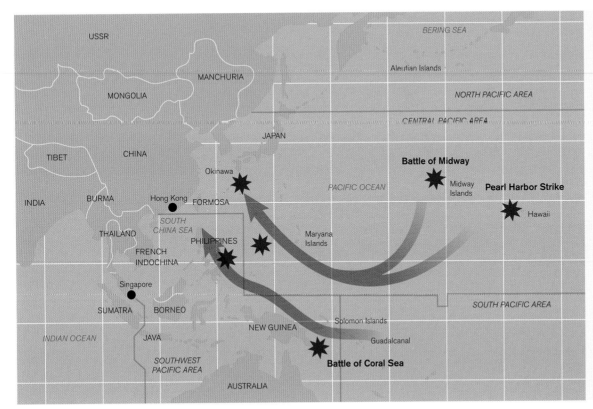

USSR

MANCHURIA

MONGOLIA

Aleutian Islands

BERING SEA

NORTH PACIFIC AREA

CENTRAL PACIFIC AREA

JAPAN

TIBET

CHINA

Okinawa

Battle of Midway

PACIFIC OCEAN

Midway
Islands

Pearl Harbor Strike

INDIA

BURMA

Hong Kong

FORMOSA

Hawaii

*SOUTH
CHINA SEA*

THAILAND

PHILIPPINES

Maryana
Islands

FRENCH
INDOCHINA

Singapore

SUMATRA

BORNEO

SOUTH PACIFIC AREA

NEW GUINEA

Solomon Islands

INDIAN OCEAN

JAVA

Guadalcanal

*SOUTHWEST
PACIFIC AREA*

Battle of Coral Sea

 Naval Battles

AUSTRALIA

FROM ISLAND TO ISLAND

General Douglas MacArthur and Admiral
Chester Nimitz jointly masterminded the
island-hopping strategy US land and naval
forces adopted in the Pacific from August
1942 onward. The idea was to capture
key Pacific islands one by one, advancing
inexorably toward Japan while bypassing
and isolating centers of Japanese resistance.
The attack was two pronged. MacArthur
pushed northwest along the New Guinea
coast and into the Bismarck Archipelago with
the eventual aim of liberating the Philippines.
In the central Pacific, Nimitz started by
recapturing the Aleutians and then hopped
his way through the Gilbert, Marshall, Caroline,
and Marianas Islands.

It was held by fewer than 3,000 Japanese. The 3rd Marine Division was the first to go ashore at Cape Torokina on November 1. By nightfall, 14,000 marines had been landed. By November 14, their number had risen to 33,861. The plan was for them to dig in and set about building air strips before the Japanese could mount any serious counterattack by land.

How the Japanese Navy would react was more problematic. Nimitz believed that the simultaneous operation he was mounting against the Gilbert Islands in the Central Pacific would deter Admiral Mineichi Koga, Yamamoto's successor as naval commander-in-chief, from committing the main Japanese fleet and its aircraft carriers to battle elsewhere in the southwest. Nimitz was correct in his assumption, though Koga did order 175 of his carrier-borne aircraft to fly to Rabaul to bolster its defense.

What Nimitz did not anticipate was how quickly Vice Admirals Sentaro Omori and Tomoshigo Samejuma, both on the spot in Rabaul, would react to the American landing. They got permission from Koga to combine their two commands into a single battle squadron, their aim being to destroy the US troop and supply transports and wipe out the naval forces supporting the landing before it could be consolidated.

CLASHES AND COLLISIONS

The Americans and the Japanese clashed on the night of November 2. Omori and his four cruisers—two heavy and two light—plus six destroyers were steaming hell for leather for Empress Augusta Bay, while Task Force 39, commanded by Rear Admiral Aaron S. Merrill and consisting of four light cruisers and eight destroyers, was racing north to intercept him.

Though the Japanese were stronger on paper, the battle went badly for Omori from the start. The visibility was poor and, unlike the Americans, he had no radar to guide him. Nor had he any idea of what forces he was up against, and the reports he got from his spotter planes only increased his confusion. The various tactical maneuvers he ordered accomplished nothing, except to throw his ships into disorder.

No sooner had battle been joined than the light cruiser *Sendai* almost collided with the destroyer *Shigure*. While taking evasive action, *Shigure* managed to sideswipe *Shiratsuyu*, her sister destroyer, and both vessels were put out of action. Meanwhile, *Sendai* was being shelled by Merrill's light cruisers. The first three salvos from the American guns set her ablaze. Confusion continued to reign among the Japanese ships as Omori tried to reform his disorganized squadron. *Haguro*, one of the heavy cruisers, narrowly missed colliding with the destroyers *Nagananami* and *Wakatsuki*, while *Myoko*, Omori's second heavy cruiser, managed to slice off the bows of the destroyer *Hatsukaze*.

THE WRITING ON THE WALL

Omori turned back to Rabaul. His failure meant that the Bougainville invasion could not be stopped, especially when Halsey was reinforced by Rear Admiral Frederick C. Sherman's Task Force 38, which included the fleet aircraft carrier *Saratoga* and the light carrier *Princeton*. When the carriers *Bunker Hill* and *Essex* and the light carrier *Independence* arrived, US naval and aerial supremacy in the Solomons was confirmed once and for all.

By contrast, Japan's naval power was in terminal decline. Between April 9, 1943, and February 14, 1944, the Japanese lost a total of 33 ships—25 destroyers, 5 light cruisers, 1 escort carrier, 1 seaplane carrier, and 1 battleship. Their shipyards were jam-packed with damaged vessels needing urgent repair. The only replacements that could be produced were three

carrier escorts, three light carriers, two light cruisers, nine destroyers, and two battleships pressed into service as hybrid aircraft carriers by the addition of a flight deck aft.

By contrast, for the landings on Eniwetok Atoll, the largest island in the Western Marshalls, in February 1944, the Americans mustered the fleet carriers *Enterprise*, *Yorktown*, *Essex*, *Intrepid*, and *Bunker Hill*, plus the light carriers *Cabot*, *Cowpens*, and *Monterey*. The force also contained *Iowa*, *New Jersey*, and four more of the USA's most modern battleships, plus accompanying cruisers and destroyers. As island after island fell to the advancing Americans, the Japanese defensive perimeter buckled. The stage was set for what was to turn out to be the decisive naval battle of the Pacific war.

▲ *Independence* was the first of nine small 11,000-ton aircraft carriers built to fight in the later stages of the Pacific naval conflict. She was originally planned to be a light cruiser, but then was converted into a carrier while still under construction. Having taken part in raids on the Japanese bases at Marcus, Wake, and Rabaul, she was a part of the task force tasked with seizing the Gilbert Islands before being damaged by Japanese torpedo planes and forced to return to the USA for repairs. Returning to the Pacific in July 1944, she fought in the battle of Leyte Gulf that October.

OPERATION HUSKY

Operation Husky—the code name for the invasion of Sicily in July 1943—was the biggest amphibious landing to be launched by the Allies in the war to date. Indeed, only Overlord surpassed it in size. It was the first step in penetrating what Churchill had christened "the soft underbelly of Europe." Victory in Sicily would open the door to the invasion of Italy itself and might precipitate, so it was hoped, Mussolini's fall.

Detailed planning for the attack began after the Casablanca Conference in January 1943. Originally, ten widely separated landings in the northwest and southeast of the island were proposed, but General Sir Bernard Montgomery's determined opposition scotched the plan. Instead, it was decided that four divisions from his Eighth Army, together with an independent infantry brigade, would be landed between Syracuse and Cape Passero, 50 miles (80km) to the south. Once ashore, the British and Canadians would seize Syracuse and its port and then secure the Italian airfields on the Catania Plain south of Mount Etna before pushing on northward toward Messina.

Lieutenant General George S. Patton's Seventh Army would come ashore west of Scoglitti on the south coast. Having captured the port at Licata, it would then seize control of the airfield at Gela before continuing its advance on Palermo. Elements of two airborne divisions—one British, the other American—would parachute behind Axis lines to capture key strategic positions a few hours in advance of the main landings.

NAVAL PLANNING

Admiral Sir Andrew Cunningham was in overall command of the naval forces assigned to support the invasion, with Rear Admiral H. Kent Hewitt commanding the naval task force in the western sector and Admiral Sir Bertram Ramset the eastern one. Between them, the American and British Admirals had 6 battleships, 2 aircraft carriers, 15 cruisers, 128 destroyers, 26 submarines, and 248 other warships under their command. Five hundred and nine troop transports and 1,225 landing craft completed the invasion fleet.

Four of the battleships—*Nelson*, *Rodney*, *Warspite*, and *Valiant*—and the carriers *Formidable*, *Indomitable*, and 4 cruisers and 17 destroyers were covering the assault in the event of any attempted intervention by the Regia Marina. Seven of the submarines were stationed off the invasion beaches to act as navigational markers. As far as the Royal and US Navies were both concerned, every possible step had been taken to ensure that the landings would go smoothly and be a success.

DISRUPTED BY A GALE

The one thing neither navy could control was the capricious weather. On July 9, the invasion fleet concentrated near Malta before heading for Sicily and its southern beaches. It was not plain sailing. As the armada steamed toward the island, a fierce 40-mile-an-hour gale, dubbed the "Mussolini wind" by the seasick GIs, whipped up the seas. The bad weather seriously hampered some of the smaller invasion craft, which battled against the wind and waves to stay on station and keep up with the bigger ships.

Despite the unexpected gale, the landings went ahead practically unopposed. According to Field Marshal Albert Kesselring, in overall command of Axis forces in Italy, this was because "the Italian coastal divisions were an utter failure." It was also at least partly due to his decision to overrule General Alfredo Guzzoni's desire to concentrate his forces in the southeastern corner of the island, which the Italian commander correctly assumed was the most likely point of attack. Instead, Kesselring opted for a more scattered defense. Also, rather than keeping his German units concentrated as a mobile reserve ready to strike at the Allied beachheads while they were still vulnerable, he divided them up into four battle groups to reinforce the Italians piecemeal.

The light cruiser *Boise* opens fire on German panzers attempting to break through to the US beachhead near Gela, Sicily, on July 11, 1943. She destroyed 24 of them. This photograph was taken from LST-325, a tank landing craft preparing to deposit its cargo of army trucks onshore. The mounted and manned machine guns ready for action on some of the trucks were intended to deter air attack. *Boise* went on to take part in the landings on the Italian mainland at Taranto and Salerno that September.

THE ITALIAN COLLAPSE

As Hitler, for one, had feared, Italian resistance was indeed feeble. Most of the Sicilians in the Napoli Division stationed on the southeastern coast ran away after firing a few token shots at the invaders. Syracuse and its important port fell undamaged into Allied hands, while the commander of the heavily fortified naval base at Augusta ran up the white flag even before he was attacked. The only serious resistance was put up by elements of the Livorno and Hermann Goering Divisions, who launched a determined counterattack on the American troops attempting to advance from Gela. The Hermann Goering Division's panzers got to within 2,000 yards

(1,829m) of the beach before supporting gunfire from the destroyer *Boise* destroyed 24 of them. The survivors fell back in disorder.

By the time Kesselring arrived in Sicily—he had to make the journey by flying boat since most of the Axis airfields on the island had been captured and put out of action by Allied bombing—the Allied bridgehead stretched from Licata to the foot of Mount Etna. All he could do was to try to establish a strong defensive line that could contain the Allied advance for "as long as possible" to gain time to evacuate the island. Thanks to brilliant organization, thousands of German and Italian troops, plus much of their equipment, made it across the Straits of Messina to safety.

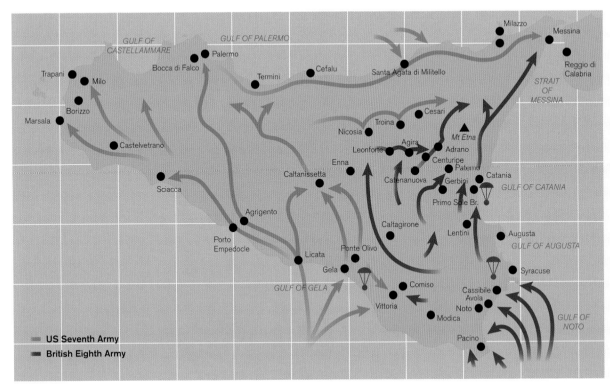

Legend:
- US Seventh Army
- British Eighth Army

THE SICILIAN LANDINGS

The Allies decided to land two invading armies in the southeast of Sicily. General Sir Bernard Montgomery's 8th Army, fresh from its North African triumphs, was to land on the beaches at Syracuse and Cape Passero and secure the port; General George S. Patton's 7th Army would come ashore west of Scoglitti, seize the port there, take Licato, and then capture the airfield at Gela. Two airborne divisions—one of them British and the other American—were to be dropped by glider and parachute ahead of the main force to capture key strategic targets. Though the airborne attack went awry, the main force met little serious opposition, except at Gela, where the panzers of the Hermann Goering Division were quickly on the scene to launch a counterattack. The Axis commanders had judged that the fierce summer storm which had broken out would put an end to any attempt at an amphibious landing.

General Vittorio Ambrosio, the Italian Army's Chief of Staff, was even more pessimistic. As early as July 19, he told Mussolini bluntly that "the fate of Sicily must be considered sealed within a more or less brief period. The essential reasons for the rapid collapse are," he continued, "the absolute lack of naval opposition and the weak aerial opposition during the approach to the coast; the inadequacy of the armament and the distribution of our coastal divisions; the scarcity and lack of strength of our defensive works; and the slight efficiency (armament and mobility) of Italian reserve decisions." He concluded grimly: "It is useless to search for the causes of this state of affairs. They are the result of three years of war begun with scanty means and during which our few resources have been burned up in Africa, Russia and in the Balkans." In his view, the final collapse of the Italian will to fight was imminent.

Certainly, the Regia Marina did not distinguish itself before, during, or after the invasion. Though on July 16 *Indomitable* was damaged by a torpedo bomber and the cruiser *Cleopatra* was torpedoed by the submarine

Alagi, both ships managed to make it back to Malta. The following day, the light cruiser *Scipione Africano* fought a high-speed engagement with British motor torpedo boats in the Straits of Messina, damaging one and sinking another. Then, on August 6 and 8, cruisers from the 7th and 8th Naval Divisions based at La Spezia attempted to attack Allied naval and merchant shipping in Palermo. Both attempts were unsuccessful.

The main Italian battlefleet remained skulking in port. It finally emerged on September 9—only to surrender. By September 11, most of it—the battleships *Vittorio Veneto*, *Italia*, *Doria*, and *Duilio*, together with the majority of its cruisers and destroyers, reached Malta. *Cesare* arrived there two days later, while the cruiser *Attilio Regolo*, three destroyers, and three torpedo boats made for Port Mahon in the Balearics, where they were interned.

Roma, however, never arrived at all. She was sunk north of Sardinia by the Luftwaffe, who attacked her with their revolutionary new Fritz-X radio-controlled glider bombs. *Italia* was damaged in the same attack.

BATTLE OF THE NORTH CAPE

Designed like the pocket battleships before them to outrun what they could not outgun, the twin battlecruisers *Scharnhorst* and *Gneisenau* were the cream of the Kriegsmarine. Their daring dash up the English Channel in March 1942, defying everything Britain could throw at them, cemented their already high naval reputation.

After that, though, *Gneisenau*'s luck ran out. While she was in dry dock at Kiel, an RAF bomb hit her directly on her foredeck. The resulting magazine explosion damaged her severely. Though she was able to make it to Gydania under her own steam, she never saw action again. The idea was to rearm her with heavier 15-inch guns, but Hitler intervened to veto the rebuilding. Instead, he ordered *Gneisenau*'s existing main armament to be removed to be used for shore batteries. The once proud battlecruiser was now little more than a hulk. The Germans scuttled her in April 1945 in an attempt to block the harbor entrance.

SAVED FROM THE SCRAPYARD

Scharnhorst was more fortunate than her unlucky sister. She escaped Hitler's axe, though, in a protracted diatribe the Führer delivered to Admiral Erich Raeder, the head of the Kriegsmarine, she, like all the other German capital ships, had been dismissed as "utterly useless." Stunned by the outburst, Raeder had resigned as commander-in-chief, to be replaced by the newly promoted Grand Admiral Karl Dönitz. Though, as a U-boat man through and through, Dönitz had almost as little time for the surface fleet as did the Führer, he persuaded him to send *Scharnhorst* to Norway to join *Tirpitz* in harassing the Allies' Russia-bound Arctic convoys once they were resumed.

The plan, in essence, was a sound one, but circumstances prevented its implementation. In September 1943, *Tirpitz* was badly damaged while at anchor by British midget submarines; the necessary repairs would take six months to complete. This left Dönitz with

Scharnhorst as the only capital ship available to mount an Arctic attack. He decided to go ahead. On December 19, 1943, he told the Führer that the battlecruiser would definitely strike at the next Allied convoy heading from northern Scotland to Murmansk.

Three days later, Convoy JW 55B was spotted by Luftwaffe reconnaissance aircraft, which began tracking its progress. On Christmas Day, *Scharnhorst*, escorted by the five destroyers of the 4th Destroyer Flotilla, put to sea from its base in Langfjord to intercept it. The Grand Admiral personally signaled Rear Admiral Erich Bey, whom he had put in command of what had been code-named Operation Ostfront: "The enemy is attempting to aggravate the difficulties of our eastern land forces in their heroic struggle by sending

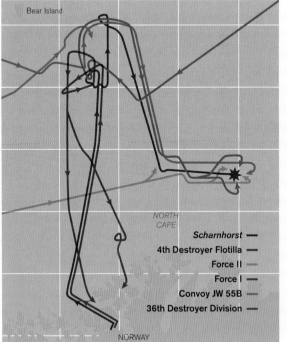

Scharnhorst —
4th Destroyer Flotilla —
Force II —
Force I —
Convoy JW 55B —
36th Destroyer Division —

TRAPPED IN THE ARCTIC

Operation Ostfront was the name given to the German plan to send the battlecruiser *Scharnhorst* and five escorting destroyers north from Norway to locate and destroy Convoy JW 55B, which had been spotted by Luftwaffe reconnaissance aircraft en route for Russia. Unbeknown to them, decoded Enigma messages had given Admiral Sir Bruce Fraser, commander-in-chief of the Home Fleet, advance warning of their intentions. His cruisers located *Scharnhorst* first, knocking out her radar. As the blinded battlecruiser fled, she steamed into the path of the battleship *Duke of York* and her destroyer escort. *Duke of York*'s first salvos silenced her opponent's forward main armament and hit her main boiler room, forcing her to slow to ten knots. She was then further crippled by torpedo attacks, while *Duke of York*, now joined by the cruisers *Belfast* and *Jamaica* kept up sustained fire on her. Battered into submission, she capsized and sank, taking most of her crew to the bottom with her.

an important convoy of provisions and arms to the
Russians. We must help."

STEAMING INTO A TRAP

What Dönitz and Bey obviously never reckoned on was
that *Scharnhorst* was being lured into a carefully
baited British trap. Members of the Norwegian
Resistance had signaled the news of her departure as
soon as she had sailed; the codebreakers at Bletchley
Park, who had cracked the Kriegsmarine's Enigma code,
confirmed that she was on her way to the Arctic and
the Barents Sea. She had therefore lost the vital
element of surprise.

Admiral Sir Bruce Fraser, commander of the British
Home Fleet, had already anticipated such an
eventuality. Using both JW 55B and the homeward-
bound Convoy RA 55A as bait, he readied two task
forces to intercept *Scharnhorst* and bring her to battle.
Force 1, commanded by Vice Admiral Robert Burnett,
consisted of the light cruisers *Belfast* and *Sheffield* and
the heavy cruiser *Norfolk*. Fraser himself led Force 2
—the battleship *Duke of York*, the light cruiser *Jamaica*
and the destroyers *Scorpion*, *Savage*, and *Saumarez*.
He was joined by *Stord*, a Norwegian destroyer, and,
later by the destroyers *Musketeer*, *Opportune*, and
Virago, which he detached from RA 55A when he
ordered it to turn north away from the approaching
Scharnhorst. Both task forces sailed for the Arctic on
December 23, two days before their German opponents
set out on their mission.

FORCE I IN ACTION

Battling the rapidly deteriorating weather, which
was severely hampering Luftwaffe air reconnaissance,
Bey started searching for the British convoys early
on the morning of October 26. Believing that he must
have missed them in the night, he detached his own
destroyers, ordering them to probe southward. In the
meantime, Burnett was closing on *Scharnhorst* from

OPPOSITE, TOP *Scharnhorst* lurks in Langfjord, waiting for the order to strike. It was thought that the battlecruiser's superior speed—she was capable of steaming at just under 33 knots—would enable her to outrun any potential opponent. Rear Admiral Erich Bey was certainly confident this would be the case. Even after he came under fire from *Duke of York*, he signaled to Dönitz "*Scharnhorst* will ever reign supreme."

OPPOSITE, BOTTOM Photographed from the aircraft carrier *Victorious*, the battleship *Duke of York*, waves cascading over her bows, is steaming at between 20 and 25 knots while escorting Convoy PQ-12 to the Russian port of Murmansk. The accuracy of her radar-controlled 14-inch gunnery, firing at a range of 10,000 yards, was the crucial factor in the sinking of *Scharnhorst*.

the northeast, aided by his radar, which first picked up the battlecruiser at around 8.30am.

Belfast was the first British ship to open fire, followed by *Norfolk* and then by *Sheffield*. The battlecruiser returned fire, but failed to score any hits. With his own radar put out of action by a British shell, Bey turned south to break off the action and then northeast in an attempt to loop around Burnett's task force and attack the convoy. Burnett shifted position to screen it.

It was not until just after noon that the British re-established radar contact with the elusive *Scharnhorst*, now steaming at close to her maximum speed of 33 knots. This time, though still radar-less, she was ready for them. She destroyed *Norfolk*'s radar and put one of her gun turrets out of action. However, Bey, bearing in mind Dönitz's injunction to withdraw if "heavy forces" were encountered, turned south again, deciding to take advantage of his ship's superior speed and make flat out for port. Burnett, who was onboard *Belfast,* steamed after him, although the other British cruisers were forced to slow down as a result of mechanical defects.

Try as she might, *Scharnhorst* could not shake off her stubborn pursuer. As Burnett shadowed her, he transmitted constant reports of her position to Force 2, which was now rapidly approaching the scene.

SCHARNHORST CRIPPLED

It was now Fraser's turn. At 4:17 p.m., *Duke of York* picked up *Scharnhorst* on her radar. Having ordered *Belfast* to fire star shells to light up the battlecruiser for his destroyers who were readying themselves to launch a torpedo attack, Fraser ordered his radar-controlled main armament to open fire. *Duke of York* hit *Scharnhorst* with her first salvo.

Bey, his forward gun turret soon out of action, turned north in a desperate effort to escape, but this only brought him under fire from *Belfast* and *Norfolk*. He changed course to the east, still trying to escape the

British trap. *Scharnhorst* hit *Duke of York* twice, damaging her radar. The battleship responded with another full broadside. A shell hit one of *Scharnhorst*'s boiler rooms, fracturing the main steam pipe to the ship's turbines. The result was instant and dramatic. *Scharnhorst*'s speed dropped to around ten knots. Though her damage control parties managed to make some repairs, her maximum speed was now only 22 knots.

This gave Fraser's destroyers the chance they need to launch their torpedo attack. Realizing his ship's desperate plight, Bey signaled: "To the Führer. We shall fight to the last shell."

THE DESTROYERS STRIKE

The end was near as the destroyers moved into the attack. *Savage* and *Saumarez* targeted *Scharnhorst*'s port side while *Scorpion* and *Stord* aimed for her starboard. Four torpedoes struck home. As *Scharnhorst* slowed again, *Duke of York*, supported by *Belfast* and *Jamaica*, closed in for the kill.

Listing severely to starboard and with her bow partially submerged, *Scharnhorst* was now limping along at just three knots. All her main armament had been silenced and she was starting to turn in circles. As more torpedoes struck home—in all, 11 out of the 55 that were fired at the ship hit their target—she was convulsed by explosion after explosion. At 7:45 p.m. a final massive detonation blew off her bow and she slipped immediately beneath the waves.

It was the end of the last surface engagement between British and German capital ships during World War II. Out of the *Scharnhorst*'s crew of 1,968, only 36 survived.

S-BOATS, MTBS, AND PTS

The Germans called their motor torpedo boats S-boats (for some unknown reason, the Allies dubbed them E-boats). The British had their MTBs, the Americans their PTs, and the Italians their MAS boats. Small, fast—their top speed was around 40 knots—and highly maneuverable, they saw action in every major theater of war. In Europe, they battled in the English Channel, the North Sea, the calmer waters of the Aegean and the Adriatic, and in the Mediterranean along the coasts of Italy and North Africa. In the Far East, they attacked the Japanese off Malaya and Burma, in the South China Sea, and, across the Pacific, played a substantial part in the naval operations leading up to the eventual liberation of the Philippines. They posed a particular threat to enemy coastal shipping. So great were the dangers of S-boat attack off East Anglia, for instance, that these waters became known to the British as "E-boat Alley."

FAST AND VERSATILE

As first conceived, the primary purpose of all motor torpedo boats was to strike at enemy coastal shipping, but they were soon employed in numerous other ways as well. Apart from escorting their own coastal convoys, they took part in commando attacks, raided harbors, landed secret agents on enemy coasts, acted as scouts, rescued downed pilots from the waves, attacked enemy submarines, and even served as minelayers, though, as they could carry a maximum of six mines, this was of little practical use. Their disadvantage was limited range, due to their high fuel consumption, and their inability to withstand punishment, either from enemy gunfire or heavy seas.

What made these craft special was their high performance, the swashbuckling audacity of their commanders and crews in the determined manner in which they hunted down their prey and pressed home their attacks. During the day, because protection had

S-BOAT

Class S-100 torpedo boat

Displacement 100 tons (max), 78.9 tons (standard)

Length 107ft 6in (32.8m)

Beam 16ft 7in (5m)

Draft 4ft 10in (1.3m)

Speed 43.8 knots

Armament Two 53.3-mm torpedo tubes, twin 20-mm cannon, single 20-mm cannon, 37-mm anti-aircraft cannon

Crew 24–30

German S-boats—referred to as E-boats by the Allies—were faster and had a longer range than the USA's PT boats and British MTBs. They were also diesel rather than petrol powered. They were most usually deployed in the English Channel and the North Sea to intercept Allied shipping heading for British ports, though they also served in the Aegean, Mediterranean, and the Black Sea. They sank about 214,728 tons of merchant shipping, 12 destroyers, 8 landing ships, 6 MTBs, 11 minesweepers, a torpedo boat, a minelayer, and a submarine as well as damaging 3 cruisers, 5 destroyers, 3 landing ships, a naval tug, and other merchant vessels. The mines that they laid accounted for 37 merchant ships, 1 destroyer, 2 minesweepers and 4 landing ships.

to be sacrificed for speed, they were vulnerable. At night, however, they came into their own.

S-BOATS

Up until early 1943, Germany's S-boats—the S stood for Schnell (fast)—were superior in terms of quality and quantity to anything the Allies could produce. Indeed, the S-boat was probably the most successful of all torpedo boat design produced by either side before and during the course of the war.

The story started in the 1920s, well before Hitler came to power, when what was later to be renamed the Kriegsmarine was already seeking ways of getting around the naval provisions of the Treaty of Versailles. What the Germans wanted was a scaled-down warship well suited for employment in a naval blitzkrieg. The S-boat was the result. Approximately twice the size of its British and US counterparts, it was better able to cope with heavy seas. It also had a longer range of a little over 800 miles (1,288km).

What began the process was a luxury motor yacht with a top speed of over 30 knots designed by the Bremen shipbuilders, Lurssen, for a millionaire American banker in 1928. The German naval high command promptly ordered a similar, but smaller, craft. This, the S-1, was completed in 1930. With a top speed of 37 knots and a displacement of 39 tons, it was armed with a 20-mm anti-aircraft gun, two torpedo tubes—a breach of the Versailles edicts—and a single machine gun. In subsequent S-boats, the tonnage went up—first to 45 and then to 78 tons—and the armament augmented. A typical 1939 S-boat was armed with two torpedo tubes, one 20-mm automatic cannon, and two, rather than one, machine guns.

The power plant was changed as well. The first S-boats were petrol driven, but soon the decision was taken to switch to diesel power. It was thought rightly that diesel-fueled S-boats were far less likely to catch

The S-boat S-204, flying a white flag of surrender, comes alongside a jetty at the British Coastal Forces base at Felixstowe, Suffolk, on May 13, 1945. She and S-205 were escorted into harbor by ten MTBs. Rear Admiral Karl Breuning, who had been in charge of S-boat operations and was onboard S-205, signed the formal instrument of surrender.

fire than were their British and American contemporaries. The three MAN diesels that were originally chosen proved unreliable, so the same number of Daimler-Benz 2,000-horsepower 20-cylinder ones were substituted. These gave a typical S-boat a top speed of well above 40 knots.

By 1939, the Kriegsmarine had 18 S-boats in service. Between then and the end of the war, the Germans built around 230 of them, Lurssen remaining the main constructor. In all, they were credited with sinking 12 destroyers, 11 minesweepers, 8 landing ships, 6 MTBs, a minelayer, a torpedo boat, a submarine, and 101 merchant ships. They also damaged two cruisers, five destroyers, three landing ships, a repair ship, a naval tug, and numerous other merchant vessels. Some 146 S-boats were lost.

MTBS AND PTS

Though the British fielded some CMBs (Coastal Motor Boats) in World War I, the program was abandoned after the German surrender. It was not resuscitated until the mid-1930s, when the British Power Boat Company, Thorneycroft, and Vosper, all vied for an Admiralty contract. Though the British Power Boat Company built the initial prototypes, it was Vosper that undertook the lion's share of the work when, following the outbreak of war, MTBs went into full production.

Vosper MTBs could make speeds of up to 40 Knots. They were generally armed with two 21-inch torpedo tubes and twin Vickers machine guns housed in a turret behind the bridge. Frequently, single and double Lewis guns were also fitted when available. As opposed to the German S-boats, the MTBs were fueled with high-octane aviation fuel rather than diesel. They were originally powered by three Italian Isotta-Fraschini engines. When the supply of these engines dried up following Italy's entry into the war in 1940, American Hall Scott ones were pressed into service as a stopgap, but they proved to be underpowered, reducing top

▼ PT boat PT-105 (below left) is captured running flat out at high speed during training exercises held off the US east coast in July 1942. Other units from MTB Squadron 5 follow their leader. British Motor Gunboats like this one (below right) frequently carried out what were termed Offensive Mining Operations to disrupt enemy shipping in coastal waters. Such operations started in June 1941 off the French and Belgian coasts; the last one took place off the French coast as late as April 1945.

speed by 11 knots. In 1941, they were replaced by Packard engines. At the same time, MTB armament started to be upgraded. The 1944 Vosper 73-foot (22-m) MTB was equipped with four torpedo tubes, a twin 20-mm cannon, and Vickers K machine guns for anti-aircraft protection.

Like the British, the US Navy turned to three different companies—the Electric Boat Company (Elco), Higgins Industries, and the Huckins Yacht Company—to produce designs for their PT boats. After a series of trials held in the waters around New York harbor in May 1941, the Elco PT boat emerged as the clear winner. The company went on to produce a total of 385 PTs for the navy during the course of the war. Higgins Industries manufactured 200, most of which served in the European theater of war. Huckins produced only 18 boats, none of which saw active service.

Elco PTs were 80 feet (24m) long with a beam of 29 feet (8.8m). They were powered by three Packard marine engines, derived from an aircraft engine design, which gave the PTs a maximum speed of 41 knots. Early boats were armed with four torpedo tubes and twin machine guns in two turrets. Subsequently, an Oerlikon 20-mm cannon was added at the stern.

The majority of Elcos fought in the Pacific. Among their primary targets were the Type A Daihatsu armored coastal barges the Japanese were using to ship troops, equipment, and supplies to their beleaguered island garrisons. As the PT boats were to discover in the battle for the Solomons, the problem was that their torpedoes were ineffective against the barges. The Daihatsus had a draft of around five feet (1.5m), but the minimum depth settings for an American torpedo was double this. The consequence was that, even if the torpedoes were on target, they speed harmlessly under the barges.

Improvisation partially overcame the problem. Future President John F. Kennedy's PT-109 had a

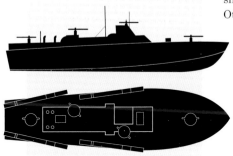

PT-109

Class Motor Torpedo Boat PT-103 class

Displacement 56 tons (full load)

Length 80ft (24.4m)

Beam 20ft 8in (6.3m)

Draft 3ft 6in (1.1m)

Speed 41 knots

Armament Four 21-in torpedo tubes, 20-mm cannon aft, 4 M2 machine-guns, 37-mm antitank gun mounted forward

Crew 17

PT-109 and her sister PT boats were the largest vessels of their type to serve in the US Navy during World War II, mainly in the Pacific theater of operations. Her most noted commander was the future President John F. Kennedy, who, as a young Lieutenant (Junior Grade), took over the captaincy in late April 1943. It did not last for long. On the night of August 2, while on patrol near New Georgia, keeping an eye out for Japanese shipping, PT-109 was rammed by the destroyer *Amagiri*. The impact sliced PT-109 in half and she sank almost immediately. The 11 survivors, including Kennedy himself, managed to swim to a nearby island, from which they were eventually rescued some days later.

single-shot 37-mm antitank gun bolted to its prow. Other skippers attached 39-mm cannons, salvaged from downed P-39 Aerocobras, to their boats. Eventually many boats had their torpedo tubes and depth charge racks removed to allow them to be fitted with 40-mm guns and, as an extra plus, some protective armor. Late in the war, some PTs were equipped with rocket launchers.

The success rate climbed. It was little wonder that the sorely taxed Japanese christened the PTs "devil craft." In the USA, the PT squadrons won themselves the nickname of the "mosquito fleet." Among the more starchy Annapolis graduates, however, they were known as the "hooligan navy"—in part because of a series of unfortunate, though accidental, mishaps.

During the invasion of New Georgia, for instance, a group of six PT boats mistook the flagship of the commanding American admiral, Richmond K. Turner, for an enemy vessel and launched a torpedo attack on it. Fortunately, there was only a skeleton crew onboard, as the ship had already been badly damaged by a Japanese air attack. On another occasion, a PT boat was attacked in daylight by a B-25 bomber, which mistook it for a Japanese barge. The PT boat fired back and shot down the bomber, killing three of its aircrew.

SLAPTON SANDS

In spring 1944, everyone knew that D-Day—the Allied invasion of northern France to launch the long-awaited Second Front   was nearing. For the Germans, the question was when and where the Allies would strike. For the Allies, it was whether or not they would manage to get ashore, avoid being driven back into the sea, and break out of their beachheads successfully. For both sides, as Field Marshal Erwin Rommel succinctly told his staff, it would be "the longest day."

As part of the preparations for the landings, extensive dress rehearsals were held, with the beaches of south Devon substituting for the ones the Allies intended to land on in Normandy. Slapton Sands, a little south of Dartmouth, was selected because it had characteristics in common with both Omaha and Sword Beaches. Operation Tiger, the code name given to the landings there, was scheduled to last from April 22 to 30. It was one of the last and largest rehearsals, with 30,000 US troops, the majority from the 4th Infantry Division, involved.

The first practice landings, which took place on April 27, were successful. In the early hours of the following day, however, an incident took place that was to turn Operation Tiger into a bloody disaster.

THE S-BOAT MENACE
The ever-increasing Allied naval activity in the English Channel, closely monitored by German radar, was mirrored by a corresponding increase in Kriegsmarine activity in the area. Several flotillas of S-boats had been stationed along the coast of northern France—mainly in Cherbourg, Boulogne, and Calais—with some based in Guernsey, one of the German-occupied Channel Islands. All of them were under the command of Kapitän zur See Rudolf Petersen, the Führer des Schellboote with his headquarters at Wimereaux near Boulogne.

Patrolling largely at night, Petersen's S-boats were formidable opponents. Powered by three triple-shafted

Daimler-Benz diesel engines with a top speed of 40 knots when supercharged, they were also heavily armed. They were equipped with twin 21-inch forward-facing torpedo tubes with two or three 20-mm cannon as standard, plus, on occasion, a 37-mm cannon or other heavy armament. Tactically, when well handled, they were almost impossible to resist. They lurked, idling on low power so as not to be detected, until they sighted a target and were ready to strike. Accelerating to full speed, they literally charged directly at the enemy. Then, after launching their torpedoes, they turned away equally rapidly, vanishing back into the darkness from which they had emerged.

As Allied naval activity in the English Channel mounted during the D-Day buildup, the S-boat presence also increased. On the night of February 5, for instance, the 5th S-boat Flotilla, operating out of Guernsey, successfully struck at Convoys PW300 and WP300, sending four Allied vessels to the bottom. On the night of April 14, the Norwegian destroyer *Eskdale* met the same fate. The Slapton Sands convoy was an irresistible target, despite Allied attempts to confuse the enemy as to their intentions and disguise the convoy's destination.

SURPRISE ATTACK
Convoy T45 sailed punctually at 9:45 a.m. on April 27 from Plymouth. Its destination was Lyme Bay and Slapton Sands. It was led by the corvette *Azalea*, followed at 2,000 yards (1,829m) by LST (Landing Ship, Tanks) 515 and, at 400-yard (366-m) intervals, LSTs 496, 511, 531, and 58, the last towing two pontoon causeways. They should have been accompanied by the destroyer *Scimitar*, but she had been holed above her waterline in a minor collision the day before and had been detained in Plymouth for repairs. For some unknown reason, her absence was not reported to higher naval command until the evening, when *Saladin* was eventually ordered to replace her. She finally sailed

US infantry take up position on Slapton Sands, a beach in Devon, during Exercise Tiger, a series of dress rehearsals for D-Day and the invasion of Nazi-occupied France. General Dwight D. Eisenhower, the Supreme Commander of the invasion forces, had told his subordinates to make the exercise as realistic as possible, down to the use of live ammunition and shellfire. What he had not anticipated was that, during the early hours of April 28. 1944, as the exercise was drawing to a close, a flotilla of nine S-boats would attack the eight landing ships convoying US troops to their mock invasion site.

at 1:37 a.m. on April 28. By the time she had caught up with the convoy it was too late.

Some precautions had been taken to deal with the threat of S-boat intervention. Lyme Bay had been cordoned off by destroyers and MTBs, while three more MTBs had been stationed off Cherbourg with orders to intercept the S-boats based there should they attempt to sail. They failed. At 11 p.m., the 5th and 9th S-boat Flotillas, consisting of six and three S-boats respectively, broke through the cordon without being detected. Traveling at 36 knots, they made rapid progress westward toward Lyme Bay. Meanwhile, the slow-moving convoy had been joined by three more LSTs as it headed into Tor Bay. The intention was for it to turn east and then south for its finally westerly approach into Lyme Bay and toward Slapton Sands.

By the time the convoy started its final turn, the S-boats had managed to evade the screening destroyers and MTBs—indeed, they never even caught sight of them. The scene was set for a classic S-boat action. Petersen, who had been alerted by Kriegsmarine radio interception to the position of the convoy, ordered the 5th Flotilla to split into pairs. The third pair, S-138 and S-136, was the first to attack.

CARNAGE AT SEA

S-138 fired a double salvo of torpedoes at the stern of what she took to be a destroyer. In fact, it was LST 507. S-131 fired single torpedoes at another unidentified target. This was LST 531. She burst into flames, turned turtle, and sank within six minutes. LST 507, which was also on fire, battled against the inevitable for 45 minutes before her surviving crew members and the troops onboard were ordered to abandon ship.

The second pair, by contrast, failed to score a hit. Though S-140 and S-142 both launched torpedoes against their respective targets, no explosions were observed. One of their commanders deduced correctly that they had aimed at shallow-draft landing craft. The first pair, S-100 and D-143, scored one torpedo hit between them. S-150 and S-139 of the 9th Flotilla attacked the same ship, while S-145 broke off to attack what her commander described as "small armed escorts."

▲ LCT-305, a tank landing craft, grounds herself on Slapton Sands. LCI9L-32C, an infantry landing craft, is alongside her. When the S-boots attacked in Lyme Bay, one LCT was hit and quickly sank. Another caught fire and had to be abandoned, while a third, though also on fire, managed to make it to the shore. It was a major disaster. Ten times more Americans died in Lyme Bay and on Slapton Sands than on Utah Beach during the actual D-Day landings.

In all probability, these were lowered landing craft. The S-boats then regrouped and withdrew from the scene without loss.

CHAOS AND CONFUSION

What was clear was that, in the confusion caused by the sudden attack, it was impossible for anyone to be certain as to what exactly was happening. The only coherent order given to the convoy as a whole was to break formation, scatter, and proceed independently. It was only later, hours after the action had been concluded, that the scale of the debacle became apparent. Not only had LSTs 507 and 531 been sunk. LST 289 had been badly damaged—her stern had been blown off by a German torpedo, though she eventually managed to limp into port. As for LST 511, it had been hit by friendly fire from LST 496 during the course of the encounter.

Casualties were high. Trapped below decks, hundreds of soldiers and sailors went down with their ships. Others leaped into the sea—there was little or no time to launch lifeboats—but many of them drowned, weighed down by their waterlogged overcoats or in some instances pitched forward under the water because they were wearing their lifebelts around their waists rather than under their armpits. Some died from hypothermia in the freezing-cold water.

In all, 749 Americans were killed or missing. Allied commanders, appalled by the tragedy, were quick to try to cover up its extent. They were particularly concerned that ten officers, known as "Bigots" because they knew which beaches had been chosen for the actual D-Day landings, were among the missing. If they had been captured by the Germans and subjected to interrogation, the fear was that the great secret might well be revealed. In fact, all ten of them drowned.

The inevitable post-mortem followed. The disaster, it opined, had been caused because the convoy's escort was simply not strong enough and because there had been a breakdown in communications between the escort and the landing craft. Thanks to a typing error, both were using different radio frequencies. No one, however, was directly to blame.

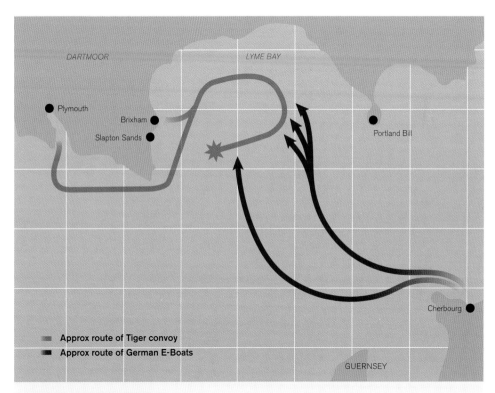

Approx route of Tiger convoy
Approx route of German E-Boats

CONVOY TO DISASTER

The ill-fated convoy sailed from Plymouth for Red Beach at Slapton Sands on April 27, escorted by a single corvette rather than the two that had been originally been allocated to the task. The S-boat attack started at 1:33 a.m. the following morning. In the chaos and confusion that followed, the ships in the convoy were ordered not to return fire as that would give away their positions to the enemy. For their part, the S-boats were convinced they were engaging a group of tankers. Many US troops drowned in Lyme Bay as they struggled vainly for survival. They had put on their life jackets incorrectly.

D-DAY

On June 2, 1944, the first wave of ships forming the D-Day invasion fleet sailed from their home ports. It was the start of the biggest amphibious operation in history. More than 4,000 landing craft and troop transport ships, escorted by more than 600 warships, including 7 battleships, 2 monitors, 23 cruisers, 2 gunboats, 74 destroyers, and 242 close support craft, were soon on the move, heading for the Normandy coast of northern France. Robert Millon, a shore-based signalman in the Royal Navy stationed in Portsmouth, watched part of the great Allied armada as it gradually assembled in the Solent. "The build up was tremendous," he wrote, "a spectacle never to be forgotten. The Solent waters gradually filled up with every type of naval craft, from battleships down to corvettes and motor torpedo boats."

The naval preparations, coordinated by Admiral Sir Bertram Ramsey, had been meticulous. More than 800 minesweepers had cleared shipping lanes through the German minefields to open the way to the invasion beaches. Each beach had two lanes—one for fast convoys and the other for slow ones. Coastal forces had been assigned to protect the invasion fleet's flanks by laying mines off Cherbourg and Le Havre. General Dwight D. Eisenhower, the Allied supreme commander, was poised to give the order for Operation Overlord to proceed. Then the weather intervened.

STORMS AND GALES

Eisenhower and his commanders had agreed that the initial landings should take place on June 5, but, for the invasion to take place at all, various weather criteria had to be satisfied. The weather in the English Channel was notoriously fickle. If it changed for the worse, high winds and rough seas could capsize landing craft, so effectively sabotaging the amphibious assault. Heavy rain could bog down the troops once they got ashore. Thick cloud cover could ground the invasion's essential air support.

The weather experts disputed and debated before reaching a cautious consensus. Group Captain James Stagg, Eisenhower's chief meteorological advisor, warned him that foul weather was on the way and that June 5 would be stormy. He advised the supreme commander that the invasion should be postponed. Eisenhower reluctantly agreed to delay D-day for 24 hours.

On the other side of the Channel, German weather forecasters had come to the same conclusion. The difference between them and Stagg was that the latter believed, though the conditions would not be ideal, a lull in the storm would allow D-Day to go ahead on June 6. The German forecasters' view was that the stormy weather would persist, making it impossible for the Allies to launch an invasion until the middle of the month at the earliest. Most of the commanders in the field agreed with them. Field Marshal Erwin Rommel, whose Army Group B was tasked with defending the Normandy coasts, was so confident that the invasion was not imminent that he went on leave to celebrate his wife's birthday at his home in Germany. Many senior officers also left their posts to travel to Rennes in Brittany to participate in the war games scheduled to be held there over the coming weekend.

EISENHOWER DECIDES

Eisenhower hesitated. He called his commanders into conclave to help him make the final decision. General Sir Bernard Montgomery, who was in overall command of Allied land forces, was adamant that the landings should go ahead. Ramsey said that his invasion fleet could not be left sitting in port and in mid-Channel for much longer. He also warned that if D-Day was postponed again, the Allies would have to wait another fortnight for the next full moon and for the tides to be suitable. Then Stagg confirmed that the forecasters were now as certain as they could be that a break in the storm was coming.

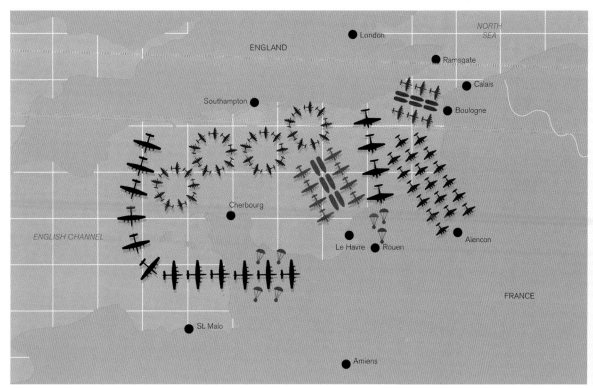

ENGLAND

London

Ramsgate

Calais

Southampton

Boulogne

Cherbourg

ENGLISH CHANNEL

Le Havre Rouen

Alencon

FRANCE

St. Malo

Amiens

OPERATION OVERLORD

Planning for Operation Overlord, the code name chosen for the D-Day landings, began in earnest in 1943. Normandy was chosen for the landings because it was well within range of fighter aircraft operating from Britain and its open beaches were not as well defended as those of the Pas de Calais, where the Germans expected the invasion to take place. It was also conveniently situated opposite the main ports of southern England.

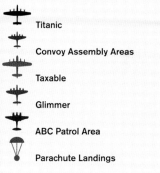

Titanic

Convoy Assembly Areas

Taxable

Glimmer

ABC Patrol Area

Parachute Landings

Eisenhower made up his mind. "OK, we'll go," he said. How confident he was underneath is a matter of dispute. It was still a gigantic gamble. On June 5, as the invasion fleet embarked on the 17-hour voyage to its destination across the Channel, he wrote a note which he planned to make public should Overlord end in disaster. "Our landings in the Cherbourg-Havre area have failed to establish a satisfactory foothold and I have withdrawn the troops," it began. "My decision to attack at this time and place was based on the best information available. The troops, the air and the navy did all that bravery and devotion to duty could do. If any blame or fault attaches to the attempt, it is mine alone."

ACROSS THE CHANNEL

As the convoys steamed in stately procession across the Channel, the final briefings were held. Major K. P.

Baxter, a British officer serving in 5 Beach Group, recorded the happenings. "Once in the docks, we were rapidly embarked on Empire Battleaxe, an LSI (Landing Ship Infantry) equipped with assault landing craft suspended in davits on both port and starboard sides," he wrote. "The vessel was one of a small group carrying the assaulting companies of infantry together with specialist units making up breaching teams and beach signal communications."

"The ship was well into the Channel when we were issued with further maps, photographs and the last briefing instructions, this time with full plane names instead of code references," Baxter continued. "Any doubts amongst the many guesses as to the true landing areas were finally dispelled."

The armada certainly made an imposing spectacle. Lieutenant Charles Mohrle, an American P-47 pilot and one of the thousands of airmen tasked with providing the fleet with air cover, set down his impressions. "Ships and boats of every nature and size churned the rough Channel surface, seemingly in a mass so solid one could have walked from shore to shore," he noted. "I specifically remember thinking that Hitler must have been mad to think that Germany could defeat a nation capable of filling the sea and sky with so much ordnance."

Mohrle was certainly right in his estimation of the sea's roughness. Though, as Stagg had predicted, the actual storm had subsided, a Force Five wind was still blowing. Bill Ryan, an infantry private in the 16th Regiment of the crack US 1st Infantry Division heading for Utah Beach, still remembered many years later how the weather had affected him and his fellow soldiers as their troop transport ship pitched and tossed. "As a result of the cramped quarters and the rough seas, most of the men were already seasick, or at the very least felt really nauseous," Ryan recalled. "Once we departed from the lee side of the transport, we were like a cork in a bathtub. Everyone who was not already sick became sick. I believe I was the only one in my boat who was not seasick."

Ralph Jackson, of the 59th Staffordshire Division, concurred. "I really have no idea how many men were aboard, but I'm quite sure everyone was just about as sick as I was," he recorded. "There were virtually no facilities on board as we were supposed to go straight to Normandy overnight. Rations were a problem; our Gunner Sergeant had suggested we bring bread with us, so we had a few loaves stored on board. That soon went mouldy! In any case, by the time we finally got to the beaches, everyone was just thrilled to get off that damned boat!"

THE NAVAL BOMBARDMENT

The fleet opened fire at around 5:30 a.m. on the early morning of June 6. It was the heavy cruiser *Belfast* that fired first; its target was the coastal artillery battery at Van sur Mer. Following *Belfast*'s lead, the great battleships turned sideways to steam parallel to the coast and joined the cruisers and destroyers in letting loose broadside after broadside against the German coastal defenses. A few LCT(R)s joined in as well, firing salvos of up to 100 six-inch rockets a time.

John Dennett, an Able Seaman onboard LST 232 which was about to head for Sword Beach, recalled how "the naval bombardment began with a deafening noise as *Warspite*, *Ramillies*, and *Roberts* opened fire with their 15-inch guns ranging at the enemy emplacements, followed by the cruisers *Mauritius*, *Arethusa*, *Danae*, and *Frobisher*. These were all close to shore as they fired their six-inch main armament." *Texas* and *Arkansas* led the naval assault on the German defenses at Omaha Beach, while *Nevada* did the same for Utah. Gold Beach and Juno Beach were similarly bombarded.

The bombardment was both accurate and effective. Many of the defenders were stunned by its sheer ferocity. Even a German military correspondent was forced to admit in a radio commentary he broadcast following the landings that its impact had been overwhelming. "The fire curtain provided by the guns of the navy proved to be one of the best trump cards of the Anglo-American invasion armies," he opined. "It may be," he continued "that the part played by the fleet was more decisive than that of the air forces because its fire was better aimed and, unlike the bomber formations, it had not to confine itself to short bursts of fire."

Though on Omaha the success of the landings was a close-run thing, by nightfall the Allies had established firm footholds along the Normandy shore. The German High Command had been taken by surprise—not least because the Allies had not landed in the Pas de Calais as Hitler, for one, had been expecting. The Kriegsmarine's S-boats and U-boats, despite their best efforts, proved powerless to check the invasion. So, too, did the Luftwaffe. On D-day itself, it managed to fly a grand total of just 391 sorties as opposed to the Allied 14,674.

A convoy of LCIs (Landing Craft Infantry) makes its way across the English Channel toward the Normandy invasion beaches on D-Day. Each LCI towed a barrage balloon for protection against attack by low-flying German aircraft, but the Luftwaffe was conspicuous in its absence. The invasion forces managed to get across the Channel largely undetected and relatively unscathed. Allied minesweepers cleared safe channels through the defensive minefields the Germans had laid, while enemy coastal radar was effectively put out of action by Allied jamming and bombing.

ARTIFICIAL HARBORS

Rommel, who had hastened back from Germany as soon as the news of the invasion reached him, was quick to take action. He wanted every available German panzer division rushed to the coast, where in his view the battle would be won or lost. He hoped, too, that the morale of the infantry manning the beach defenses would be strengthened by the presence of such elite armored formations in the battle beside them.

The trouble was the panzers were not under Rommel's direct control. Nor were they at the disposal of Field Marshal Gerd von Rundstedt, the overall commander-in-chief in France. Before the invasion, Hitler had insisted on dividing them up. Rommel was given three of the nine available panzer divisions, only one of which—21st Panzer—was within striking distance of the Normandy coast. The other two were deployed north of the Seine. Three more were sent to the south of France, while the remaining two were held in a general reserve commanded by General Leo Geyr von Schweppenburg.

Only the Führer could decide when, where, and how the panzers could be employed. When he finally was advised of the Allied landings late in the afternoon of D-Day—he had taken a sleeping pill, fallen asleep, and his staff refused to wake him—he procrastinated. He believed that the Normandy landings were a deception and the main ones would come later in the region of the Pas de Calais. He stubbornly refused to allow the bulk of the panzers to move.

One of the reasons for Hitler's lack of decision was his belief that time was on his side. Unless, he opined, the Allies gained control of a major port—and the German garrisons in Le Havre and Cherbourg had been ordered to hold out to the last man—their troops would be starved of the reinforcements and supplies they needed in order to take the offensive, break out of their bridgeheads, and press forward into the heart of France. Such a delay would also give him the chance to bring his new V weapons into play.

The Führer, however, had once again underestimated Allied technological ability. After the experience they had gained in the abortive raid on Dieppe in August 1942, the invasion planners had come to the conclusion that it would be impossible to capture an existing port on the Normandy coast quickly. Therefore, as part of the D-Day preparations, the Allies set about prefabricating two floating harbors—one for the Americans to be situated off St. Laurent and the other to support the British and Canadians off Arromanches.

TOWED ACROSS THE CHANNEL

Much of the early prefabrication work was carried out in Conway, North Wales. Once enough sections of the two harbors were ready, they were floated up the coast to Garlieston in Wigtown Bay in Scotland where they were put together and tested. The military requirement was for a mile-long pier that would be capable of withstanding gale-force winds and be able to berth large freighters and transports. Floating roadways, linking the harbors with the beaches, would ensure the rapid unloading of war material. It was calculated that each harbor would have the capacity to handle 7,000 tons of supplies a day.

Seagoing tugs towed the two Mulberries across the Channel from Lee on Solent to the French coast. Simultaneously, blockships, which were to be scuttled in predetermined positions to protect the harbors from high seas and adverse tides, left Poole for Normandy. Once they reached their destination, the Mulberries were soon in operation. Although the American Mulberry broke up as a result of a fierce storm on June 19, the British one continued to operate until the Allied advance made it redundant.

The Mulberries were a triumphant success. After the war, Albert Speer, Hitler's Armaments Minister, commented ruefully: "To construct our own defenses, we had in two years used some 13 million cubic meters of concrete and 1.5 million tons of steel. A fortnight

▲ One of the concrete caissons used in the construction of the Mulberry prefabricated harbor at Arromanches is about to be towed across the English Channel to its destination on the Normandy coast (top left). The caissons were sunk to form the main breakwater (top right). Note the anti-aircraft guns mounted on platforms to protect the harbor in the event of an aerial attack. The annotated photograph (bottom) shows the completed harbor.

PIPELINE UNDER THE SEA

Following D-Day, the Operation Pluto pipeline the Allies laid on the seabed under the English Channel fueled the advance through France, Belgium, and into Nazi Germany. The first undersea pipeline, which ran from Shanklin in the Isle of Wight to Cherbourg, became fully operational on August 14, 1944. As the armies moved inland, the pipeline was transferred from the Isle of Wight to Dungeness in Kent to shorten the supply route. Ultimately 17 pipelines were operating between Britain and the Continent. By March 1945, a million gallons of fuel were being delivered daily. In total it was estimated that 172 million gallons of fuel passed through PLUTO between August 1944 and the end of the war.

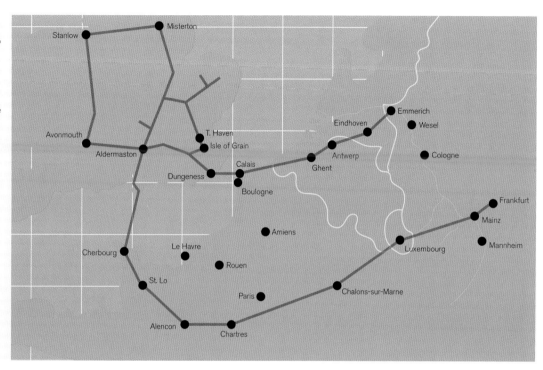

after the Normandy landings, this colossal effort was brought to nothing by an idea of simple genius. As we now know, the invasion forces brought their own harbors with them."

A PIPELINE UNDER THE SEA

Petrol was another essential that Hitler believed would be in short supply for the Allies. Standard procedure would have been to ship fuel by tankers into the war zone. Not only would this have meant the tankers running the risk of being attacked by the Luftwaffe and Kriegsmarine; the supply could easily have been interrupted by vagaries in the weather.

The answer was PLUTO (Pipe Line Under The Ocean). In the weeks and months following D-Day,

thousands of gallons of petrol were pumped under the Channel for onward road transportation directly to the advancing armies. The feat, said Eisenhower, was "second only in daring to the Mulberry harbors." Between August 1944, when PLUTO went into operation, and the end of the war in Europe in May 1945, more than 172 million gallons of fuel were pumped to France. From the moment the Allies broke through the German defenses and fanned out into France, they never paused until they reached the Reich's western frontier.

ENDGAME

By the end of 1944 the naval war in Europe was winding down. On November 12, RAF Lancaster bombers, armed with 12,000-lb (5,443-kg) "Tallboy" bombs sank the already badly damaged *Tirpitz*; the rest of the German surface fleet was now largely in the Baltic, where soon it was helping to evacuate refugees and providing artillery support for the hard-pressed Wehrmacht as it reeled back into the fatherland. The U-boats had been forced out of the Atlantic. The advent of revolutionary new submarines with their vastly increased underwater speed was too little and too late. In the Far East, what remained of the Japanese navy proved itself unable to check the inexorable American advance across the Pacific toward the home islands, despite its admirals' promises that it would fight to the last man.

BATTLE OF THE PHILIPPINE SEA

By spring 1944, US naval and land forces in the Far Eastern theater of war were firmly on the offensive in the central, southern, and southwestern Pacific. The Japanese, by contrast, had been thrown firmly onto the defensive. Rather than trying to check the American naval advance, most of their Combined Fleet was sitting inactive at anchor in Truk Lagoon, Lingga Roads off Singapore, or in the Inland Sea of Japan.

Admiral Soemu Toyoda, who had succeeded Admiral Minechi Koga as commander-in-chief of the Combined Fleet, was not prepared to remain passively on the defensive. He resurrected Yamamoto's original strategy of dealing a death blow to the US Pacific Fleet in one decisive battle. If he continued to fight the naval war piecemeal as had happened at Truck that February, he faced eventual, but certain, defeat. For him, the choice was as simple as that.

OPERATION A-GO

The catalyst that prompted Toyoda into acting was the American invasion of Saipan, the largest island in the northern Marianas, in June 1944. It was an island the Japanese had to defend at all costs, for, if it and the adjacent fell, US long-range strategic bombers based on them finally would be within striking distance of Japan herself. Toyoda immediately activated Operation A-GO.

It was a gamble against the odds. Vice Admiral Jisaburo Ozawa, whom Toyoda had put in command of the Japanese carrier striking force and the First Mobile Fleet, had 5 fleet carriers, 2 light cruisers, 5 battleships, 11 heavy and 2 light cruisers, and 28 destroyers at his disposal. Admiral Raymond A. Spruance and Vice Admiral Marc A. Mitscher, in command of the US Fifth Fleet and Task Force 58, fielded 7 fleet and 8 light carriers, 7 battleships, 8 heavy cruisers, 15 light cruisers, and 69 destroyers between them. In terms of ships, Ozawa was outclassed in every category, with the

ESSEX

Class	Essex-class aircraft carrier
Displacement	33,000 tons (full load)
Length	840ft (256m)
Beam	93ft (28.3m)
Draft	28ft 6in (8.7m)
Speed	33 knots
Aircraft carried	80–100
Armament	12 5-in anti-aircraft guns, 68 40-mm anti-aircraft cannon, 52 20-mm anti-aircraft cannon
Crew	3,448

Twenty-three more Essex-class aircraft carriers followed Essex into service between 1942 and 1945. They were built in two groups, with ships in the second group featuring a lengthened bow to give their forward 40-mm anti-aircraft guns better fields of fire. Despite being involved in many major naval actions in the Pacific, not one Essex-class carrier was actually sunk by the Japanese, though some were seriously damaged. Franklin, hit by two 500-lb (227-kg) bombs that smashed through her hangar deck, starting huge fires and causing aircraft, aviation fuel, and bombs to explode, was the classic example. Despite the major damage she received—casualties numbered 832 dead and 270 wounded—she managed to get back to Pearl Harbor for repair.

exception of heavy cruisers. When it came to aircraft strength, the contrast was even more apparent. The Japanese could put 473 carrier-borne planes into the air; the Americans 956. US fliers were also far better trained than their Japanese counterparts. It took the former two years and at least 300 hours of flying time before they were considered ready for active service. The time allowed for Japanese pilot training was at most six months. Some of Ozawa's pilots had been flying for only eight weeks before they were pitched into battle.

Despite these drawbacks, Ozawa was confident of victory. To counterbalance American aerial superiority, he intended to give battle only when the 500 or so land-based aircraft the Japanese had stationed on the islands of Guam, Yap, and Rota could be called upon to support his own planes in the attack. Ozawa also knew that his carrier-borne planes had a longer range than their US counterparts. They could scout for up 560 miles (901km) and attack at up to 300 miles (483km) away from their carriers. The Americans could manage only between 325 and 350 miles (523km and 563km) when scouting, and not much beyond 200 miles (322km) when attacking.

THE BATTLE BEGINS

Even before the battle of the Philippine Sea started, things started to go wrong for the Japanese. Vice Admiral Kakuji Kakuta, in command of the land planes, managed to only get 50 out of the 500 aircraft he had promised to Guam. His airfields elsewhere were coming under almost constant American aerial attack.

Ozawa was never made aware of the debacle. Unbeknown to him, he now was forced to rely solely on his carrier-borne aircraft to take on the US carriers. He had been counting on Kakuta's planes to sink one third of them before mounting any such attack. Moreover, his fleet had been spotted by US submarines, which had alerted Spruance and Mitscher to its approach.

The *Essex*-class aircraft carrier *Bunker Hill* is seen in the distance, narrowly escaping being directly hit by clusters of Japanese bombs dropped close beside her. Shrapnel fragments scattered across the ship, killing 2 and wounding over 80 of her crewmen. She fought on, her planes helping to sink one Japanese carrier. She was less fortunate the following May. While supporting the invasion of Okinawa, she was hit and badly crippled by two Japanese kamikazes.

Concerned that holding his present course would leave him open to a Japanese night attack, Mitscher asked Spruance if he could steam just far enough west to launch an air strike at dawn. Spruance turned him down. Instead, he ordered Task Force 58 to protect the Saipan landings by interposing itself between Ozawa and the island.

At around 5:50 a.m. on the morning of July 19, a Japanese Zero fighter scouting from Guam managed to signal Ozawa Task Force 58's position before being shot down. Almost simultaneously, Japanese planes began taking off from Guam; Grumman F6F Hellcat fighters from *Belleau Wood*, *Cabot*, *Yorktown*, and *Hornet* were scrambled to intercept them. An hour-long dogfight over and near Guam ensued, during which the Hellcats managed to shoot down 35 aircraft. They were then recalled to defend their carriers against another Japanese aerial attack.

THE "GREAT MARIANAS TURKEY SHOOT"

What exultant American aviators later christened the "Great Marianas Turkey Shoot" was about to start. Ozawa's first wave consisted of 16 fighters, 45 fighters carrying bombs, and 8 torpedo bombers. They were intercepted by 220 Hellcats approximately 55 miles (89km) away from the US carriers—Spruance had sent every fighter he could to deal with the Japanese attack.

The Japanese were massacred wholesale. Out of the 69 planes Ozawa despatched, 42 were downed in less than 35 minutes. Only one managed to get past the screening Hellcats and score a bomb hit on the battleship *South Dakota*, causing minor damage. The all-important carriers were left unscathed. The second wave, which was launched at 10 a.m., fared even worse. It consisted of 34 dive-bombers, 27 torpedo bombers, and 48 fighters. Only 31 of them escaped being shot down. Around 20 made it as far as Rear Admiral Ellis A. Lee's battle line, where they narrowly missed hitting three

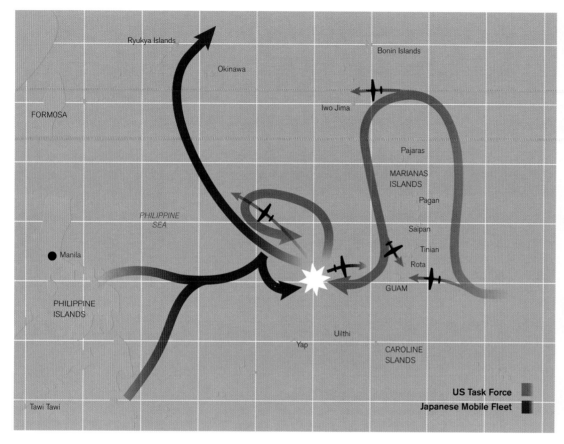

Ryukyu Islands

Okinawa

Bonin Islands

FORMOSA

Iwo Jima

Pajaras

MARIANAS
ISLANDS

PHILIPPINE
SEA

Pagan

Saipan

Manila

Tinian

Rota

PHILIPPINE
ISLANDS

GUAM

Uilthi

Yap

CAROLINE
SLANDS

US Task Force
Japanese Mobile Fleet

Tawi Tawi

OUTNUMBERED AND OUTFLOWN

Vice Admiral Jisaburo Ozawa, commanding the First
Mobile Fleet, was confident that his carriers could
cripple their American opponents by drawing on
land-based planes to reinforce his carrier-borne
aircraft. He was wrong. The former never got into
action and the latter were decimated. Admiral
Raymond Spruance, Ozawa's counterpart, split his
carrier task force into four groups, his aim being
to stop Ozawa slipping round him. Despite striking
first, the Japanese suffered devastating aerial
losses. Many of their planes were shot down by the
battleships, heavy cruisers, and destroyers Spruance
had ordered to form a defensive battle line and never
got anywhere near his carriers.

battleships, but only six got as far as the American
carriers where they were downed by the determined
US fighters and heavy anti-aircraft fire.

The third wave, which took off at 10 a.m. from *Junyo*
and *Ryuhu*, was more fortunate, but only because most
of the planes in it—15 fighters, 25 fighters armed with
bombs, and 7 torpedo bombers—failed to find Task
Force 58 at all. Only seven of its aircraft were lost. At
11:30 a.m., Ozawa launched a fourth strike. It was his
final throw. This time, only 9 of the 87 planes involved
made it back to their carriers; 49 of them tried to land
on Orote Field on Guam, but were pounced on by 27
Hellcats from *Cowpens*, *Essex*, and *Hornet* as they
approached the landing strip—30 were shot down; the
other 19 were forced to crash-land.

These were by no means Ozawa's only problems as
the battle developed. Critically, two of his aircraft carriers
had also been sunk. The US submarine *Albacore* was
the first to strike. Managing to get past his screening
warships, she torpedoed *Taiho*, Ozawa's flagship and
the newest and largest carrier in the Imperial Japanese
Navy. Then 20 minutes or so after, the second wave was
launched. The mortally wounded carrier finally sank
at 5:28 p.m., two hours after a massive explosion tore
right through her. She was preceded to the bottom by
Shokaku, which Cavalla had hit with four torpedoes at
12:22 p.m. At 3:10 p.m., the fire raging onboard reached
her magazines. She blew up and sank immediately.

The greatest carrier battle of the war was now
nearing its end. It had lasted for over eight hours.

Ozawa had lost 346 aircraft to the American 30. Two of his carriers had been sunk. The Americans had sustained a single bomb hit on a battleship which inflicted only superficial damage. It was a clear-cut American victory.

HUNTING DOWN THE JAPANESE

The hunter now became the hunted. It was not until 3:40 p.m. the following day, however, that a scouting plane from *Enterprise* spotted Ozawa's fleet some 275 miles (443km) away heading northwest. It was in the middle of refueling. Spruance and Mitscher decided that, despite the risks of attacking at extreme range and in the dark, their best course of action was to order an all-out night attack on the Japanese.

US planes started taking off from their carriers at 4.20pm. Within the space of just ten minutes, 85 fighters, 77 dive-bombers, and 54 torpedo bombers were airborne and heading for Ozawa's last reported position. The Japanese admiral managed to get 100 planes into the air to oppose them.

The first US aircraft reached Ozawa's fleet, which was now dispersed into three groups, at 6:40 p.m. In the 20-minute attack which followed, *Hiyu*, a battleship that the Japanese had converted into a makeshift aircraft carrier, was sunk, together with two tankers. *Genyo Maru*, a third tanker, became unnavigable and had to be scuttled by the Japanese themselves. *Zuikaku* and *Junyo* were extensively damaged, together with *Chiyoda* and the heavy cruiser *Maya*. *Shigure* was hit by a small bomb while *Haruna* suffered one direct hit aft, two on her quarter deck, and two near misses on her port bow.

The action cost Ozawa 65 of the planes that had managed to survive the "Turkey Shoot." US losses amounted to 80 aircraft. The bulk of these losses occurred when their pilots ran out of fuel while trying to locate their carriers in the dark, even though Mitscher tried to help them by ordering the carriers

to shine all their searchlights vertically skyward to act as beacons.

The Americans finally called off the chase on June 21 at 4:20 p.m., when they turned back toward Saipan. Ozawa made it back to Okinawa Bay the following day with only 35 serviceable planes left out of the 430 that he had started with. The "Great Marianas Turkey Shoot" effectively had put an end to any possibility of a future threat by Japanese carrier-based aviation.

▲ The Japanese carrier *Zuikaku* and two escorting destroyers dodge the US carrier planes attacking them during the late afternoon of June 20, 1944. Despite being hit by several bombs, *Zuikaku* managed to make her getaway. She was luckier than *Taiho* and *Shokaku*, which were torpedoed by the submarines *Albacore* and *Cavalla* earlier in the battle. *Shokaku* sank within minutes of being torpedoed three times; *Taiho*, the newest and largest aircraft carrier in the Japanese fleet, blew up and sank shortly after 2:30 p.m. in the afternoon.

TOP AND BOTTOM A kamikaze torpedo-bomber breaks apart in flames in midair, shot down while trying to crash-dive into an American carrier. At Okinawa, out of 193 kamikaze attacks, 169 planes were destroyed. Nevertheless, the kamikazes that got through sank 21 ships and damaged a further 66. Their score would have been much greater if more planes had managed to reach their targets.

OPPOSITE The US carrier *Belleau Wood* on fire after she was hit by a kamikaze suicide plane off the Philippines on October 30, 1944. Flight deck crew members are shifting undamaged TBM planes away from the flames while others fight the fires. *Franklin*, also hit by kamikazes during the same attack, is seen on fire in the distance.

STRANGLING JAPAN: PACIFIC SUBMARINE WARFARE

When General Hideki Tojo—Japan's premier for much of the war—was asked, after his country's unconditional surrender, what reasons he could give for the Japanese defeat, he said that there were three of them. On top of the list he put the decimation of the Japanese merchant fleet by US submarines.

The loss did more than sap Japan's economic and industrial strength. By 1945, it had brought the country close to starvation. It was the result of a long, but unremitting, campaign of attrition in which US submarines had played the principal part. By the time the war came to an end, they had sunk almost five million tons of enemy shipping—more than sixty percent of the entire Japanese merchant marine. Japan could not possibly withstand such losses.

SINK ON SIGHT

From Pearl Harbor onward, American naval policy in the Pacific was clear and straightforward. Admiral Chester Nimitz, the new commander-in-chief of the Pacific Fleet, ordered his submarines to sink any ships they came across without warning and on sight. It was unrestricted submarine warfare with a vengeance— exactly the same type of warfare Dönitz's U-boats were employing in the battle of the Atlantic.

There, however, the similarity ended. US fleet submarines did not hunt in wolf packs. Nor did they look to supply submarines—the Germans called these "milk cows"—for fuel and supply replenishment. On the whole, they were larger, more comfortable—they were fitted with air-conditioning, for example—and possessed greater endurance than their German counterparts. With a cruising range of 10,000 miles (16,093km), a surface speed of 20 knots, and an underwater one of nine knots, they carried enough supplies for a patrol lasting 90 days. Maximum underwater endurance was 48 hours.

US submarines were also well armed. At first, they were equipped with six to ten 21-inch torpedo tubes,

I-400 SUBMARINE

Class I-401 STO Class submarine

Displacement 5,220 tons (surfaced), 6,560 tons (submerged)

Length 380ft 6in (116m)

Beam 39ft 6in (12m)

Draft 23ft (7m)

Speed 18.5 knots (surfaced), 6.5 knots (submerged)

Armament Eight 21-in bow torpedo tubes, one 5.5-lb deck gun, ten 25-mm anti-aircraft cannon in three triple and one single mount

Aircraft 3 Aichi M6A1 seaplanes

Crew 100

The giant I-400 class submarines the Japanese built toward the end of World War II were the largest in the world until the coming of nuclear submarines in the Cold War era. One of their unique features was the three seaplane bombers they carried. These were launched by a fixed catapult running out over the bows from their watertight deck hangar. Three I-400s were completed in all. Two never saw action—their planned kamikaze mission was cancelled—while the third was converted into an underwater oil tanker while she was under construction.

a single three-inch deck gun, and two machine guns. More deck guns were added later. From August 1942 onward, they were also fitted with air warning and surface search radar. The latter was an especially important innovation. Neither Japanese submarines nor surface escorts possessed radar of anything but the most primitive kind. This left US submariners in a class of their own, fighting by night or in poor visibility.

DEFECTIVE TORPEDOES

Unfortunately for the American submariners, there were major problems with their torpedoes, whose depth control mechanisms and magnetic exploders both proved to be defective in action. All too often, a torpedo would run ten feet (3m) deeper than it was set, so missing its intended target altogether. Even when a hit was scored, the fragile nature of the firing pin in the exploder meant that the impact of hitting a ship distorted it, so that it failed to act. As if this was not enough, American torpedoes were also prone to explode prematurely.

It took almost two years to fix the faults, especially since some high-ranking officers in the submarine command and the Bureau of Ordnance refused to admit there was anything major wrong with the existing torpedoes. Captain Ralph Christie, who had superintended the magnetic exploder's development before the war, and Rear Admiral Charles Lockwood, who took over from Rear Admiral Robert H. English in charge of submarine activity at Pearl Harbor after the latter died in a plane crash, were both particularly vehement in defending it against all costs.

It was not until October 1943 that US submarines started to be re-equipped with new and improved contact torpedoes. *Halibut*, commanded by Lieutenant Commander Ignatius "Pete" Galantin, who himself had suffered from the appalling performance of his torpedoes on a previous war patrol, was the submarine chosen to test them. He sailed from Pearl Harbor to the

The *Gato*-class submarine *Halibut* began its first war patrol off the Aleutians on October 2, 1942. Commander Philip H. Ross commanded this and her next four war patrols, after which Lieutenant Commander Ignatius J. Galantin took the boat over. On her tenth war patrol, *Halibut* was seriously damaged by depth-charge attacks in the Luzon Strait. Though she managed to limp back to Saipan and then to Pearl Harbor, she never saw action again. Her pressure hull had been distorted by the attack, so it was now unsafe to dive her.

small Hawaiian island of Kahoolawe, where he fired six of the new torpedoes into the vertical cliffs to strike the rock at 90 degrees. All of them detonated successfully.

PACIFIC SUCCESS

Finally armed with reliable torpedoes, US submarines immediately began making massive inroads into Japanese shipping. In September 1943 alone, a record 31 merchantmen totaling 135,000 tons were sunk; two months later, they set another record, sinking 47 merchant ships totaling 228,000 tons.

By the end of the year, the Japanese had lost 1,335,240 gross tons of merchant shipping. It was a rate of loss they could not possibly afford to sustain. Belatedly, they started taking steps to protect their maritime lifeline. It was agreed that their shipping losses had to be cut to under a million tons a year, about half the current rate. To achieve this, they decided to build 40 new escort vessels. It was too little, too late. The US submarine force was now over 150 strong and increasing at the rate of six boats a month.

Month by month, the total of tonnage sunk grew and grew, especially after Lockwood introduced his own version of wolf-pack tactics into the Pacific. In the first six months of 1944, US submarines sank over a million tons of merchant shipping and 125,000 tons of warships. In July, the Japanese lost a further 220,000 tons of merchant shipping. In October, the total was 320,906 tons, the highest monthly score of the war.

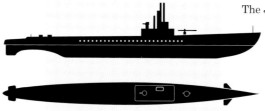

TANG

Class *Balao*-class submarine

Displacement 1,490 tons (surfaced), 2,070 tons (submerged)

Length 311ft 1in (94.8m)

Beam 27ft 5in (8.4m)

Draft 16ft 1in (4.9m)

Speed 20.5 knots (surfaced), 8.75 knots (submerged)

Armament Ten 21-in torpedo tubes, six forward, four aft, one 5-in deck gun, 40-mm and 20-mm anti-aircraft cannon

Crew 78

Balao-class submarines were improved versions of the *Gato*-class boats that preceded them. A 5-inch deck gun became standard equipment, replacing the 3-inch guns that had been fitted on *Gato*-class vessels. In addition, the amount of fuel that could be carried went up from 389 to 472 tons. As a result, range and endurance were both increased. In total, 120 *Balao*-class submarines served in the Pacific, of which 11 were lost.

In November, another 214,506 tons were sunk. The Japanese were reduced to desperate measures in an attempt to reduce the loss rate. Admiral Naokuni Nomura, commanding the Grand Escort Fleet, issued orders that convoys in danger areas were to proceed only by day, hiding by night in suitable anchorages. It was all in vain. By the beginning of 1945, US submarines were effectively blockading Japan, cutting imports of oil, raw materials, and food to a trickle. The oil and aviation fuel tanks were running dry, industry was in chaos, and the Japanese reduced to subsisting on average on less than 1,700 calories of food a day.

VICTORY AFTER VICTORY

By now, US submariners were breaking records with monotonous regularity. Commander Richard O'Kane, captain of *Tang*, was a prime case in point. On his first four war patrols, he sunk 20 Japanese vessels. On his fifth, which began on September 24, 1944, he added nine more to his score before closing in on yet another Japanese convoy in the Formosa Strait exactly a month later. Having shadowed the convoy patiently through the night, O'Kane surfaced at daybreak and maneuvered *Tang* into position for his attack.

The first six torpedoes O'Kane fired all hit their marks, sending two tankers and a destroyer to the bottom and badly damaging a troop transport. With just two torpedoes left, O'Kane decided to finish off the transport. The first torpedo he fired ran straight and true toward its intended target. The second did not. It turned full circle and headed back toward *Tang* instead. All attempts to steer away from it failed. It hit *Tang* abreast of the after torpedo room close to the maneuvering room bulkhead.

Tang went down stern first at terrifying speed. O'Kane and eight of his bridge crew who had been thrown into the water by the blast from the initial explosion watched her vanish as they floundered in the

The *Balao*-class submarine *Tang* returns to Pearl Harbor after her second war patrol in May 1944. She was sunk in the Formosa Straits on October 24, 1944 as a result of the malfunctioning of one of her own torpedoes, which, after being fired, swung around in a circle, eventually striking *Tang* abaft of her forward torpedo room. She started to sink within seconds, taking most of her crew to the bottom with her. Commander Richard H. O'Kane, her captain, survived. He was the most successful US submariner of the entire Pacific war.

At 72,000 tons the largest aircraft carrier built during World War II, the still uncompleted *Shinano* was spotted by *Archerfish* as she zigzagged down the Japanese coast toward Kure, where it was hoped she would be safe from US heavy bombing attack. *Shinano*'s vastly superior speed should have easily enabled her to outrun her enemy, but problems with her propeller bearings forced her to slow down dramatically. *Archerfish* torpedoed her four times. Within minutes, *Shinano* was developing an ever-increasing list to starboard. She stopped dead in the water, capsized, and sank.

sea. Only four survived, to be joined later by eleven more, who had managed to get out through the dying submarine's escape chamber. The rest of the crew were asphyxiated by smoke from a fire that had broken out in the battery compartment and deadly chlorine gas leaking from the batteries themselves.

O'Kane and his fellow survivors were picked up by a destroyer and shipped to Japan where they ended up in a prison camp until the Japanese surrender. By that time, only 9 of the original 15 survivors—including O'Kane himself—were still alive. It was a tragic end to what Rear Admiral Lockwood later called "one of the greatest submarine cruises of all time."

O'Kane was one hero of the submarine campaign. Commander Joseph F. Enright, captain of *Archerfish*, was another. On November 29, 1944, he made the biggest single kill of the entire submarine war when he torpedoed and sank the new 60,000-ton *Shinano*, originally intended to be a sister-ship to the great battleships *Yamato* and *Musashi*, but converted into a giant aircraft carrier while still on the stocks. She had taken more than four years to build and was reckoned by the Japanese to be unsinkable. Enright was to prove them wrong.

Escorted by three destroyers, *Shinano* had sailed from Tokyo Bay at 6 p.m. the previous evening to escape the threat of US bombing. Enright, who had been patrolling outside the bay, made radar contact with her only two hours later and started to follow her southward. Though the carrier was faster than he was, her zigzags meant he could just keep up with her, although he could not maneuver *Archerfish* into a favorable position to launch an attack. Then, at 3 a.m., she suddenly altered course and headed straight toward him, thus presenting him with the perfect target. Enright fired six torpedoes at her, four of which hit.

GATO

Class *Gato*-class fleet submarine

Displacement 1,525 tons (surfaced), 2,424 tons (submerged)

Length 311ft 10in (95m)

Beam 27ft (8.3m)

Draft 17ft (5.2m)

Speed 21 knots (surfaced), 9 knots (submerged)

Armament Ten 21-in torpedo tubes, six forward, four aft, one 3-in deck gun, 40-mm and 20-mm anti-aircraft cannon

Crew 70

Gato-class submarines were largely responsible for the decimation of Japan's merchant marine and a large portion of the Imperial Japanese Navy during World War II. Though only one boat—*Drum*—was actually in commission when the Pacific war started, US shipyards were soon churning out around three *Gatos* a week. Many racked up impressive war records. *Flasher*, *Rasher*, and *Barb* were the three top-scoring boats in the entire US submarine fleet in terms of the amount of enemy shipping tonnage sunk.

In theory, *Shinano* should have survived. In actuality, she did not. Because she had put to sea so hastily, some of her watertight doors had not been fitted, while others leaked. Nor was she equipped with her full complement of pumps. The dockyard workers onboard to complete her panicked. A few hours later she rolled over and sank, taking most of her crew to the bottom with her.

The sinking was symbolic of just how important a weapon the submarine had become. Admiral Nimitz summed it up neatly. At a press conference he held in September 1945, a month after Japan's surrender, he said: "Battleships are the ships of yesterday, aircraft carriers are the ships of today, but submarines are going to be the ships of tomorrow." At the time, it was considered a remarkable prediction. Time was to prove it correct.

LEYTE GULF

In September 1944, after much debate, the Allied Joint Chiefs of Staff meeting in Quebec decided on the next major step in the Pacific campaign. Acting on the advice of Admiral William "Bull" Halsey, whose carrier raids on the Philippines had highlighted the weakness of Japanese aviation, the existing plans to island-hop to the Philippines were scrapped. US amphibious forces would now go straight for the jugular and invade Leyte itself.

General Douglas MacArthur and Admiral Chester Nimitz would be in overall command of the assault. Naval support would be provided by Admiral Thomas Kincaid's Seventh Fleet and Halsey's Third Fleet, together with Vice Admiral Marc Mitscher's Fast Carrier Task Force. Vice Admiral Theodore "Ping" Wilkinson commanded the Southern Transport Force and Vice Admiral Daniel E. Barbey the Northern Transport Force. The landings were set for October 20, though the operation actually began three days earlier with the seizure of three small islands commanding the eastern approaches to Leyte itself.

THE JAPANESE RESPONSE

The Japanese fully expected a new attack, but were unsure where the Americans intended to strike. It could be in the Philippines, Taiwan, or even the Ryukyus, even closer to Japan itself. Wherever it turned out to be, they were determined to fight to the last ship and the last man. Admiral Soemu Toyoda, commander-in-chief of the Combined Fleet, prepared three separate battle plans for each eventuality. Then, he got the clue he needed.

On October 18, two days before the landings, US minesweepers were spotted in operation off Leyte, clearing shipping lanes for the approaching invasion fleet. It was the clue he needed. Toyoda immediately activated SHO-1. This plan called for practically all of Japan's naval strength to be thrown into one last decisive battle.

Toyoda split his fleet into three task forces. The Northern Force, commanded by Vice Admiral Jisaburo

Ozawa and consisting of four aircraft carriers—*Zuikaku*, *Zuiho*, *Chitose*, and *Chiyoda*—the two hybrid battleship/carriers *Hyuga* and *Ise*, three light cruisers, and eight destroyers, would approach the Philippines from the north. It was to serve as a decoy, to lure Halsey and his fleet out of position. Vice Admiral Takeo Kurita's Center Force—5 battleships, including the super-battleships *Musashi* and *Yamamoto*, 9 heavy cruisers, 2 light cruisers, and 15 destroyers—would then emerge from the San Bernadino Strait, sail down the coast of Samar, and engage the US invasion fleet from the northeast. Simultaneously, Vice Admiral Shoji Nishimura and Vice Admiral Kiyohide Shima with their respective squadrons of the Southern Force would debouch from the Surigao Strait, rendezvous with Kurita, and fall on the transports congregating off the invasion beaches.

It was an ambitious plan, but the odds were stacked against it succeeding. Fuel shortages meant that it took a week for the ships making up the task forces to assemble and steam to Leyte from Lingga Roads off Singapore and Japanese home waters. By the time they arrived, MacArthur's troops were already well established onshore. The Japanese were also dependent on Philippine-based planes for air cover. Ozawa's carriers between them had only 116 aircraft onboard. That was why they were deliberately chosen as a decoy—or maybe even a sacrifice. Toyoda seems to have been pinning his hopes on winning an old-fashioned ship-to-ship surface action.

THE BATTLE BEGINS

Battle started in the Palawan Passage in the early hours of October 23. As Center Force steamed at 15 knots into the passage, it was spotted by *Darter* and *Dace*, two patrolling US submarines. Having transmitted a sighting report to Halsey, the Americans maneuvered into position for an attack.

Darter struck first, firing six torpedoes at the heavy cruiser *Atago*, Kurita's flagship. Four torpedoes struck home. *Darter* then swung around and fired a second salvo at *Takeo*, scoring another two hits. *Atago* caught fire, settled by the bows, and sank. The badly damaged *Takeo* stopped dead in the water. Meanwhile, *Dace* had scored four hits on the cruiser *Maya*. She too quickly sank.

Kurita, who had been rescued from the water by a Japanese destroyer, shifted his flag to *Yamamoto* and stuck to his course, entering the Sibuyan Sea and heading north as planned. The hoped for air cover did not appear. Instead, wave after wave of American aircraft swarmed into the attack. The strikes—five of them in all—began in mid-morning and lasted until late afternoon. Their main target was *Musashi*, which was hit by 13 torpedoes and 10 bombs on her port side and 7 torpedoes and 7 bombs on her starboard. Even this supposedly unsinkable battleship could not withstand such punishment. She slowed and fell back behind Kurita's force, eventually ending up 20 miles (32km) astern of it. She sank at 7:35 p.m.

Musashi was not the only ship to be savaged by the American planes. *Yamamoto* took two bomb hits, but the list she developed was soon corrected. The two direct hits on the battleship *Nagato*, one of which penetrated her port boiler room, forced her to slow down until the damage was repaired. The heavy cruiser *Tone* and the destroyers *Kiyoshimo*, *Fujinami*, and *Uranami* also suffered hits and near misses. The temporarily unnerved Kurita reversed course. Believing him beaten, the impetuous Halsey ordered his fleet to sail northward to engage Ozawa's carriers. He left the San Bernadino Strait unguarded and Kincaid's Seventh Fleet unsupported.

ROUTING THE SOUTHERN FORCE

In the Surigao Strait, Kincaid was fighting his own battle. Warned that Nishimura's Southern Force was approaching, he ordered Rear Admiral Jesse B. Oldendorf to intercept them before they could close for action. Oldendorf baited his trap carefully. He stationed

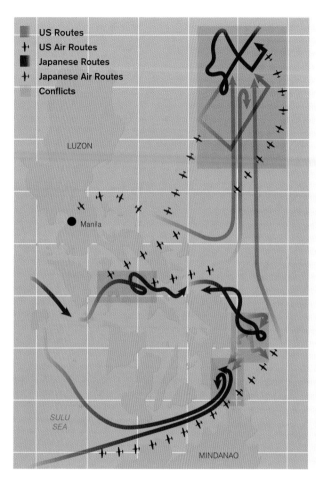

US Routes
US Air Routes
Japanese Routes
Japanese Air Routes
Conflicts

LUZON

Manila

SULU
SEA

MINDANAO

JAPAN'S LAST THROW

To defeat the invasion of the island of Leyte in the Philippines, the Japanese planned to use Ozawa's carriers as bait to tempt Admiral Halsey and his task force out of position, so opening the way for a two-pronged attack on the US invasion transports via the San Bernardino and Surigao Straits. Though Halsey succumbed to the temptation, the Japanese scheme fell apart. Admiral Kurita, commander of the First Strike Force, found himself bereft of air cover, while Nishimura's Force C ran into an ambush set by Rear Admiral Jesse B. Oldendorf. The battle ended with the destruction of most of what remained of the Imperial Japanese Navy.

39 PT boats far down the strait as his first line of defense and 28 destroyers farther up it. If Nishimura got past these, he would then face Oldendorf's five battleships—*Mississippi*, *Maryland*, *West Virginia*, *Tennessee*, *California*, and *Pennsylvania*—plus his heavy and light cruisers.

All went according to Oldendorf's plan. Though Nishimura succeeded in running the gauntlet of the

The Japanese First Strike Force sails from Brunei Bay, Borneo, on February 22 en route for the Philippines and Leyte Gulf (top left). From left to right, the battleships *Nagato*, *Musashi*, and *Yamato* are visible steaming in the distance, together with the heavy cruisers *Maya*, *Chokai*, *Takao*, *Atago*, *Haguro*, and *Myoko*. *Yamato* (opposite) and other ships take evasive action while being attacked by US Navy carrier-borne aircraft in the Sibuyan Sea. The shadow of one of the attacking planes is visible on a cloud (lower right center). The great battleship finally took two bomb hits, the more serious one in her port-bow anchor room (bottom left). She took on 2,000 gallons of water and started to list, but effective counterflooding quickly righted her. *Musashi* was less lucky. Torpedoed from the air 13 times on her port side and seven on her starboard and hit by ten bombs to port and seven to starboard, she sank that evening.

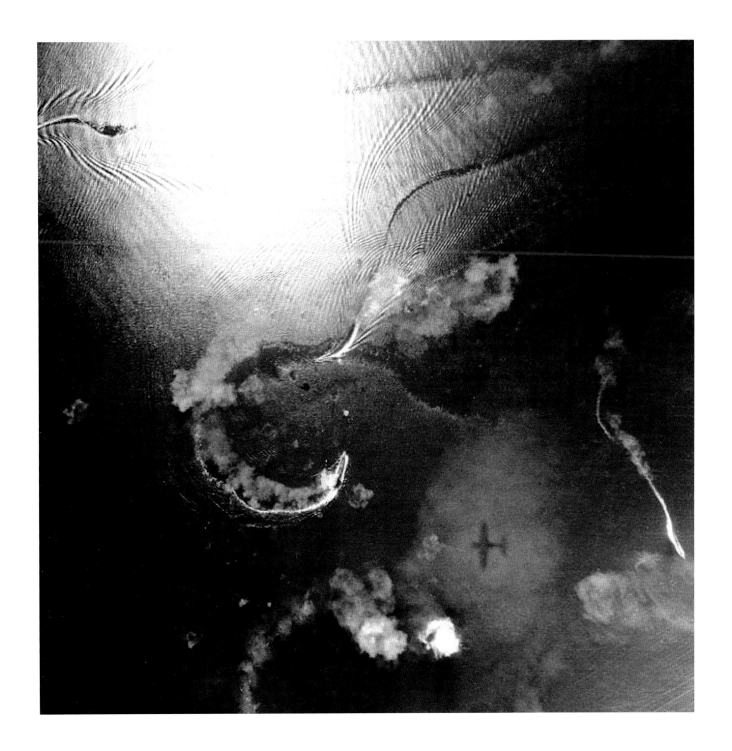

PT boats without suffering any damage, it was a different matter when he ran into the destroyers. *Fuso* was the first Japanese ship to be sunk, followed by *Yamagumo* and *Michishio*. *Asagumo*'s bow was ripped off and *Yamashiro* was hit as well. Then the cruisers and battleships joined in. The resulting clash was one-sided. Oldendorf's ships sank two battleships and a heavy cruiser. The remnants of the Southern Force turned back to make good their escape. So, too, did Shima, whose ships never got into action.

KURITA RETURNS

The battle was not yet over. As Oldendorf was concluding the action, he received the news that Kurita had returned to the attack. Under cover of darkness, the Japanese admiral had debouched undetected from the San Bernadino Strait and taken Rear Admiral Clifton A. F. Sprague's six lightly armed escort carriers stationed off Samar by surprise. They, three destroyers, and three destroyer escorts with them were all that stood between Kurita's battlefleet and the invasion beaches.

Sprague's carriers were not built to take part in heavy surface fighting. Nevertheless, given the situation, Sprague decided he must fight a delaying action. While the carriers launched all their available aircraft and started steaming toward the rest of the Seventh Fleet, he ordered his destroyers to attack as Kurita began a slow loop south, driving Sprague's Task Group toward Leyte Gulf. As he did so, he came under almost constant aerial attack.

Kalinin Bay was the first of Sprague's carriers to be hit, but, despite heavy damage, she managed to stay in formation. The destroyers *Johnston* and *Hoel* were not as lucky. Both of them were sunk along with the destroyer escort *Samuel B. Roberts* as they literally charged at the Japanese battleships and heavy cruisers.

The battle was nearing crisis point. *Chikuma*, *Tone*, *Haguro*, and *Chokai*, Kurita's four remaining heavy cruisers, closed the range on the American carriers.

Chikuma began to pound *Gambier Bay*, which dropped astern and began to sink. However, the Americans were quick to retaliate; *Chokai*, *Chikuma*, and *Suzuya* all went down, sunk as a result of determined aerial attacks.

Sprague's harried carriers were now coming under battleship as well as cruiser fire. Then, much to the Americans' amazement, the heavy cruisers broke off their pursuit. Soon it was clear that the entire Center Force was withdrawing. Kurita had decided to retire back through the San Bernardino Strait to save his ships from further punishment. He had lost one of his two super-battleships and five heavy cruisers. Two more heavy cruisers had been crippled and practically all his force had sustained some form of damage. He also knew that Nishimura's force had been destroyed. Withdrawal now seemed to him to be the only sensible option.

THE FINAL BATTLE

Ozawa meanwhile had been carrying out his part of the plan. When, however, he learned that Kurita was retiring, he also began to withdraw north. Then Toyoda signaled to him Tokyo ordering him to head south again. He and the Northern Force were back on a collision course with Halsey and his fleet.

Halsey's scouting aircraft sighted the two groups into which Ozawa had divided his force at around 2 a.m. on October 25. Mitscher told his carriers to prepare to launch a first strike at earliest light. In the meantime, Ozawa flew off most of his planes to Clark and Tuguegarao Fields on the Philippines. This left him with just 13 fighters with which to take on the American aircraft when they attacked.

Mitscher's first wave struck at around 8 a.m., followed by a second one an hour and three-quarters later. The first wave sank *Chitose* and a destroyer. It also badly damaged the Pearl Harbor veteran *Zuikaku*, forcing Ozawa to shift his flag to the light cruiser *Oyodo*. The second wave set *Chiyoda* on fire and disabled her engines. An attempt to take her in

▲ The light carrier *Princeton* blazes as *Birmingham* steams alongside trying to help fight the fires raging onboard. The carrier's destruction was the work of a lone Japanese pilot, who dropped a 500-lb (227-kg) bomb squarely between six armed torpedo bombers being readied for take-off on her flight deck. Though her crew fought as hard as they could to save her, *Princeton* had to be abandoned before she eventually exploded after being torpedoed by one of her escorts. Her sinking was one of the only successes the Japanese enjoyed during the battle.

failed. Eventually, the Japanese abandoned her to be sunk by Halsey's cruisers late that afternoon.

The third strike was the biggest and equally devastating. The sorely tried *Zuikaku* was hit by three torpedoes simultaneously and promptly capsized and sank. *Zuiho* was badly damaged, though it took planes from the fourth strike to finish her off. Two more strikes after that caused relatively little damage.

Halsey was now readying his surface ships to take over and deliver the knockout blow. Before he could get into action, however, his cavalier decision to leave Kincaid in the lurch caught up with him. Nimitz himself intervened. Much against his will, Halsey turned back to speed to Kincaid's assistance, though in the event he arrived too late to make any difference. Kurita seized the opportunity to escape.

The Battle of Leyte Gulf was over. In all four of its actions, fought in the Sibuyan Sea on October 24, Surigao Strait on the 24th and 25th, off Samar on the 25th, and off Cape Engano from the 25th to 26th, the Americans had emerged victorious. In terms of the number of ships involved, it ranks as the greatest naval battle of all time. It was also the Imperial Japanese Navy's swansong. After it, the Combined Fleet was

never again an effective fighting force. Their great naval victory enabled the Americans to secure their beachhead on Leyte, so opening the door for the liberation of the whole of the Philippines. This in turn cut the Japanese off from their conquered territories elsewhere in Southeast Asia, reducing the flow of vitally needed supplies of foodstuffs, oil, and other raw materials to the Home Islands to a trickle. In the fighting, the Japanese had lost four aircraft carriers, 3 battleships, 8 cruisers, and 12 destroyers. More than 10,000 sailors and airmen had been killed. American losses were much lighter. A light aircraft carrier, two escort carriers, two destroyers, and one destroyer escort were sunk and 1,500 men were killed.

OPERATION TEN-GO

When as the final precursor to the projected invasion of the Japanese Home Islands, US troops landed on Okinawa on April 1, 1945, the Japanese were determined to resist to the death. A month before the landings, Emperor Hirohito himself had convened a meeting of the High Command to discuss its plans for a last stand.

After being told how the army proposed to defend the island with 100,000 troops and hundreds of kamikaze planes, Hirohito asked what the navy would be doing to defend Okinawa when the Americans launched their assault. "And where is the Navy?" he demanded. The navy chiefs were nonplussed by the Emperor's question. Was it possible that he did not realize that the once-mighty Combined Fleet had now been reduced to just a handful of ships? Did he not know that there was nothing the navy could do to change the situation?

Hirohito's meaning, however, was clear. It was unthinkable that, while the army was making the ultimate sacrifice, what remained of the navy's surface ships stayed out of combat. The fate of the Imperial Japanese Navy had been decided.

SAILING TO DESTRUCTION

Admiral Soemu Toyoda, the commander-in-chief, and his planners quickly threw Ten-Go together as their response to Hirohito's unspoken demand. It was a kamikaze-style operation, in which the super-battleship *Yamato*, the light cruiser *Yahagi*, and eight destroyers—all that Toyoda could scrape quickly together as a fighting force—would sortie through the Bungo Strait, fight their way through the American invasion fleet, and eventually beach themselves on Okinawa. Once aground, the ships were to act as shore batteries until their destruction, at which point their surviving crew members were to disembark and fight as infantry in the massive counterattack the army had already planned.

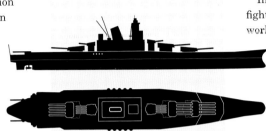

YAMAOTO

Class	*Yamato*-class battleship
Displacement	71,660 tons (full load)
Length	800ft 6in (244m)
Beam	127ft 9in (38.9m)
Draft	35ft 6in (10.8m)
Speed	27.5 knots
Armament	Nine 18-in guns in three main turrets, 12 6.1-in guns in six turrets, 12 5-in anti-aircraft guns, 24 25-mm cannon, four 13-mm machine guns
Crew	2,500

Yamato and her sister-ship *Musashi* were by far the largest battleships ever built. At 71,600 tons fully loaded, their displacement was nearly twice as much that of their Allied contemporaries. Their massive 18-inch main armament outranged all Allied warships, while their massive armor was also truly formidable. However, they were not unsinkable. *Musashi* was sunk from the air during the battle of Leyte Gulf; *Yamato* met the same fate while on a last-ditch suicide mission to Okinawa in April 1945. She was a decoy, the intention being for her to draw off as many US carrier planes as possible, thus leaving the Allied surface fleet open to a large-scale kamikaze raid.

In theory, *Yamato* was an extremely formidable fighting machine. By far the largest battleship in the world, she was some 863 feet long, displaced 72,908 tons when fully loaded, and had a maximum speed of 27.5 knots. Her main armament consisted of nine 18.1-inch guns firing 3,200-lb (1,451.5-kg) shells and with a range of 22.5 miles (36km) and 150 anti-aircraft guns. Her complement was 2,767 officers and men. In practice, the operation she was now being ordered to undertake was a suicide mission right from the start.

Yamato had only enough fuel for a one-way trip and *Yahagi* was provisioned for just five days. Vice Admiral Seiichi Ito, in overall command, made it clear that he opposed the mission, arguing that it was a waste of precious resources. In reply, Vice Admiral Ryunosuke Kusaka, Toyoda's Chief of Staff, told him and his equally doubting subordinate officers that it was the Emperor's personal wish Ten-Go went ahead. There could be no questioning of the imperial authority. On April 6, the squadron sailed.

MITSCHER ATTACKS

At 4 a.m. on April 7, Ito entered the North Pacific southeast of Kyushu. It was not long before US scouting planes spotted him heading south. He immediately changed course westward, hoping to stay out of range of Mitscher's carrier-based aircraft, before steaming south again. Admiral Raymond A. Spruance had already taken precautions against any such breakthrough. He had ordered Vice Admiral Morton L. Deyo and his force of 6 battleships—*Massachusetts*, *Indiana*, *New Jersey*, *South Dakota*, *Wisconsin*, and *Missouri*—plus 7 cruisers and 21 destroyers to ready themselves for a surface engagement if Mitscher's airstrikes proved unsuccessful.

Shortly after noon, Mitscher's first wave of fighters, dive-bombers, and torpedo planes swept into action. Soon, Ito and his ships were under almost continuous

Yamato's last battle began at 12.32pm when she and her escorts—a light cruiser and eight destroyers—opened fire with all their guns on the first of three waves of US dive-bombers and torpedo planes approaching them. The dive-bombers scored their first hits at 12.40pm; the torpedo planes fired two torpedoes into her port side ten minutes later. Soon, more hits were being scored—eight to port and two to starboard. The last torpedo struck home at 2.17pm, after which *Yamato*'s ever-increasing list became uncontrollable.

attack. Rear Admiral Kosaku Aruga, captain of *Yamato*, ordered his gunners to open fire. Gunfire from his screening ships echoed from across the water. The hitherto gloomy sky turned bright with multicolored shell explosions.

The Japanese ships increased speed to 25 knots and started to take evasive action. Their zigzagging did them little good. *Yahagi* was hit in her engine room by a torpedo. Stopped dead in the water, the light cruiser took 6 more torpedo and 12 bomb hits before sinking at 2:05 p.m. The destroyers *Isokaze* and *Hanakaze* accompanied her to the bottom. *Suzutsuki* was on fire and *Sasumi*, her rudder jammed, was out of control, steaming slowly in circles. Both were subsequently scuttled by the Japanese themselves.

Yamato, maneuvering for her life, was struck by at least 8 torpedoes and up to 15 bombs. Lieutenant John Carter, piloting an Avenger torpedo bomber, recorded what happened after four other Avengers, flying low and fast, dropped their torpedoes in a spread. "As luck would have it," he later recalled, "the big ship was turning to port, thereby exposing the full broadside expanse of her enormous hull to the converging torpedoes." Carter saw at least three of them strike home, two detonating so close together that the result looked like a single massive explosion.

YAMATO SINKS

The great super-battleship was now listing heavily to port. Despite attempts to right her by counterflooding, the list grew worse and worse. Then, at around 2:10 p.m., Aruga felt yet another torpedo smash into his ship's stern. The main rudder immediately jammed hard to port. *Yamato* could no longer be steered. Aruga ordered what remained of her crew to abandon ship. At 2:20 p.m., *Yamato* rolled over completely and sank after being torn apart by one last massive internal explosion. Aruga and Ito went down with their ship. Only four battered destroyers managed to escape the debacle and

make it back to their home port. Toyoda's last throw had come to an inglorious end.

In Japan, news of the disaster was kept a closely guarded secret from the public. It fell to Navy Minister Mitsumasa Yonai to inform the Emperor. With downcast eyes, Yonai stood before Hirohito and reported that Operation Ten-Go had failed. It had cost the Japanese between 3,700 and 4,250 dead as well as *Yamato*, *Yahagi*, and four destroyers. American losses were 12 men killed and 10 aircraft downed.

The emperor seemed not to understand. He peered at Yonai through his spectacles. "What about the navy?" he asked. "What is the status of the fleet?" There was no fleet, Yonai told him. The once-invincible Imperial Japanese Navy had ceased to exist as an effective fighting force.

Yamato photographed from the air moments after she succumbed to the massive bomb and torpedo damage her attackers had inflicted on her. As she finally rolled over and sank, she was torn apart by two massive internal explosions as the fires onboard reached her aft magazines. The explosions sent a majestic mushroom cloud of smoke billowing into the air thousands of feet above her.

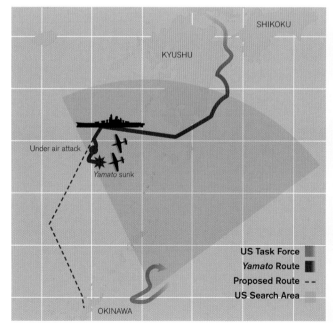

SHIKOKU

KYUSHU

Under air attack

Yamato sunk

US Task Force
Yamato Route
Proposed Route --
US Search Area

OKINAWA

THE LAST VOYAGE

Yamato was spotted by the patrolling US submarines *Threadfin* and *Hackleback* while navigating the Bungo Strait shortly after leaving port at Tokuyama, and tracked all the way from Japanese home waters to her final battleground in the North Pacific 175 miles (282km) south of Kyushu. The plan was for the battleship to fight its way through to Okinawa, where she would beach herself and use her giant 18-inch main armament to provide artillery support for the Japanese ground forces battling against the invading Americans. She had been supplied with just enough fuel to make the one-way trip.

BIBLIOGRAPHY/FURTHER READING

In an all-embracing survey like this, the problem is to decide what is worth including and what could be omitted. The books listed here hopefully will encourage readers to investigate specific subjects in more depth and detail. For reasons of space, though, it has been impossible to credit all the Internet resources that have been consulted.

Ballantyre, Iain
Killing the Bismarck
Pen & Sword Maritime

Barnett, Correlli
Engage the Enemy More Closely
Penguin

Brescia, Maurizio
Mussolini's Navy
Seaforth

Bennett, G. H.
Hitler's Ghost Ships
University of Plymouth Press

Frank, Richard B.
Guadalcanal
Penguin

Lavery, Brian
Churchill's Navy
Conway Maritime

Dull, Paul S.
A Battle History of the Imperial Japanese Navy
Naval Institute Press

Hornfischer, James D.
Neptune's Inferno
Presidio Press

Kennedy, Paul M.
The Rise and Fall of British Naval Mastery
Palgrove Macmillan

Konstam, Angus
Bismarck 1941
Osprey

Konstam, Angus
The Battle of North Cape
Pen & Sword

Lowry, Thomas P. & Welham, John
The Attack on Taranto
Stackpole

Mallmann-Showell, Jak P.
A Companion to the German Navy
History Press

Marriott, Leo
Fighting Ships of World War II
Airlife

Middlebrook, Martin & Mahoney, Patrick
Battleship: The Loss of the Prince of Wales and the Repulse
Penguin

Morison, Samuel Eliot
History of United States Naval Operations in World War II
Little Brown, 15 volumes

Morison, Samuel Eliot
The Two Ocean War
Little Brown

O'Hara, Vincent
On Seas Contested
Naval Institute Press

O'Hara, Vincent
The German Fleet At War
Naval Institute Press

Padfield, Peter
Battleship
Birlinn

Padfield, Peter
Dönitz: The Last Führer
HarperCollins

Padfield, Peter
War Beneath the Sea
Wiley

Parshall, Jonathan
Shattered Sword
Potomac Books

Potter, John Deane
Fiasco
Macmillan

Robinson, Terence
Channel Dash
Pan Macmillan

Santarini Marc
Bismarck and Hood
Fonthill Media

Simmons, Mark
The Battle of Matapan
The History Press

Spurr, Russell
A Glorious Way To Die: The Kamikaze Mission of the Battleship Yamato
William Morrow Paperbacks

Stille, Mark
The Imperial Japanese Navy in the Pacific War
Osprey

Stille, Mark
The Naval Battle of Guadalcanal
Osprey

Symonds, Craig L.
The Battle of Midway
OUP USA

Tillman, Barrett
Clash of the Carriers
New American Library

Tolk, Ian W.
Pacific Crucible
Norton

Walling, Michael
Forgotten Sacrifice
Osprey

Wilson, Ben
Empire of the Deep
Phoenix

Williams, Andrew
The Battle of the Atlantic
BBC Books

Woodman, Richard
Arctic Convoys
Pen & Sword

Woodman, Richard
The Battle of the River Plate
Pen & Sword Maritime

Van der Vat, Dan
Pearl Harbor
Basic Books

Van der Vat, Dan
The Atlantic Campaign
HarperCollins

Van der Vat, Dan
The Pacific Campaign
Hodder & Stoughton

Vego, Milan N.
The Battle for Leyte
Naval Institute Press

Zimm, Alan D.
The Attack on Pearl Harbor
Casemate

INDEX

Page numbers in **bold** include photographs or maps. Ship names are shown in *italics*.

PHOTO CREDITS

All other images featured are public domain.

Every effort has been made to credit the copyright holders of the images used in this book. We apologize for any unintentional omissions or errors and will insert the appropriate acknowledgment to any companies or individuals in subsequent editions of the work.